CLIVE WOODWARD

The Biography

CLIVE WOODWARD

The Biography

ALISON KERVIN

ORION

Copyright © Alison Kervin 2005

The right of Alison Kervin to be identified as the
author of this work has been asserted by her in accordance
with the Copyright, Designs and Patents Act 1988.

First published in hardback in Great Britain in 2005 by
Orion Books
an imprint of the Orion Publishing Group Ltd
Orion House, 5 Upper St Martin's Lane,
London WC2H 9EA

1 3 5 7 9 10 8 6 4 2

A CIP catalogue record for this book is
available from the British Library.

ISBN: 0 75286 857 8

Printed in Great Britain by
Clays Ltd, St Ives plc

Every effort has been made to fulfil requirements with
regard to reproducing copyright material. The author and publisher
will be glad to rectify any omissions at the earliest opportunity.

www.orionbooks.co.uk

For George – my beautiful blue-eyed blond –
and in memory of my grandmother who passed away
during the writing of this book.

Contents

Section Four

Section Five

Section Six

Acknowledgements

To my agent – Sheila Crowley at AP Watt, an Irish rugby supporter but in all other respects a woman who displays flawless judgement. A great friend and confidante. Her simple comment, 'You should write a book about Clive Woodward,' set me off on this path to discover all I could about the football-loving, modern-thinking, sleep-evading maverick whose eclectic, electric touch brought sparks to the England rugby team. Thanks to Ian Marshall, Lorraine Baxter, Marion Paull and all at Orion Publishing and to my dream team of researchers – Alan 'peerless' Pearey and Niamh Dyar. Thanks also to Peter 'red pen' Kervin for reading the final version in record time and pointing out the bits that made no sense whatsoever.

Thanks to all at Easingwold School, especially Bill Bell, Malcolm Milne and Gerry Kershaw, to all at the Old Conways Society and everyone at Merseyside Maritime Museum in Liverpool, to Basil Lord and those who cast their minds back to try to remember the period, especially Colin Goodey, Vaughan Atkinson (who was dodging bullets in Iraq as we communicated), Dave Yates, Tom Rowlands, Lance Mitchell, Richard Coombes, Phil van Bergen, Nick Faignez, Alan Burns and John Holme.

Thanks to Dr Steve Bull, sports and business psychologist, and Dr Adrian Atkinson MA, MSc, PhD, CPSYCHOL, business and clinical psychologist, for their perceptive observations. Thanks to Sir John Harvey-Jones, Simon Clifford, Stuart Farmer, Sir Alan Sugar and enormous thanks to the delightful Humphrey Walters – charm personified.

Thanks to all at Harlequins, especially to Nick Cross, the staggering statistician who can raise one eyebrow and recall every game ever played at the club. I don't know how you can do it, but I'm glad you can. Thanks to Bob Hiller, Earle Kirton, Colin Herridge, David Cooke, Roger Looker and Val Bendall.

At Loughborough, thanks to Jim Greenwood, whose afternoon drink in the sunshine was interrupted by my questioning, Sue Campbell, Stuart Biddle, Rex Hazeldine, Lord Sebastian Coe, David Bunker and Rod Thorpe.

At Leicester, a big thank you to Chris Goddard and the *Leicester Mercury*. Thanks to the club, to Angus Collington, Peter Wheeler, Dusty Hare, Paul Dodge, Chalkie White, Steve Kenney, Ian Smith (and Oakham School). Thanks to Kevin Williams for his generosity and honesty and to Tim Buttimore for his support.

Thanks to Terry Burwell, Tony Bond, Mike Weston, Ray Gravell, John Beattie, Derek Quinnell, Tim Barnwell, Willie John McBride, Robert Norster, Peter Winterbottom,

John O'Driscoll and to Don and Sue Rutherford for time, help and a beautiful lunch. Thanks to Roger Uttley for his absolute honesty. Thanks to all at the RFU, Pennyhill Park Hotel and all of Clive's England and Lions team-mates who gave their time and racked their brains to come up with such funny stories. Thanks to Fran Cotton, Bill Beaumont, Martyn Thomas, Cliff Brittle, Graeme Cattermole and Francis Baron, to Jack Rowell and Geoff Cooke. Thanks to the England players from the past who added their thoughts to the mix and thanks to Pennyhill Park Hotel.

To Paddi 'they all think I'm crazy but I'm not' Lund (he is) – thank you for your time and I hope the Latin dancing is going well. Thanks to Fletcher Potanin for guiding me through the Lund business practices and to Alan Jones, the Australian answer to Jeremy Paxman. Thanks to Alan King and Peter Russell and to those at Fuji Xerox who helped me to track them down. Thanks to David Parker and Manly Rugby Club, to Philip Cox and Thomas Dooner. Thanks to the Manly Pacific Hotel and to Richard Holt, the manager, who kindly showed me round the hotel, including the provocatively named 'war room'.

Thanks to everyone at the Imperial War Museum, the Royal Navy, Royal Air Force and the State Library of New South Wales. Thanks to all at Henley Rugby Club, especially Noel Murphy, Mike Poulson and Nigel Dudding, and to all at London Irish Rugby Club – Paddy Lennon, Conor O'Shea, Colin Hall, Kieran McCarthy and Brendan Quirke in particular. Thanks, too, to Bath RFC and to Caroline Inman and all at the BBC for their help.

Thanks to the England management team and those coaches from other countries who added their voice to the debate, and to all the current players who spoke with such honesty – Andy Robinson, Dr Simon Kemp, Louise Ramsay, Richard Prescott, Lawrence Dallaglio, Martin Johnson, Jonny Wilkinson, Martin Corry, David Rees, Matt Perry, Will Green, Jason Leonard … all of them. Thanks, too, to the Royal Marines and to Lt Col George Matthews RM in particular.

Thanks to Clive's family, friends, acquaintances and colleagues who took time to reflect on the man (Ann Heaver and Steve Holdsworth – thanks very much). From Ely via Yorkshire, North Wales, London, Loughborough and Leicester, thoughts and feelings have been captured and, I hope, accurately reproduced here. For all the funny stories about Hawaiian huts, car phones, big nights out and broken bones, to those who told me 'not to be published' stories – about diamonds, beer and rocking cars – thank you for telling me, but I wish you'd let me include them.

Most of all, thanks to Sir Clive Woodward whose reaction to my declaration that I planned to write a biography about him was staggering. 'I'm flattered,' he said. 'I don't have any issues at all.' He has dealt with my intrusions, questions and turning up at functions, unannounced and unwelcome, with the same stoicism and strength of character that defined him throughout his time with England. He even had the grace to smile. 'There she goes,' he cried once, as I walked through a rugby lunch, clutching a large holdall. 'See that bag? – it's full of secrets and stories about me.' It was – and here they all are…

'Mr Lely, I desire you would use all your skill to paint your picture truly like me, and not flatter me at all; but remark all these roughness, pimples, warts, and everything as you see me; otherwise I will never pay a farthing for it.' Oliver Cromwell to his portrait painter

Snapshots of a complicated man

In the hotel's lobby, a huge fire is burning. Leather chairs and comfy sofas fill the air with old world charm. I have just had dinner with Sir Clive Woodward. It is now past 11 p.m. but he has another meeting before he can retire for the night, and he will be in his car and on the way to the next assignment by 5 a.m. Sleep will be fitted in somewhere. Lying down with closed eyes is not high on Clive's list of priorities. He walks me to the door. A uniformed attendant moves to join us.

'It's cold out there, ma'am,' ventures the man, rubbing his gloved hands together. 'Let me get your car for you.'

My car is in a dimly lit car park some two hundred or so metres from the hotel's main door. His offer is kind and I am inclined to accept. The doorman turns to Clive.

'Is that OK?' he asks, sheepishly, as if I were a teenager he had just asked out on a date.

'Of course,' says Clive. 'Yes. Get her car for her.'

I hand over my car keys and the man disappears into the dark night.

'Why did he ask you whether he could get my car?' I ask. It seems odd.

'I'm a bit funny about things like that,' Clive says, smiling a crooked smile and raising his eyebrows in a manner that betrays a little embarrassment. 'I don't let the staff get the players' cars for them. Ever. It's not fair. The players are more than capable of walking a few yards to their cars. I won't have the hotel's staff running around after them. I don't think international sportsmen should behave like that. If I catch the players being impolite or exploiting the goodwill of the staff here, they know I will be cross. They should have more respect. They *must* have

3

more respect if they are in Team England.' He shrugs. 'That's just the way I am.'

I am left wondering, not for the first time, how on earth he will survive in football. 'They'll show respect, too,' he says.

🏈

At Harrow School, Roger Uttley is edgy. The former England forward, England coach and England manager, the man who was the powerhouse of the national game for so long, does not care to talk with the tape recorder whirring. He does not really care to talk at all, if the truth be known. He finds the whole thing too painful, too difficult. He was reluctant to have anything to do with the project, but I asked only for honesty and he agreed. He says he's not bitter about the time he spent working with Clive. He says he bears no malice, but those few years were the most dreadful of his life. He seems changed. I knew Roger years ago. He was confident, strident, forceful, an authoritative figure, but today he seems quiet, a little reticent and hurt. Mainly, though, he seems sad.

He was cast aside by the England establishment. He thinks it was because Clive saw him as a threat. Roger was the England team manager and Clive was England coach. Clive was full-time and Roger part-time, but Roger's role, in principle, was the lead role. Roger recalls conflict after conflict until the power struggle between the two of them reached fever pitch.

Roger remembers a meeting they had when it all came to a head. Clive invited him for coffee. 'I remember us sitting down to have a chat about things in the café at the Petersham Hotel in Richmond. Clive said, "I think I should have complete control," and I didn't feel I had any choice but to let him have it.'

Inevitably after that, Clive called and said he wanted to talk to Roger. He drove to Harrow School and explained that the England manager's services were no longer required.

🏈

'Dear Clive, First of all, I would like to congratulate you and the England squad for bringing home the World Cup. I watched the match with other players from the England Deaf Rugby Team. We all enjoyed it very much and have to say that we completely agree with your views on the referee. It probably didn't occur to you that anyone could hear when you were shouting inside the coaches' box but, you see, the advantage of being deaf is the ability to lip-read…'

'I'm not a homosexual, but I realise now that I loved Clive Woodward. He started a war and he became the enemy. I ended up hating the guy, hating him, because of the statements he sometimes made, not about me but about the French. I think now, though, that he is adorable.' Bernard Laporte, coach of the France team, swoons.

'People say I'm mad. I'm not mad. I'm quite a sensible bloke. Not that I mind the tag too much. I'd rather be called "half madman, half genius" than "the mad professor", though. I don't like being called a mad professor for lots of reasons – but mainly because I'm not.' Clive on Clive, 2003.

'He's a mad professor.' Martin Johnson.

'He is a mad professor.' Dusty Hare.

'He was like a mad professor.' Paul Dodge.

'People call him a mad professor, don't they? It's not hard to see why.' Jason Leonard.

'Some would describe Clive as a lunatic, others as an eccentric. He's a mad professor.' Ian Smith.

Kieran McCarthy sits looking out over the London Irish training pitch and allows himself a quick giggle. Clive was the coach of London Irish for just a couple of years, but those years are remembered as if they happened yesterday. 'He was great, lots of bright ideas, but he was hard work. He was really demanding and slightly mad. I'm sure he won't mind me saying that. You know who he reminds me of?' McCarthy smiles as he speaks. 'Van Gogh. He's got that artist's temperament. You'd not be a bit surprised if Clive Woodward went and cut his ear in one moment of madness, then about ten seconds later he'd be saying, "What the hell did I do that for? I can't hear a thing now."'

Steve Holdstock, a close friend of Clive's and a colleague at Rank Xerox, recalls a funny moment when Clive was in his twenties and taking a group of employees to dinner in a noisy restaurant. He told the waitress he'd like to order wine. She came over and presented him with the wine list. As Clive looked up and asked what the house wine was, someone at the table asked a question about the music. The waitress said, 'It's Chris de Burgh,' and Clive thought she was answering his question. 'We'll have four bottles of that, then,' he replied.

'I remember sharing a room with Clive in South Africa (on tour with the British and Irish Lions). One evening, Clive took a call and said, "Hang on." He put the receiver down and waited for a minute, then picked it up and carried on. After he put the phone down, I said, "What was all that about?" He explained that at Rank Xerox he'd been trained always to be in control of the conversation. He would have been about twenty-three at the time. I just thought, "Wow." ' John Beattie, former Scotland and Lions number 8.

'I may be in a minority of one but that does not mean I'm wrong.' Clive in 2004, at his final press conference.

Introduction

On two rainy evenings on the other side of the world, the reputation of Sir Clive Ronald Woodward was made and broken, lifted beyond recognition and smashed beyond reason. It is the essence of sport that reputations twirl on its wobbly axis – years of previous work is irrationally tarnished or bolstered over the course of days, hours or minutes. One missed penalty, one dropped goal, one dropped pass – a reputation hinges, swells and deflates on such things.

When I began writing this book, Clive had just won the World Cup. He was the greatest rugby coach in the history of the world – a genius, the nation's hero, one of the best coaches that England had produced across any sport, ever. His management talks attracted capacity crowds and his views were sought on everything from creating élite teams to motivation and leadership. He was knighted and feted, respected and admired.

Two years later, as the book was being finished, Clive took the British and Irish Lions on tour to New Zealand, confidently predicting victory. Despite the team having spent just a few weeks together, they boarded the plane full of self-belief. Clive sat at press conferences and announced that they would win. He gave television interviews and proclaimed that this was the best-prepared Lions team ever to leave these shores. It was certainly the largest and most expensive squad to do so. They lost 3–0 and Clive returned with his reputation in tatters.

His management style and even his understanding of the game were subject to debate. His very character was under the microscope. What sort of man would take Alastair Campbell on a rugby tour? What sort of man would spend all that money without delivering? He was colder, more calculating and infinitely more self-obsessed than we'd ever realised. He had gone not only from success to failure, but from good guy to bad guy.

The three Test defeats hit home one after the other – bang, bang, bang. The world shifted a little on its axis with every pounding New Zealand victory. It was the most fascinating thing to witness – to see a man who had brought the World Cup to England and inspired the nation to rise in celebration just two years previously, suddenly demonised and being stripped of every ounce of credibility. Where did that leave my biography of him?

I had to address some key questions. Is Clive really a fundamentally different person as a result of the defeats in New Zealand? No. Did he become a different person when England won the World Cup? No. He was more respected after the World Cup and less respected after the Lions tour – all that really changed was the public perception of him as a winner. His aims did not change and his hopes for the future did not change. The things he did and the views he holds, the influences on him, and the thought processes he goes through, they are all the same. The World Cup victory and the Lions tour failure undoubtedly help to reveal facets of Clive's character but they do not define his character. That is something infinitely more complex.

The aim of this book is to deal in facts and reflect thoughts and opinions in a balanced and rational way in order to create a text that looks carefully at the life and personality of Clive Woodward. One of the many beauties of writing a book is the chance for sober reflection and perspective – they are luxuries denied to a journalist who must rush to a view on a daily basis.

I could easily write two books, one proclaiming Clive to be the most successful coach in history and one declaring him the worst coach in history. I could tuck them away and produce them from time to time over the next twenty-five years, and they would both be right in any one moment. The truth, of course, is much harder to uncover.

This book aims to analyse the personality of the man who brought the World Cup to England in 2003, dramatically resigned from his position as head coach, took the Lions to New Zealand on their worst tour, then switched codes entirely and went to work at Southampton Football Club. It is the tale of a little boy sent away to boarding school on his own and struggling for acceptance and love in a cold, authoritative and frustrating institution. It is about the expression of that frustration through an extraordinary gift for sport. The book tells the tale of his time in Australia, and how he returned to England to establish his own company and combine business and sporting skills to transform two rugby clubs. Above all, it tells the story of how he shook English rugby up over seven years, and made everyone in the national side believe they could be winners.

There have been high points and low points. Many people speak fondly of Clive; many do not. It is the tale of a complex man driven by a need to be successful, a man who is fiercely competitive and very private, very much an individual but fascinated by the dynamics of the team, a risk taker, a man who sometimes appears blindingly self-confident and at other times appears strangely vulnerable. He is well liked, but often not so well understood.

Researching and writing this book has been a fascinating experience, a roller-coaster ride at times but never dull. I have learnt much about what it takes to be successful at the highest level, and much about coping with failure and fighting back. My sincerest hope is that the reading will be as enjoyable as the writing.

Alison Kervin, August 2005

SECTION ONE

Chapter One

The Legacy

'If you think you can do a thing or think you can't do a thing, you're right.' **Henry Ford**

The drive up to Pennyhill Park Hotel is long and winding, the route adorned by freshly mown borders, artfully planted daffodils and immaculately pruned rhododendron bushes. It's like some fairytale driveway to a magical castle where wishes come true and dreams are realised. On the right is the golf course, on the left a rugby pitch, partially hidden, but the huge H posts are visible above the neat bushes, redwood trees and chestnut-tree saplings. Inside, the hotel offers a spa area where players can receive recuperative treatments – massages, ice baths and steam – and a gym, designed with the England rugby team's precise needs in mind. Even the restaurant staff are aware of the specific requirements of modern, international players. They understand the complicated six meals a day eating habits and have designed menus around the food lists provided to them by England nutritionists. So many egg-white omelettes are made in this place that they have started buying egg whites in tubs, ready prepared. Prior to that, some poor soul in the kitchen spent most of his working life separating the whites from the yolks.

Then there's the pitch, where horses once roamed, positioned by the entrance to the hotel. The pitch was developed by Keith Kent, the head groundsman at Twickenham, and built by the same team who laid the Twickenham turf. It's in immaculate condition and used only by the

England team. Players don't have to leave the hotel grounds for rugby training now – just a few steps from bed and they're there. It's perfect. Who ever thought of putting a full-sized pitch in the 120-acre grounds of a luxury hotel? Sir Clive Ronald Woodward.

I'm on my way to have dinner with Clive at this hotel, which symbolises everything about his tenure as England coach, and much about the man. Even the slightly fantastical, mythical appeal of the hotel has something of Clive about it. There are so many tales about him – like the time he moved the entire England team, locks, props and barrel, from the Holiday Inn's Garden Court Motel in Newlands to the Pink Palace, one of the most glamorous hotels in South Africa. He made the move when England were on tour in 1998 because he didn't think the one they were in was good enough even though it was selected by their hosts. The Lions team had stayed there the previous year but such detail held no interest for the new England coach. The hotel wasn't good enough, so he moved the team. He paid for the extravagance on his own credit card, and almost with his job.

In the lead up to the 2003 World Cup, his determination to have the absolute best for his men reached fevered heights. He established that the one thing missing at Pennyhill Park was somewhere close to the pitch in which to store the team's equipment. Woodward asked the RFU for more money to fund it. 'We can't haul the equipment up to the pitch every time we want to train. We're wasting time,' he said. There are many things you could accuse Clive of, but being a time-waster is not one of them.

The RFU's refusal did not mark the end of the line, but the beginning of a new one. This is a common theme. Nothing marks the end of the line if you want the prize enough. It's just a matter of creative thinking. Clive spoke to Frank McCartney on this occasion. McCartney is an old friend from London Irish. He's the man who used to organise all the catering (and, significantly, catering marquees) at the club. McCartney took the call, heard the request and smiled to himself at the cheek of the man. Within days he had arranged for a large marquee to stand next to the rugby pitch. The players no longer had to haul all the equipment up to it. Precious time and effort were saved. The marquee was so huge that they laid out an entire gym inside it. The players were in that gym by 7 a.m. every morning in the run-up to the World Cup – throwing heavy weights around as loud music pumped out, disturbing the tranquility of this rural idyll. It is these little details that matter. Detail, detail, detail. Finding an edge and doing things as well as you can. Never compromising. Every 1 per cent increase is a per cent worth having.

When Clive wanted Dave Campbell, the chef at the hotel, to accompany the team to the World Cup, the RFU refused to pay. They said it was a personnel demand too far. The England coach thought they were being shortsighted. He thought they didn't fully appreciate the complexities of managing an élite sports team. He wanted the chef on tour, so he got him, persuading Uncle Ben's Rice to pay for Campbell's trip.

Clive grew used to getting his own way. He became immensely adept at the political manœuvring and out-manœuvring that so frequently separates the intelligent and well-meaning from the successful. His method with England was to alter the very fabric of the team. He took a group of fantastically talented players and made them think differently. He altered their approach, their expectations and even their shirts. He appointed cultural architects within the team to help him build his successful side, and recruited experts from business and across sport to help him develop the elusive winning mentality.

He worked hard over seven years to transform the national side. Then he moved on to coach the Lions – a peripatetic workforce with whom he had just ten days' training. He raised expectations and worked to create the winning mentality but to no avail. The result was three defeats. Clive simply couldn't play to any of his strengths. With the benefit of hindsight, he should not have taken on the role. His greatest successes have come when he has had maximum exposure to players. Clive, by his own admission, is not a charismatic, 'charge in and make a million alterations on the first day' sort of coach. He needs time and likes to make substantial changes to every area of the team. His greatest successes came in club rugby where he had twice-weekly access to players. This bodes well for his role at Southampton Football Club, where he will see the players every day, but means he was never going to be able to perform at his best on the Lions tour.

Woodward walked away from his job as head coach of the England rugby team for a number of reasons, but mainly because he felt he didn't have enough time with the players. Why, then, would he take on the Lions? It was madness for him to have tried, but he was flattered by the offer and lured by the prospect of trying to achieve the impossible.

You need talent and time to win in rugby. He had both with England, and was willing to go to extraordinary lengths to succeed. Soon after he started as national coach, the RFU dithered over the buying of four rugby league players that he wanted in his squad. Clive rushed home and announced that he would like to remortgage the house to buy them himself. Those close to him have lost count of the number of times he has suggested remortgaging his family home to fund some project to give England 'the edge'.

When the RFU refused to pay for the computer programme developed by Sherylle Calder, the visual awareness coach who became the unprecedented final member of the coaching dream team, Clive paid for it himself. Unlike the hotel-swapping scenario, he never got the money back. It doesn't seem to bother him too much. Financial benefit is not his primary motivator. It's fascinating to consider what is – perhaps prestige, control, power. Perhaps he's still trying to prove, to no one who can hear him, that the little boy sent away to boarding school is worth something.

Clive is a few minutes late for our meeting. This, in itself, presents an unusual state of affairs. Clive prides himself on his punctuality, forcing the team to adopt 'Lombardi Time' – always arrive everywhere ten minutes early. Vince Lombardi, the legendary coach of the Green Bay Packers American football team, is one of the many men from whom Clive takes inspiration and ideas. Central to Lombardi's coaching ethos was an insistence that players should conduct themselves respectfully at all times and they should strive for perfect execution. He would demand 'obedience, dedication and 110 per cent effort' from them. The Green Bay Packers were American football's perpetual losers when Lombardi took over as head coach, aged forty-five. They'd won just one game in the previous year but he told them, 'If you obey my rules and use my methods, I will make you a championship side.'

Three years later, they won the National Football League championship. During his nine-year reign, they had nine winning seasons. They won six division titles, five NFL titles and two SuperBowls. He did things differently. He once changed his players' jersey numbers before a game to confuse his opponents, the Chicago Bears. Clive followed this strategy as he sought to encourage his players to play fifteen-man rugby and not rely on their shirt numbers to direct their input and role in matches.

In 1998, a year after starting as England coach, Clive travelled to America to take a look at how two American football clubs organised themselves. He spent time with Colorado University and Denver Broncos, and these set-ups inspired him to think differently about rugby. 'It opened Clive's eyes,' says England defence coach, Phil Larder. 'Clive saw how the Broncos' coach delegated to specialists in various areas. That's the approach Clive has brought to England so successfully.' He returned from Denver and changed his job title to 'head coach' to mimic several American football teams (Lombardi was always called head coach). The RFU should be grateful that he didn't call himself 'Executive Vice President of Football Operations', a title rejoiced in by Mike Shanahan of Denver Broncos.

I sit by the fire to wait for the former Executive Vice President of Rugby Operations (you must admit – it does have a certain ring to it). The doormen hustle and bustle around, lugging bags and assisting guests. I am carrying a pile of notebooks with 'Clive Woodward notes', 'Clive Woodward – childhood', 'Clive – the England Years' written on the covers. It wouldn't take a genius to work out why I'm here. One of the porters spots me and rushes over.

'He's in the bar – shall I get him?' he asks.

'There's no rush,' I reply. 'Perhaps you could just tell him I'm here.'

A few minutes later, Andy Robinson, the current England coach, heaves into view, speed walking through reception like one of those cartoon characters with fast-spinning wheels for legs. He is being followed by a member of the public, who is clutching a tatty, dog-eared piece of paper and a pen. He proffers the paper towards Robinson's fast-retreating back, while a young boy chases at his heels. There's no chance that he's going to catch Robinson and get the autograph he wants unless he starts running, which of course, he doesn't want to do.

This is a peculiarly English scene. The man does not want to draw attention or make a nuisance of himself by shouting. What if Robinson won't give him an autograph? He'll look a complete lemon if he runs after him only to be turned down. So he walks fast but in a self-conscious way, like a man rushing to catch a train but not wanting anyone to know that's what he's doing – slowing down as the train pulls out, nonchalantly sauntering along the platform and flicking open his newspaper as if he didn't really want to catch it anyway. In America, they'd throw their briefcases in the air in fury and shout unashamedly at the departing train. The Englishman carefully looks around to check no one has seen him and waits patiently for the next train to arrive. The man in pursuit of Robinson is not prepared to raise his voice or run, so the little boy does not get his autograph.

This trait of avoiding embarrassment at all costs and seeking to avoid failure, or even the appearance of any kind of failure, is something that Clive rails against. If you are directed by the need to avoid failure, you become risk-averse and predictable – the two enemies of success. The willingness to fail, upset people or make himself look ridiculous in pursuit of victory is a key part of Clive's make-up, and his ability to make that understood by all who controlled his destiny at the RFU was a key part of England's World Cup victory.

Clive took huge risks, as player, coach and businessman. He played out his tenure as England coach like a man who wasn't afraid of anything. He says he learnt more from the failures than he did from the victories. He was risk-embracing and even under the most pounding criticism, he stayed true to his beliefs. Sure, defeat hurt but he didn't ever believe that the failures made *him* a failure. That is a crucial difference between Clive and the other dozens of coaches who either resign or are sacked every four years as their teams fail to come up to scratch in the World Cup.

Losing is important. Surrounding yourself with people who believe in you despite the defeats, and learn from them with you, is a huge factor in eventual victory. Consider this – the top ten richest Americans have failed at least three times in business. Head-hunters in the USA today look for signs of business failure as an indication of ambition, drive and determination. The new policy in the US is to leave names, addresses and education details off curriculum vitae because they can lead to prejudice. What employers are looking for is 'balls' – the ability to make mistakes, learn from them and bounce back. It doesn't matter where you were educated or what your name is – will you take the tough decisions? Will you risk everything in pursuit of greatness with intelligence, conviction and consistency?

If you look at the heads of businesses at the top of the Fortune 1000 companies in the United States in 2004, over 80 per cent have failed in their careers at least once. The adage in the USA is 'you don't fail forever'. In the UK, the temptation is to think that people are either successes or failures whereas the truth is that the great successes are usually bouncing back from failure. To achieve the winning mindset you need to have experienced failure but there's a real fear of failure in this country. In the United States, one in ten people attempt to set up their own business. In Australia, it's one in twelve. In the UK, it's one in thirty-four. Why?

'It's all down to fear of failure,' says Adrian Atkinson, leading business psychologist.

'Quite simply, fear of failure,' echoes Steve Bull, psychologist to the England cricket team and British Olympic team.

There's a stigma associated with failure. Everyone's heard stories about the businessman sitting in the park all day with his briefcase rather than confess to his family or peer group that he has been made redundant, so great is his shame about what has happened.

'In the US, business failure is seen as a necessary part of learning and subsequent success,' says business speaker and television presenter René Carayol. 'American entrepreneurs tend to see their personal standing rise after a business failure, provided they learn from their mistakes. A failure is more a Purple Heart.'

Clive doesn't entertain the notion of 'fear of failure'. In the pursuit of victory, he never stops to consider the impact or implications of defeat. The Lions tour is the most obvious example. A million questions spring to mind. Why did he do it? Why not carve out a successful and lucrative career on the public-speaking circuit? Why not sit back and advise others instead of throwing himself into the arena again? Clive could have been held up forever as the man who won the World Cup. Why on earth risk his reputation on an unlikely expedition to New Zealand? Probably because a reputation is worth nothing if it cannot stand up to the onslaught of fresh challenges. What about being made to look a fool if he lost? Clive makes no plans based on an assumption that he will lose.

Well, Clive lost in New Zealand and he looked a fool. It's not the first time. He's looked foolish before and if he keeps challenging himself, he's bound to look foolish again. Unless you consider temporary foolishness to be a small price to pay for victory, you should probably leave the arena.

Clive did losing before he did winning as well as after, which is often forgotten, given the Webb Ellis trophy, the knighthood and the public adulation. In fact, he did quite a lot of losing before winning. He says now, with the benefit of hindsight and a little time for sober reflection, that those defeats helped him to win the World Cup. The tour to hell of 1998? The back-to-back Grand Slam defeats? 'We wouldn't have won the World Cup without them.'

Remember 1999 when Clive's confident prediction 'judge me on the World Cup' was blown into a million pieces? The tournament was being held in Britain and France for the first time since 1991, the year in which England had come so close to victory that the mere mention of the final match against Australia – in which they threw it all away – still sends shivers down the spines of all those Englishmen who competed. The tournament in 1999 was to be payback time. The first professional tournament with professional players and coaches was to be England's moment in the sun. Their coach had as much as promised us that, but on a sunny day in Paris in the quarter-final, South Africa's fly-half booted drop goal after drop goal, and England's World Cup dreams crashed.

A million Englishmen dropped their shoulders and sank their faces into their pints, miserable beyond compare. Forget 1966 and all that – England had never won the rugby World Cup. At least football fans had the memories of Geoff Hurst and Bobby Moore to console them. For the rugby fraternity, it was more like 1999 years of hurt.

I wrote a feature covering the back page of *The Times*, screaming 'Woodward Should Go'. I thought he should. Others did, too. He seemed to have alienated himself, and didn't seem to be fronting up to what had happened. He'd demanded and demanded with the promise of success and it had all come to nothing. But while those like me were wondering about this man at the helm of the England team, the man himself was having his finest moment. He was showing quite brilliant leadership qualities.

'The team were feeling terrible, but Clive stood in front of them and told them how well they'd done,' recalls Humphrey Walters, the management expert retained by Clive to help work with the team. 'He praised them, said how proud he was of them and that this was the beginning. They were to forget about 1999 and begin thinking about 2003. He told them they would win the next World Cup. He said this defeat marked the beginning of something great for English rugby. I've never heard him give a speech like it and to this day I don't know how he did it. He must have been feeling awful, but he managed to rise above it and in that moment the seeds for 2003 were sown. I watched and thought, "He's done it. He's completely turned them round." I knew in that moment that England would win the next World Cup.'

When it comes to defining what makes someone great, the ability to turn adversity to strength, to overcome defeat and continue the search for victory must be high up there. You simply can't avoid defeat and any efforts to do so will hamper your progress. You have to deal with it. Victory is the ultimate definer, but on the road to victory lie all manner of hurdles and locked gates. If you can bounce back from defeat as sure-footedly as Clive did, there is a good chance that you will overcome most of them.

We sit in the far corner of the restaurant and pick up the menu. Clive orders a salmon starter and Caesar salad. I had lunch with Clive once and he had a ham sandwich. I'm not sure why I remember that but, as a writer, one is inclined to note down all the details – just in case you need them. A friend, also a writer, had previously been at a function with Clive at which he had a ham sandwich. A straw poll of Clive's luncheon companions revealed that he always has a ham sandwich. 'It's a work thing,' he says. Ham sandwiches are triggers. He's big on things like that – keeping himself in a work mindset, doing everything to stop himself being distracted. He makes a clear delineation between work and play – an almost cruel delineation, as many of the players found out. He is uncomfortable when the thin line separating the two becomes smudged. When he's working, he opts for functionality over extravagance. The 'most expensive champagne you have' moments come when the work is done.

'Did you enjoy your childhood?' I ask. I'm intrigued by this question, because everyone I talk to seems to recall Clive, even when he was young, as being 'mature beyond his years' and 'an old head on young shoulders'. People recall a seriousness and world-weariness even in the young boy. I wonder whether his recollections of childhood are different.

He smiles and looks down at the menu in a manner that says, 'Wow – don't get too close and personal.' Clive has an interesting body language. If you ask him questions about business, rugby, management or leadership, he looks you straight in the eye and answers you with authority and knowledge. His shoulders are back and his chin is up. This is not arrogance – it's confidence. He's on safe ground in a results-orientated world of facts and figures. Ask him about his personal life and his body language closes in.

As an interviewer, I have watched body language closely – sometimes the unspoken reaction to a question has a clarity and eloquence that the spoken word does not. Once the body language changes – the arms fold, the legs cross and the eyes flit to the side – I back off. There is no point in pursuing a line of questioning that closes the interviewee down. What is unusual about Clive and distinct from all the other people I've interviewed (except Prince Edward, who has spookily similar traits in this respect) is that he closes down at the mere mention of anything remotely personal. He feels instantly uncomfortable.

When Humphrey Walters first began working with England, he asked Clive to fill out a simple questionnaire in order to determine what personality type he was. The questionnaire identified three primary social motives – the need to achieve, the need for affiliation and the need for influence. Guess which two motivated Clive the most? Yep – the need for achievement and the need for influence.

The personality type indicated by this is someone with a 'low need to form friendships. This may cause this person to be seen as "hard" and not interested in people. Achieving results is satisfying for them and getting others to achieve results is also satisfying. They are often successful, although subordinates may find them difficult people to get to know because of their relatively low interest in developing close personal relationships.'

Although Clive undoubtedly has many intense, close personal relationships – not least with his wife, Jayne, and family – one of the common themes in the Woodward story is Clive's ability to end relationships quite suddenly when something happens that he doesn't like. The 'somethings', usually business situations that most people would consider rather minor, appear to wound Clive to such an extent that he cuts all ties with the person immediately, in some cases after friendships that have lasted over a decade. He allows previously close friendships to disintegrate rather than address the issues and try to come to some sort of understanding.

Steve Holdstock was once an extremely close friend of Clive's. They spent a lot of time together in Sydney and Steve worked for Clive's business when the two came back from Australia. As Clive's business grew, Steve began to feel isolated. He was based in the Midlands instead of in the south with the rest of the sales force, and he thought he was no longer playing a key part in the firm. So he decided to leave and set up his own company and some of the contacts he had made went with him. This is, of course, a traditionally sticky point between parting employee and employer. Even hairdressers are barred from taking clients from one salon to the next – it's the clients who make the choice. Clients follow hairdressers, solicitors and public relations experts, and they follow salesmen, too. Holdstock insists that the clients who joined him in his new company wanted to work with him because he'd formed good relationships with them. Clearly this is Holdstock's version of events. Clive would not be drawn to comment.

'Not a day goes by when I don't think of him. I really loved the guy,' says Holdstock. 'I think he would be amazed if he knew how much he hurt me. He can make people do anything for him and feel they are part of his world. Then he suddenly drops them if something goes wrong. It can really hurt. I still feel he's a fantastic person, but he does have this ability to cut people off.'

Is this because of Clive's motivation – achievement rather than friendship? If the friendship challenges Clive's ability to achieve, the friend goes.

Clive worked at Rank Xerox in Leicester and Fuji Xerox in Sydney for a while. His boss there, Alan King, also found himself cut out of the picture when a business decision went wrong. 'I didn't speak to Clive for years because of it. He just wouldn't have anything to do with me. Then I heard he was moving back to England from Sydney, so I called him to see if he fancied a beer before going. He didn't.'

Clive has a reputation for not being able to forgive and forget easily but, at the same time, and with considerable foundation, for absolute loyalty. If you are in his camp, you are truly in his camp. Ann Heaver has worked for Clive for the last fifteen years. After meeting him in Australia, she came back to England and has worked for him in various capacities, latterly as his personal assistant. She describes Clive as 'a fantastic friend' and cites many examples of times when he has been a huge personal strength to her.

'He has been there for me through some pretty difficult times, including the death of my parents and the break-up of my marriage. He's part of our family and I feel like I'm part of his.'

Lawrence Dallaglio was the most public and obvious recipient of Clive's unswerving loyalty. When the former England captain fell foul of the *News of the World* for telling the paper's reporters that he had been involved with drugs on the 1997 Lions tour, his life was in tatters. His girlfriend had just given birth and was struggling with sleepless nights while he was front and back of all the newspapers and followed everywhere by reporters and photographers. He denied that he had actually taken drugs and continues to deny this. That was enough for Clive. The England coach stepped in to offer support. The finest lawyers were marshalled, including the late, magnificently flamboyant George Carman QC, and Clive offered a safe retreat and all the help he could to Dallaglio and his young family. He never stopped to doubt, he just acted with a kindness and fervour that Dallaglio will remember for the rest of his life.

Contrast this with the story of Richard Cockerill, who was dropped immediately and without explanation when he wrote a book about life within the England team. Cockerill's fairly low-profile book, which he claims was an honest insight into life with England, seems a far lesser 'crime' than Lawrence's high-profile sex, drugs and rock'n'roll headline-grabbing tour stories. To the outside world, the effects of the Cockerill story were as nothing compared to the devastating effects of the Dallaglio escapade. Understanding why Clive backed the captain and not the hooker is key to understanding how Clive's mind works.

In Clive's view, Dallaglio let *himself* down by lying to reporters, who were pretending to be marketing managers from Gillette, when he told them colourful tales about what he got up to on tour. What Cockerill did was unforgivable – he let *the team* down. By betraying the trust of his team-mates when he wrote his book, he broke the most important rule of all.

Cynics might say that the only reason Clive backed Dallaglio so passionately and with such conviction was that Dallaglio was an invaluable player and Clive needed him in the team. Cockerill was not in the same position. Whether this had any impact on his thinking or not, there is no doubt that Clive feels passionately about the bonds that bind a team. The Royal Marines, who welcomed Clive and the team to Lympstone in 1999, just before the World Cup, to undertake leadership and team-building tasks, recall a man very keen on the concepts of teamship and loyalty.

'When he first came down to Lympstone to have a look round, we talked to him about the buddy-buddy system,' says Lt Col George Matthews RM. 'Once he heard about that, you could see by the look in his eye that he was interested. He found the concept very appealing.'

The buddy-buddy system is the set-up whereby soldiers look after each other as much as they look after themselves.

'If you're in Norway, for example, when it's minus twenty-five, you have to check your buddy's ears to make sure he's not getting frost-bitten. If he gets frost-bitten and loses an ear, it's your fault,' says Matthews. 'That's the level of responsibility that guys in our teams have. Your responsibility is to your buddy and that spins out to your section and the troop. The buddy-buddy system was what Clive wanted to instil in the squad. At the end of eighty minutes of rugby, he wanted them to be able to look each other in the eye and say, "I did everything I possibly could." I think he liked that mindset. He went to a military school, didn't he? Wasn't his father in the military?'

Clive still hasn't answered me. 'Did you enjoy childhood?' I ask again. He looks out of the large glass windows behind me.

'I enjoyed the early part,' he says, with a half-smile. 'I was very happy then.'

Chapter Two

Early learning

---

*'None of us are born equal ... rather we are born unequal ...
some of us are born with an inherent and competitive drive.'*
Vince Lombardi

Clive remembers the sun-dappled fields outside his home in Yorkshire
most of all. The beautiful garden backed on to endless rolling grass
fields where he would run around with his football from early in the
morning until late at night. Clive was eleven years old when he went to
live on the RAF base at Linton-on-Ouse with his parents, his elder
sister, Linda, and younger brother, Colin.

The Woodwards' house, 24 The Paddock, was built at the end of the
landing strip and planes would come in low over the roof as they
descended. Clive would pick up his ball and look up at the trainee
pilots. His father, Flight Lieutenant Ronald William Woodward, trained
naval officers to fly Chipmunk planes. The trainee pilots always waved
at the little boy with the ball and the little boy waved back. Clive
remembers a happy time, running around outside, living 'an ideal life'
full of community spirit, fun and adventure. There were lots of children
to play with and all the fun of being on a big airbase in the North Yorkshire countryside.

By the time they arrived in Yorkshire, the family had already moved
house twice – such is the curse and adventure of life in the services.
Clive was born 200 miles away from Linton-on-Ouse, on 6 January
1956, in the RAF hospital, Ely, in Cambridgeshire. Clive's father was
then a Flight Sergeant (equivalent to Sergeant Major in the Army)
serving at RAF Ely. From their East Midlands base, the family moved

to Edinburgh where Clive began his schooling at Corstorphine Junior School. Ronald Woodward was promoted to Flight Lieutenant in 1962 and, in 1967, the family moved to Linton-on-Ouse where he took up his role as a Master Pilot Instructor and Clive began his senior school education in nearby Easingwold Grammar, just a bus ride away. It was a large, sporty place where Clive's love of football was encouraged and developed. He adored it.

By the time Clive started at Easingwold, football totally dominated his life. He had never played rugby – the sport had not even registered on his radar. The England stars of the time – Geoff Hurst, Bobby Moore, Alan Ball and especially Martin Peters, who played in midfield like Clive – absorbed the youngster's thoughts and figured in his dreams. They formed the cornerstone of his fantasies. Their pictures filled his walls and his mind – constantly. He recalls an unusually tender moment with his father when England won the 1966 World Cup final, the year before they headed for Yorkshire. He remembers seeing his father shrug off the constraints of his office and rush out into the garden – leaping around and dancing in celebration of the World Cup victory over Germany. He recalls everyone rushing out of their houses and hugging each other. He remembers the joy that the victory brought and the closeness to his father that the victory engendered. His overriding aim, over thirty years later, when he took charge of the England rugby team, was 'to inspire the nation'. Certainly, one of the seeds of the dream was sown on that happy day in 1966 when he hugged his father and ran out into the streets in sheer delight.

In September 1967, Gerry Kershaw was a rather nervous twenty-one year-old trainee physical education teacher, starting at Easingwold Grammar. He was a football and rugby league specialist, drawn to the school because of its impressive sporting reputation. His first day was also the day that a thin young boy called Clive Woodward arrived.

'You arrive at a new school and hope you'll spot some great new talent, but I suppose you don't really expect to. Then this scrawny eleven-year-old kid comes along. He was a real bright light in the sporting section of the school. Anything he touched, he succeeded in.

He was just so good at everything. You had the feeling that anything he wanted to do, he could do and would be successful at. If he'd taken up rowing, I'm sure he'd have been good at that. But Clive loved football and that's what he did. He was extremely talented.'

Malcolm Milne was also a PE teacher at the school. He remembers the eleven-year-old coming to the Under-13s football group practices: 'It was easy to see that he stood out. He had class, balance and pace. He was like Ian Botham, someone with real flair. He was a natural. Everything about him was a class or two higher than the rest. I had him in my side for a year and he had real talent.'

Away from the football field, the recollections are of a well-mannered, confident boy, although he was quite quiet and something of a loner. He would always do as he was told. Academically, he was nothing out of the ordinary – in the second stream for most subjects.

'Competent, but he didn't shine academically,' says Bill Bell, head of PE. 'He had a few close friends but wasn't in any of the gangs. He spent most of his time playing soccer. He was a mature boy.'

Bell coached the Under-15s side. 'I remember an occasion when one of the players was unavailable for a Cup match, so I put young Woodward in, even though he was two age groups down. I remember that he didn't look out of place. He shone, in fact. He had confidence about him, verging on arrogance. He wasn't like the other country lads at all. He always had an old head on young shoulders. The lad was a hell of a player. He oozed class. He was just very, very talented.' Bell remembers Clive's parents coming to watch him on the football field. 'His father was proud of him, always watching him play. He seemed really to enjoy it.'

That recollection is interesting, given that Clive spent just two years at Easingwold Grammar before being moved to a military boarding school, HMS *Conway*, in North Wales. Clive is sure that the move happened precisely because of his father's wish to suppress his interest in football, and to urge him to focus on the academic side of school life. Clive's banishment to HMS *Conway* at the age of thirteen caused a rift in his relationship with his father that was never properly mended. Perhaps it is worth knowing a little more about Clive's father.

Ronald William Woodward was born in Battersea in 1925. He was fourteen when the Second World War broke out and he enlisted in the Royal Air Force in 1942, halfway through the war, aged just seventeen. He saw active combat and remained with the Force until 1949 when, aged twenty-four, he was moved to the reserve (the part of the RAF not committed to immediate action in military engagement). In December 1950, Woodward Senior re-enlisted in the Royal Air Force and rose through the ranks. In 1956, the year of Clive's birth, he became an officer, appointed to a permanent commission as a Pilot Officer.

This promotion had social as well as career implications. Woodward was forging a successful career, having been made an officer at the age of thirty-one. To win such a commission in the RAF in the 1950s with little education, no privileged background and having joined the ranks as a teenager, was a massive achievement. The commission would redefine his life and the lives of his family. Their standing in the community was vastly improved, their accommodation and income raised to match. They would have officer housing, be invited to officers' functions and have a life markedly different from that of a non-commissioned family.

The promotion put Ronald Woodward into daily contact with influential men. Many of those with whom he mixed as an officer had far more privileged backgrounds. There are no precise figures relating to what percentage of RAF officers in the 1950s had degrees, but in 1968, RAF policy stated that all permanent officers must have degrees. Based on that evidence, the RAF Information Department officials say, 'It would be safe to conclude that there were very, very few officers who did not have higher education degrees. Those without them must have shown exceptional promise.'

Woodward Senior had been on the front line when he was a teenager and had risen to the rank of Squadron Leader by the time Clive was fifteen. He wanted a better life for his children.

The Woodwards were not a large extended family. Clive has met neither his maternal nor paternal grandparents. 'I don't know quite what happened there,' he says. 'I just never met any grandparents. There was always the five of us.' Until he met his wife, Jayne, he did not have a clear sense of how the layers of a family work together, or even how they define themselves. Concepts such as cousins, nephews, aunts and uncles were meaningless.

The family travelled around a lot when Clive was younger, making new friends at each new base, then upping sticks and moving on. It was a peripatetic lifestyle without the anchors most families have. The small details of family history, the blood that binds a family to its own despite geography or social positioning, those were all missing as the five of them moved from base to base with none of the children aware of why no other relatives were introduced or were part of their lives.

In early 1969, aged thirteen, Clive was presented with a fantastic opportunity. Scouts from Everton would be visiting the school to watch an Under-15s football match in which he had been selected to play. Scouts from York City often attended the school's games but it was unheard of for an Everton scout to descend on them. Clive was playing above his age group in the match, so he knew that if he played his best, he would be sure to impress them.

Clive recalls that he turned up for the match full of excitement and prepared to dazzle. He wanted a career in football and thought this might provide him with his route to the big time. In the event, he never heard what the scout thought of him. He would never know whether his boyish dreams of running out in front of a packed Goodison Park could have come true because, while he was playing, his father had a chat with Robin Gilbert, the school's headmaster, about Clive's progress. Gilbert told Flight Lieutenant Woodward that his son was bright but not applying himself academically because of his fascination with football. Gilbert suggested that Clive would struggle at school if his academic ambitions did not take precedence over his sporting ambitions. These words stuck in the mind of Woodward Senior, and he began to fear that his son might throw away his education on a distant dream, a whim. For Flight Lieutenant Woodward, determined that his children should attend university, this was a risk he could not take.

A few days later, Woodward found himself sitting next to the Commanding Officer in the base canteen. He shared his fears for his son with his CO and, in the interests of offering a real solution, the Commanding Officer made a suggestion that changed the course of Clive's life. He suggested that Ronald might send his son to HMS *Conway*, the military boarding school that he had attended. It was a rigorous, disciplined establishment where they would actively encourage the boy's academic development. When he explained that Woodward need not be out of pocket because it would all be paid for as part of his officer's benefits, a plan was hatched. Clive was summoned by his father and told the news – he would go to a non-football-playing boarding school in a remote part of North Wales. Clive was devastated. By taking football away from him, his father was denying him the one thing he loved more than any other.

Even years later, Clive still regrets the decision his father made. 'Not knowing how the football would have turned out is something that will always be with me, and something that clearly has had a major effect on developing my character,' he says.

In Clive's thirteen-year-old mind, the move to HMS *Conway* was a dreadful blow because it was inextricably linked with the denial to him of football, a game that he adored, but it had more implications than that. It prevented him from enjoying not just football, but also a normal family life. He would be the only one to be sent away. While his brother and sister were allowed to grow up at home, Clive spent his formative years at a cold, austere boarding school in North Wales.

Dr Adrian Atkinson is a clinical and business psychologist. His forte is identifying 'stars' in an organisation, men and women whose talents are quite extraordinary. 'There are certain core traits that all entrepreneurs have,' he says, 'and usually things have happened in their backgrounds to develop these traits.

Being "sent away" is a hugely traumatic experience. I have worked with lots of people who struggle throughout their lives to come to terms with the fact that they were sent away from home. Of course, boarding school can provide great memories for many children, but if they are sent against their will, the consequences are there, later in life. We are all walking wounded, to one extent or another. Perhaps the fact that Clive had no other close relatives to talk to would not have helped him in this situation – just his father and mother, and they appeared to be rejecting him.'

Others at Easingwold are surprised at this news. Gerry Kershaw in particular expresses a degree of confusion. He thought he knew Clive quite well. He also thought he knew Robin Gilbert, having worked with the headmaster for many years and known him for thirty-eight (Kershaw spent his entire career at the school he joined as a callow twenty-one-year old). He is quite shocked to discover what happened.

'We were all told that he left when he was thirteen because his father had a new post and was moving from the area. There was great disappointment. Linda, his elder sister, had just finished her A Levels and went off to university, so we assumed that it was an appropriate time for his father to get a new posting.'

It may seem pointless to examine and analyse the detail and implications of events that took place over thirty-five years ago, but it is essential to understanding Clive's absolute determination to be a success. The effect of going to HMS *Conway* believing that he had been sent there specifically to deny him the thing he most loved had a massive effect on him and has been crucial in the development of his character. It was a landmark moment.

I refer at this point to the words of Edward Hallett Carr. He is the historian whose slim book *What Is History?* ruined my teenage years. His philosophical and analytical approach to the concept of historical study was highly advocated by my father, while his daughter's view of A Level history was that one should learn the bare bones as speedily as possible without elevating oneself to debate or analysis of any description.

Carr writes: 'It used to be said that facts speak for themselves. This is, of course, untrue ... a fact is like a sack – it won't stand up until you've put something in it. The only reason we are interested to know that the battle was fought at Hastings in 1066 is that historians regard it as a major historical event.'

So whether Clive went to one school or another is of no great importance *per se*. It is given importance because of Clive's reaction to it. Clive has 'put something in' to this fact. He has used his sending away to boarding school while his brother and sister were allowed to stay at home as a huge motivator. It was a life-changing moment – the day he became independent and strong, forced to rely on himself and his own quick thinking and make the absolute best of every situation he was in.

Adrian Atkinson says, 'It seems that Clive's belief that he was sent away to boarding school because his father did not want him to play football led to all manner of psychological issues, such as anger, hostility and feelings of rejection and failure, which could leave him searching for the love and acceptance that he never felt he had as a child. These feelings of rejection and failure provide a fertile ground for the development of characteristics that lead to success. In fact, if someone says to me, as they often do, "What do most successful people have?" I would say precisely those feelings at exactly that age.'

Do all successful people have damaged backgrounds?

'Not all, but the vast majority do. There's usually something in their past that has left them feeling a need to prove themselves time and again.'

In Yorkshire, Gerry Kershaw went on to become a senior rugby league referee long after Clive's departure, which brought the two men back into contact with one another. 'I turned up to referee a match at Warrington and found I'd been banned from the boardroom,' says Kershaw. 'I had no idea why and was quite put out. It seemed to be very rude. No one else appeared to be barred from there. I went to see the chairman and complained, but they wouldn't let me in the room.' He remembered the incident for a long time and took it as a personal slight. It coloured his view of Warrington and led him to pen a series of angry messages to the chairman, protesting at his treatment by the club officials.

Years later, Clive went back to Easingwold to open a new cricket pavilion. In casual conversation, Kershaw asked his former pupil whether he'd ever been tempted to play rugby league. Clive admitted that yes, he had. He confessed that the day in Warrington on which

Kershaw had been banned from the boardroom was because Clive was in there negotiating a move to league that never came off. Rugby union was an amateur sport at the time, and any transgression of the amateur regulations, such as being seen at a rugby league club, was not tolerated. Clive had glanced in the match-day programme, seen Kershaw's name down as referee and, knowing that Gerry would recognise him instantly, told club officials. They thought it best to hide Clive away. The obvious place to hide him? The boardroom.

Chapter Three

Return to the legacy

'Silly things do cease to be silly if they are done by sensible people in an impudent way.' **Jane Austen**

Clive settles himself at the dinner table in Pennyhill Park Hotel's restaurant. He removes his cream jacket and takes his mobile phone from his inside top pocket. 'Excuse me,' he says, as he places the garment neatly over a chair at the next table. He looks down at his phone, which is flashing away in his hands. The reluctance is tangible. To answer that little device's bleeping sirens, as we all know, is to engage oneself in a series of questions and problems that one simply need not engage oneself in. Don't play the messages. He decides, to my relief, not to answer it.

Clive adjusts his shirt, pulling the shoulders up and back where the weight of his recently removed jacket had flattened them. He's not wearing a tie today, which is somehow significant. Out of the tentacle-like grips of the Rugby Football Union and the International Rugby Board, and he's already shrugged off that most traditional aspect of male attire.

It's unusual to see him tie-less. Clive has always embraced the sartorial symbols of the businessman. He was keen to mould himself in that image. The early photographs of him arriving to manage the England rugby team in his neat suits always jarred. We'd been used to seeing the nation's sporting coaches chewing gum in the dug-outs. He looked more like a man planning to spend his day stamping tickets at the local library and relieving flustered mothers of 10p for the late return of their children's Harry Potter books than a man planning to turn the

England rugby team into the greatest in the world.

With his owlish glasses and a sensible haircut, which grew shorter as his time in office grew longer until he finished his England management tenure with less hair on his head than Jonny Wilkinson has on his chin, he looked like a successful building society manager. The image was emphasised by his smart but inoffensive attire, the slightly wonky smile, the dimpled chin and look of utter concentration at all times. He dispensed with the glasses but the severity remained. His shoes always shined, his shirt was always ironed. He wore cuff links, for God's sake. Cuff links! Who ever heard of cuff links outside banks, legal firms and small, suburban estate agents?

Clive's drive to dress well has not always stood him in good stead in his career. When he went to work at the NatWest bank in Richmond as an eager eighteen-year-old, he wore a tweed suit, much to the amusement of his smartly dressed colleagues. Then, when he went to work in Australia, he swung completely the other way, turning up for his first morning at Fuji Xerox wearing a wool suit and silk tie in an office full of sun-tanned men dressed in short-sleeved shirts and flip-flops. Clive was forced to accept that the new environment in which he found himself demanded new and different attire. He tempered his sartorial tastes and, at one stage, rather curiously turned his office into an Hawaiian hut in order to encourage those who worked for him to indulge in a little playfulness as he disguised the fact that his sales targets for them were throat-clutchingly ambitious. He, of course, matched his Hawaiian hut by wearing the required flowery shirts.

When Clive took over as manager of the England rugby team, he immediately insisted upon raising the awareness level among players and managers of their conduct in public. Players and management should be appropriately attired. The definition of 'appropriately' was clearly explained by Clive, as was everything else, in the documents, emails and, most significantly, the 'bible' that England players were presented with as a rite of passage upon selection.

Clive has always believed that players should act with a level of decency befitting international athletes. He was keen to put this into writing in the form of a 'bible' – a document that would encapsulate all the hopes, dreams and required behaviour of an international player. I have a copy of the original version. It has a worn, brown leather cover

and a sticker sporting the flag of St George, with ENGLAND embla-
zoned across the centre. Inside, it outlines the code of conduct of the
team, the policies and procedures, objectives and a 'who's who' guide,
including the names of the players' wives and girlfriends, with the
amusing warning 'subject to change – frequently in some cases' underneath the list.

The 'bible' offers a pathway into Clive's thinking. It illustrates with
crystal clarity his demand for respect, both in the behaviour of his team
and of others towards them. The interesting thing here is that Clive is
not on some sort of moral crusade – it is his genuine belief that if
people raise their standards of behaviour off the pitch, there will be a
corresponding rise in the expectations they have of themselves on it.
Dress is one manifestation of this. In the 'bible' it says, 'You are reminded to be suitably dressed at all times in the team hotel.' Language must
be clean in public. 'You are representing England at ALL times – not
just when you arrive in the hotel. The highest standards are required
and expected at all times.'

He believes there is more to international rugby than the eighty
minutes on the pitch, or even the twenty odd days a year on England
duty. The Royal Marines declare that 'leadership is a lifestyle – you're
never off duty if you're a Marine – you're always representing the
service'. This is an ethos shared by Clive. Players must always be on
time (élite time is Lombardi time – ten minutes early, remember) and
they must return phone calls to players and management within
twenty-four hours. This shows respect. The code of conduct means
that players raise themselves to a higher level.

The 'bible' was one of the first things to bring Clive into conflict
with the RFU. He told Don Rutherford, the technical director of the
Union, that they would cost £275 each. 'Whaaaattt?' screeched
Rutherford, well aware that the Union's new signing had already
punched great big holes in the budget. 'Can you not produce them any
more cheaply?' Clive said not, and stood his ground. He won. He had
his budget-busting 'bibles'. Throughout his time in office, Clive drove
large, heavily armoured tanks through all the financial boundaries laid
before him. That he was able to do this, and get away with it, has much
to do with his extraordinary abilities as a politician. Dr Simon Kemp,
the England team doctor, describes it as an ability to manage upwards

as well as downwards. 'He doesn't just manage us, he manages those above him, too. There was never one occasion when, if I needed a piece of equipment, Clive couldn't get the money for me to have it. As long as I could justify it to Clive, he would do the rest. He's a consummate politician.'

Clive was able to redirect the RFU budget towards Team England because he had the ear and trust of Cliff Brittle, chair of the management board, and Fran Cotton, deputy chair of the management board. When Francis Baron became chief executive in 1998, he became another ally initially. Clive would approach them with his excessive demands and they would take responsibility for convincing a highly sceptical board to back him.

Clive says that he was not the extravagant spender that everyone considers him to have been and that many of his projects were independently financed. This is undoubtedly true, but it is also true that he saw the budget as standing between him and what he wanted, and therefore as something to be overcome. He was frustrated at the lack of money available for him to spend.

'That's all there is,' Don Rutherford said once. 'If you think you need more, why don't you do your own budgets next time? Sit down, work out what you need and we'll try to get it cleared through the committees. Then, as long as you stick to it, everything will be OK.'

It wasn't of course. Clive cleverly avoided this trap and was thus free to explode through the budgets that other people had prepared. Never lay down on paper something that may later be taken and used in evidence against you. Clive was the scourge of the accountants wherever he worked.

'If you could find someone halfway between Don and Clive in terms of dealing with budgets, you'd have exactly the right approach,' says Cliff Brittle. 'Clive was just way too far one way, and Don way too far the other way. We all knew there'd be a certain amount of spending to produce a team great enough to win the World Cup, but there's not a person on the board who didn't choke at the level of expenditure coming through from the England team.'

The 'bibles' were a classic Woodward production, falling into the category 'critical non-essentials' – the things that aren't essential to the process of playing a game of rugby, but are critical to creating the right climate in which to encourage the winning mindset.

The concept of 'critical non-essentials' was lifted from a crazy Brisbane dentist, Dr Paddi Lund. Lund worked out that none of his clients (he never calls them patients) understood dentistry. No one knew what work was being done inside their mouths. The only way to make dentistry more agreeable was to make the experience of visiting a dentist pleasanter, so he set up a practice quite unlike any other. It features a large, silver cappuccino machine as its centrepiece, with Royal Doulton china, beautiful furniture and classical music in small waiting lounges. People are invited to come for afternoon tea rather than explicitly told that their six-month appointment is due. Lund has taken the sting out of dentistry and become a massive success. Clive fell in love with the idea.

Lund's philosophy is that details matter. They are important. This ties in rather neatly with Woodward's philosophy that attention to detail spawns greatness. He has always believed that winning is about 'inches not miles'.

Dave Reddin, the England fitness coach, says that Team England is 'a positive place to be'. He recalls how Clive explained his 'details count' theory. He did not believe that any player could suddenly improve by 30 per cent, so Reddin's task was to make as many 1 per cent increases as possible. No improvement was too small. Every tiny little step in the right direction would take them to where they wanted to be.

'I've just got to make a quick call,' says Clive. 'Sorry. I promise that I'll switch the thing off then.' He starts squinting at the mobile phone and pressing a sequence of buttons as if he doesn't really know what he's doing. He reminds me of my mum when she first got her phone and shouted into it at such volume that she didn't really need the phone at all.

For Clive, making calls in public places, or in front of a guest, is not strictly speaking out of the Clive book of exceptional manners – hence the apology. In the 'bible' it says that no mobile phones are to be taken to any team meeting or training session or to be used around the team hotel – 'Leave mobiles in your rooms and answer messages at appropriate times. It is rude and irritating for others to have your phones ringing in public places.'

He calls Sherylle Calder, the England team's visual awareness coach. She was another to fall into the 'critical non-essentials' category. No other rugby team had one and there was much eyebrow raising when Clive announced her appointment. She proved to be a valuable member of his team. Now he faces the task of creating a new band of experts – a 'dream team' of specialist coaches to move into football with him. He has big plans in football and he knows that if he succeeds, he will transform sports coaching forever. He has absolute confidence that he will succeed. He just knows he can't fail. His head must be a nice place to be. It must be fabulous to have such vast quantities of unshakeable, all-consuming belief. It would make anything possible. 'Anything is possible,' says Clive, as if reading my mind. 'It just depends how hard you're willing to work for it.' It turns out he's willing to work pretty hard.

The restaurant at Pennyhill Park Hotel is almost empty. Just a couple of other tables are occupied, far away from us as we sit in the corner. Clive is facing the window, looking out on to the crop of new buildings and grass beyond. He seems quite relaxed. He smiles and orders more wine.

'What was HMS *Conway* like?' I ask, and the mood changes – a seismic shift. It would take a blind man not to read the change in body language here.

'The dark years,' he says, arms folded, eye contact gone, smile gone, brow furrowed. He looks out of the window as if the answers lie on the freshly mown grass outside. 'God, I hated it there.'

Chapter Four

HMS Conway

*'It has been my experience that folks who have
no vices have very few virtues.'* **Abraham Lincoln**

On a bright, autumnal morning in 1969, Flight Lieutenant Ronald and
Mrs Joyce Woodward climbed into the family car with their disconso-
late teenaged son, ready for the four-hour drive from Yorkshire to
North Wales. Clive was to start the following morning at the HMS
Conway Merchant Navy Cadet School, an institution based in Angle-
sey, near Llanfairpwllgwyngyll. It must have been a proud day for
Woodward Senior, delivering his elder son to be educated at a school
attended by, and recommended by, the Commanding Officer of his
base. His own elevated position in the RAF had secured the place in
this exclusive school. Clive would have the education that his father
had always dreamed of giving him.

Clive sat quietly in the back of the car. He didn't want to go to
school in North Wales. He had never been to Wales before. He'd been
born in the Midlands, been to junior school in Scotland and to secondary school in Yorkshire. At Linton-on-Ouse he'd finally felt at home.
Ahead of him lay five years at a school that had modelled itself on, and
allowed itself to be defined by, a narrow and desperately old-fashioned
notion of masculinity. Rugby was good. Football was bad. Creativity,
freedom of expression and challenging the status quo were bad. Strict
discipline and adherence to rules above all else were good. This was
how it had to be in times of conflict, so this is how it would be in the
school that was set up to train men for such conflicts.

HMS *Conway* had been established in the 1850s to train naval officers, and it had an impressive reputation. A total of 1,450 old boys are known to have served in the forces (apart from the thousands who served in the Merchant Navy). The school produced sixteen Admirals, two Air Marshals, four Victoria Cross holders, one George Cross, one George medal, a poet laureate (John Masefield) and an Archbishop of Wales. Clive was at school with, but not in the same year as, Iain Duncan-Smith, the former leader of the Conservative party. In Britain in the 1960s, however, the school was desperately out of step with the way in which academic institutions were being organised. Clive, the football-mad, slightly unconventional teenager, simply didn't fit in.

Clive remained silent as the car wound its way through the country lanes. His first sight of HMS *Conway* did nothing to arrest his growing concern at what lay ahead. The school building reeks of austerity. It looks more like a prison or military hospital than a lively boarding school for young boys. Even today, thirty years after Clive left, it still harbours a sense of foreboding, consisting of long narrow buildings with small windows running the length of them, all sharp corners and flat walls with everything in lines, characterless, like 1960s prefabs. It was as if the architects' plans were based entirely on functionality, with not so much as a nod towards the physical appearance of the place. Today, the buildings are owned by Cheshire Education Authority. They run outdoor pursuit and holiday courses for boys and girls at the school, taking advantage of the countryside nearby and its close proximity to the sea.

When Clive first arrived at the school, his parents were told he was a 'new chum' – the delightful name given to all new arrivals. Mums and dads would happily hand over their sons to the care and attention of an 'old hand' assigned by the school to look after each boy.

'But once the parents left, you discovered that the real name given to new boys was "plebs", not "new chums",' explains Vaughan Atkinson, the man who had the dubious honour of being Clive's 'fag' later in Clive's school life. The name 'pleb' is based, naturally enough, on 'plebeians' – the lowest form of life.

'The "old hand" would show you the school, run through the rules, then dump you like a hot brick into the starboard dorm where you'd sink or swim on your merits,' added Atkinson.

Clive was appointed 'fag' to an older boy, Paul Heaver. Heaver would re-enter his life later, when the two met up in happier circumstances on the sun-kissed beaches of Manly, when Clive moved to Australia to play rugby in the Sydney suburb. For now, though, Clive was stuck with cleaning Heaver's shoes, ironing his trousers and generally kow-towing to the older boy.

The school had a complicated set-up, using naval terminology that was incredibly baffling to all new arrivals. This created an immediate 'them and us' situation between the boys at the school, who under-stood the language, and the new boys, who did not. This distinction was further exacerbated by the fact that all dormitories were split into two – starboard for new cadets, as the pupils were called, and port for older cadets.

There were around a hundred boys at the school when Clive joined. They wore Royal Naval midshipman uniforms when outside and on Sunday parades. The rest of the time they wore working rig referred to as 'eights'. The school building was always called 'the ship', as are all naval buildings. It had a 'quarter deck', and was divided into four dor-mitories, referred to as 'tops'. There was Maintop, Mizzentop, Foretop and Forecastle. Clive was in Foretop.

A typical day at HMS *Conway* started at 6.30 a.m. when a bugler sounded reveille. If you had misbehaved the day before – including being late for lessons, not concentrating in lessons, anything deemed worthy of punishment by the older boys – you would be up at 5.30 a.m. in 'early heave-out' and have to clean the school, including the toilets and floors, and do exercises until the rest of the school awoke. The wake-up for the majority of the school was followed by the clean-ing of the living quarters ready for inspection, known as rounds. Then the divisions fell in on the parade ground for an inspection by the headmaster, Basil Lord. The boys marched around the parade ground with a full band playing, while Mr Lord looked on.

After this lively introduction to the day, came the lessons, following the normal O Level and A Level curriculum. Afternoons were filled with sports that were deemed appropriate for young men – rugby, sailing and orienteering were favourites. Training was also done for the breeches buoy competition – a school contest in which the 'tops' competed against one another in transferring a 'survivor' across the deck using a rope contraption called a breeches buoy. Further lessons took place between 3 p.m. and 6 p.m., followed by recreation in the evening, division inspections and lights out, again by bugler, at 10 p.m.

In addition to naval traditions, boarding school traditions were also upheld at the school. Vaughan Atkinson recalls that 'beans were called fart pellets, the female cooks who came to work at the school were called galley trogs, and there was this thing we always had to do. If you wanted to pass through a dormitory that was not your own and were refused by the occupants of that dormitory (this could mean having to go down four floors, along the long alleyway and back up four floors), you'd say the sacred word "hut" to gain admission.

'The black boxes that we kept sports gear in were called Boris boxes, and Boris scrubbing was when smelly individuals were forced naked into the showers and scrubbed with Vim and yard brushes by others who objected to their lack of cleanliness.'

Clive had no desire to go to sea and, from day one, did not respond well to this naval regime, but it was the school's approach to football that he hated the most. All of HMS *Conway*'s worst characteristics were distilled in its attitude to, and opposition to, football – the snobbery, stubbornness and arrogance. One teacher – Colin Goodey, who taught football outside school and maths in it – came to Clive's rescue. Goodey recognised Clive's frustrations at a system that prevented him from playing football and decided to try to help by turning PE sessions that should have had rugby at their core into football lessons.

'Life at *Conway* was tough,' recalls Goodey. 'You had to fit in with the routine and traditions. Any deviation away from them and a cadet would suffer the wrath of a senior cadet captain and be forced to pay a visit to the gun room, where most punishments were administered.

'I remember that Clive was a shy, quiet but very intelligent boy, who was away from home for the first time. From a maths point of view he gave me no hassle and proved, according to my old marks book, to be above average. He worked hard for me as soon as he realised that I was a soccer player and was player/coach of a North Wales team.

'I didn't want to coach rugby and Clive didn't want to play it, so every Wednesday afternoon when we were supposed to be doing just that, we used to head for the pitch farthest away from school, well out of sight of both the captain and the headmaster. The conspiracy was hatched. We did rugby football training but with a little more emphasis on football. Woodward was delighted. It was fun and the cadets were having exercise and fresh air.

'I can promise you, it's not easy to make accurate passes or dribble with a rugby ball, and that's when I saw just how good Clive was as a potential soccer player. He just swept down the pitch controlling that ball as if it was a round one. I had posted a cadet who was, I think, asthmatic at the entrance to the pitch and his job was to blow a whistle should any senior member of staff approach. Then the oval ball would be immediately "handled". I will always remember Clive's face when, on our second or third Wednesday, I took a brand-new Mitre soccer ball out of my rucksack. That was possibly the first time a soccer ball had touched *Conway* soil. We had fantastic fun and some wonderful games, but Clive was in a league of his own and technically superb – a natural.

'I was short of a fast and fit centre-forward or winger for my Welsh coast side and it soon occurred to me that here was the star that could make my side champions. I divulged my plan to Clive, knowing that it would not be easy to pull it off. He was mad with excitement.

'The initial plan was for him to be allowed out of school to join our training sessions and watch a few games prior to me bringing him on as a substitute. The hurdles were immense. First, we would have to gain the head's permission. Second, his parents would have to agree.'

Clive approached Basil Lord and asked whether he might play football for Mr Goodey's team. Mr Lord's reply has stayed with him for over thirty years – 'If you don't stop all this nonsense, I will take the teaser to you.'

As Goodey recalls, 'Clive was thrashed and plummeted into unhappiness, and as a consequence ran away from school. For my part, I was told in no uncertain terms to end "this nonsense". Clive ran away again later but eventually succumbed to the tradition of the ship – rugby football.'

In fact, Clive ran away from school three times in total. On every occasion, his father would meet him at the door, and frogmarch him back to the station. Basil Lord, though, does not remember it this way.

'I remember a very talented rugby football player who had a natural gift for the game. If he wanted to play football, it would have been very difficult for him to do so because it wasn't played at the school, but there was no suggestion of banning him. I'm surprised to hear all this about him running away. I'm eighty now and my memory has been better, but I don't remember that side of Woodward at all. I just remember him being a fine rugger player.'

What is certain is that Clive was not allowed to play football in any formal capacity. What is also clear is that his efforts to do so resulted in him being quite seriously beaten with a three-foot marine rope known as the 'teaser'. This was the primary form of discipline at HMS *Conway*. For the most part, discipline was enforced by the older boys, which was, of course, a double-edged sword. Most of those with the authority to administer disciplinary measures were indoctrinated into the culture and philosophy of the school, and sought to treat those whose punishment was in their hands with the same severity as they had been treated. 'Show me a child-beater,' says Adrian Atkinson, 'and I'll show you a beaten child.'

There is something democratic and fair about allowing the boys themselves to mete out discipline and something utterly despicable about it. As boys entered the system, so they became anaesthetised by it. They saw their role models indulge in violence and they too would rise to positions whereby they could beat young boys for the simplest transgressions. It was *Animal Farm* meets *Lord of the Flies*. All animals were equal when they arrived, and equally appalled at the severity, but some coped and thrived in the 'stick rather than carrot' system, and others did not. They retreated into themselves and got through their years at HMS *Conway* as best they could while longing for the moment of release. By the end, some animals were infinitely more equal than others. It was the most equal of the animals who were handed the conch.

Discipline was doled out by cadet captains who lived in the gun room where the boys went for physical punishment, or to appeal against punishment. Appeals would earn thrashings as surely as the crimes themselves. Older boys would roam the dormitories, beating younger boys and inflicting quite serious injuries on them. All beatings administered by the 'teaser' were known as 'cuts'.

'The teaser was a vicious little weapon made from tarred hemp with an eye splice at one end and a six-foot back splice at the business end, known as the dog's bollocks. The back splice, which thickened and strengthened the rope, was "whipped" using a very thin twine to give it further strength and make it less flexible. It was stored in a bottle of salt water, which gave it the consistency of a metal bar. Sometimes there was metalwork in the whipping. This rope was then used to beat cadets as a punishment,' says Atkinson.

No boy felt able to relax fully at school for fear of late-night thrashings. I interviewed eighteen boys who had attended HMS *Conway* at the same time as Clive. Fifteen of them described the night-time fear and said they had not quite got over it. All fifteen said they would prefer me not to quote them or refer to them by name on this subject. They said, 'It makes me look like I was weak and I don't think I was,' and, 'I'd hate my children to read it and think I was a cry baby.'

Former *Conway* students agree that very few, if any, boys would have made it through school without coming into contact with the teaser at some stage. That was clearly great progress – twenty years before Clive's time, the teaser was used with such regularity that boys were lucky to walk anywhere in the course of a day without encountering it. They even had semi-public floggings when boys were caught doing anything that threatened to impinge on the reputation of the school – such as drinking in a local bar. The boys would all gather round while the older, bigger boys hit the younger ones with such ferocity that the scars stayed with them for life.

Chapter Five

A first taste of sweet success

'It's not enough that we do our best; sometimes we have to do what's required.' **Sir Winston Churchill**

One of the most fascinating questions about Clive Woodward is why, having been banned from playing football at HMS *Conway*, did he fall into line and play rugby to such a high level instead? Surely, any self-respecting teenager, having been barred from doing something he loved by the masters of an institution that he held in great contempt, would rather smoke, drink and pierce his own ears than conform so mightily to what the hated teachers wanted. Rugby would be forever the sport that stopped him playing football. Understanding why Clive said to himself, 'Right – if I can't play football, then I'll be the best bloody rugby player you ever had instead,' is one of the keys to understanding the man.

Dr Adrian Atkinson sits in his Central London office in front of a whiteboard with a complicated arrangement of arrows strewn across it, all linking back to the word 'personality' scrawled across the middle. Atkinson works with businesses to identify individuals with unique skills, finding the entrepreneurs in an organisation and explaining the psychology of entrepreneurial behaviour to company directors, encouraging them to look for and nurture it.

'Many successful people have a high need for achievement. Although the chance to play football was taken away from Clive, the need for achievement remained,' explains Atkinson. 'He would still have felt the urge to be successful and to achieve something. Given his sporting talent and natural physical skills, it makes absolute sense to me that, rather than mourn the fact that he couldn't play one sport, he threw himself into another.

'Most successful people have a belief that they are in control of their own destiny. They feel that it is they who will decide what they do.'

So rolling over in a self-pitying fashion and blaming rotten luck would not have been on Clive's agenda. Instead, he would take control where he could. Having tried and failed to play football, he would naturally and instinctively have done something else rather than not succeed at anything.

'People with a high need for achievement tend to see their lives as plans or projects. They want to be number one in their reference groups and have strong self-discipline. They choose what they want, plan and go. If football was off the agenda, the drive to succeed wasn't, so it's no surprise that he played rugby instead.'

In fact, the denial of football may, paradoxically, have contributed to Clive's rugby success.

'The burning frustration has been perhaps the best motivator for me,' says Clive. 'This is probably why I have become so driven. It is critical to what I believe and how I operate. It taught me never to compromise on second best and to stand up for what you believe in. This determined stance has caused controversy and some people view me as selfish and volatile.'

Clive played rugby with some reticence at first but he was 'an absolute natural' according to his coach. Once Clive realised this, and worked out that his successes in the sport afforded him a smoother path through the school, he threw himself into it with gusto. Being a winner at rugby, better than his peers, would have been alluring enough to the most mild-mannered and unambitious of cadets, but for Clive, ambitious to the core, it was like a drug.

Clive is recalled as being a small, wiry boy when he arrived at the school. He began his rugby by playing scrum-half (called half-back at

HMS *Conway*) and made an immediate impression. The sublime skills that had been so evident on the football field, transferred to the rugby field. Those who played with him describe his 'absolute lack of fear'. Without the fear of being tackled to hinder him, and with his glossy footballing skills, he became one of the school's star players, making his mark alongside Iain Duncan-Smith at fly-half. In his first term, he went from having begun school without understanding rugby at all, run through an active dislike of it because it replaced football, to becoming so skilled at it that he made the top team in his year group.

Mr Lord remembers, 'He was very, very quick on the rugby field. Not just a quick runner but he had a remarkably quick recovery, and he put in second tackles every time. Everything about him was just that bit faster and slicker.'

Dave Yates, a fellow pupil, remembers him when he first played: 'I would play on the wing and never touch the ball, whereas every time Clive got hold of it he scored. He had the skills to change the result of a game. He was a special player from early on.'

Yates also remembers one of the more onerous tasks for any boy representing HMS *Conway* – the school's own very embarrassing version of the New Zealand haka.

'We stood in a circle with our arms around each other, and we chanted, "Pieces of eight, pieces of eight, pieces of nine and ten. We'll cut the throats of any man and sew them up again. Dead men tell no lies." Then we all jumped up. Rather than intimidating the opposition, I think it rendered them useless with laughter!'

In 1974, his final year at HMS *Conway*, Clive went to the Welsh schoolboy trials with Nick Faigniez, the team's vice captain. These trials were open to anyone living in, being schooled in or in any other way qualified for Wales. For a boy from HMS *Conway* to attend the trials was rare. The school preferred to keep its boys to itself, wanting them to play for the school rather than risk any clash with Welsh schoolboy fixtures that would deplete their slender resources. HMS *Conway* prided itself on its sporting reputation, enjoying a healthy fixture list with such schools as Pangbourne College. The school had a reputation for being tough. Alan Burns, editor of the *Conway* Club newsletter says, 'An old friend, Bob Weighill, England captain and one-time secretary of the Rugby Football Union, was at Wirral Grammar

School in the 1930s. He once told me that his school had cancelled their fixture with *Conway* because *Conway* teams were too rough.'

By the time Clive made it into the sixth form, the school was not long for this world. It was going to close in two years and no new pupils were being admitted. Just sixty boys remained and most of them were de-mob happy. Many of the old rules and constraints ceased to apply. Woodward was cleared to attend trials. Clive recalls that the coach from the North Wales schoolboy side took him to the trial, where he faced deep opposition because he wasn't Welsh. He says he was not considered by the selectors because his parents were English. It left him with a dislike for all things Welsh to layer on top of his fundamental dislike for North Wales because his despicable school was based there. After leaving HMS *Conway*, he never went back to North Wales. He has changed his views since then, of course. The experiences of touring with Welsh players in Lions teams, as player and coach, have mellowed his views.

Clive's sporting skills were not confined to rugby. He also played for the hockey team and was captain of the tennis team, described by *Conway* magazine as, 'Perhaps our best player, ever.' Tom Rowlands, a friend from *Conway*, says, 'My key memory of Clive was of a fantastic all-round sportsman who was slightly embarrassed at how easy it was for him to win.'

Phil van Bergen 'bunked up' next to Clive and remembers, 'a quiet, thoughtful boy – always doing sport'.

Richard Coombes, a year or so older than Clive, was junior cadet captain (prefect in charge of dormitories) when Clive joined. 'He was a strong-willed sort of a boy. At boarding school there's a certain amount of bullying that goes on. I remember Clive as being someone who always stood up for himself. He didn't seem scared and I remember thinking how well and how quickly he settled in to school life. He was a popular boy but he kept himself to himself. He was a good all-round sportsman, which helped with meeting people and making friends.'

Away from sport, Clive also excelled, although not academically. He is described as 'average' by most who knew him. However, Mr Lord protests that he was 'far from average – he was a bright boy who deserved his university place.' In the social structure of the school, however, there is no question that he rose to the very top. His leadership skills took him to the position of deputy chief cadet captain (the equivalent of deputy head boy) and to a second-place finish in the Queen's *Conway* Gold Medal award – the highest accolade offered at HMS *Conway*. Coming second is not something that Clive is overly keen on but, given the nature of the award and the fact that he was spending more time running around on sports fields than reading books, he did exceptionally well.

'To be picked by one's peers,' says Lord, 'to show officer-like qualities. These are the things for which we searched at the school. The prize was to encourage such qualities as cheerful submission to superiors, self-respect and independence of character, kindness and protection of the weak, readiness to forgive offence, a desire to calculate the differences of others, and above all, fearless devotion to duty and unflinching truthfulness.'

'I was close to Clive at school,' says Lance Mitchell. 'He was talented. Sports-wise he was the best the school had ever seen. Every sport he did, he was good at. If he'd played for England at tennis or cricket or hockey, no one would have been surprised.

'He was a natural leader. When we were in the colts rugby team, we went up to the top fields to be coached in the art of sidestepping. On the way back down to the main school, we walked past the tennis courts and I clearly remember Clive grabbing the ball and saying, "I think this is a much better way of doing it." He demonstrated his own way and we were all using the Clive Woodward method by the time he'd finished rather than the way we were taught.'

Once Clive became the DCCC of the school, life got a little easier. He had his own cabin and someone to attend to menial tasks for him. Clive's little helper, Vaughan Atkinson, remembers Clive as 'quite mature, sometimes very serious, but he also liked to have a laugh and joke. He was always very appreciative of what I did for him and was a well-liked individual.

'I had to clean his shoes and press his uniform among other tasks. This was considered a good job because it meant I did not have to do all the other mundane tasks that cadets were subjected to. My memories of Clive are that he was very fair, and allowed me to have a lot of free time.'

Dave Yates recalls, 'Everyone at HMS *Conway* had a nickname and for some reason his was "Claude". I remember him as a very fair man in a very tough regime. In our final year, Clive was the DCCC. I was once called into his study over some misdemeanour and didn't get a beating, which was commonplace with other cadet captains. Instead, I had to get up early the next day in my gym kit and do some roly-polies up a hill in the snow, which seemed very fair at the time.

'Cadet captains carried teasers. I don't remember ever seeing Clive use one. There was also a *Conway* experience called the "crucifixion". The quarter boys would select victims on their way to class and put a broom handle through one sleeve of the naval officer's jumper we wore, push it across his back and out through the other sleeve rendering his arms useless. They would then lift the victim up and hook him on the coat hooks that adorned the corridors by his webbing belt. There he stayed until a caring soul took him down. I would like to think Clive was more of a "getter downer" than a "putter upper"!'

Clive was also a success in areas that one might not expect. In June 1970, when he had been at the school for ten months, the *North Wales Chronicle* covered the school's play *One for the Pot*. Clive played Amy Hardcastle, resplendent in tight black dress. 'The best attempt at "drag" acting ever seen from the *Conway* company,' extolled the newspaper. His father must have been so proud!

Once a week, girls would be brought, trembling, into the very masculine environment of HMS *Conway* for what were laughingly called dancing lessons. These amounted to nothing more than the girls being stepped all over by the boys. It is with great sadness that I bring you the news that no one can remember what Clive was like in Miss Edmonson's dance class. We can only wonder. Certainly, the teenaged Clive had something of a way with the ladies.

'He actually went out with my sister,' declares Lance Mitchell, 'when we were eighteen and my sister was a year and a half younger than us. Clive went out with her when she came up to school to visit me.' So far, so good. 'But, apparently, he asked her for a goodnight kiss and she ran away.' So far, not so very good.

There is no question that, despite his dislike of the school, Clive was a huge success there. There is no question, either, that for many of the boys who attended HMS *Conway*, it was a very positive experience. Lance Mitchell's memories are infinitely brighter than Clive's.

'I'm amazed at what Clive says about his time at school. Just remember, Clive was deputy chief cadet captain. He led as close to a role-model life as any schoolboy could. He would not have got to that position unless he was enthusiastic about the school. I thought it was a great place. It was hard but a great learning experience.'

Memory can be a most imperfect servant and perceptions can be vastly different. One boy's attitude to school life can differ greatly from another's. Many other boys who attended the school agree with Clive's version of events – the school was unnecessarily harsh and had a brutality they had never encountered before or since.

'But there was fun, too,' says Mitchell. 'A whole bunch of us were really good friends at school – Clive was in the group. I can remember us all meeting up for New Year's Eve the year after we left. We went to Trafalgar Square, had some drinks and went to the Strand, ending up at the Seaman's Mission. Three of us were left at the end, including Clive. We dossed down there at seven in the morning, and then went to Wembley to see a Watford match in the afternoon. It was great. We had a lot of fun and talked about school days.'

Dinner is over, and I climb into my car and prepare to take the long winding road out of this hotel. But, on the drive away from Pennyhill Park, things look different. The rhododendron bushes are an alternate colour. These remarkable plants have varying leaves and are planted in such a way that you see a different colour on the way out from the one you observed on the way in. How dramatic and artistic. Rugby players arrive at the hotel, spend time with Team England – changing their attitudes and improving their belief and self-confidence then, when they leave, everything looks different. Wonderful. It would be fabulous to report that Clive planted these bushes himself with this in mind, digging down into the earth with his bare hands until his fingernails were broken and his knuckles raw. Sadly not. 'It was the gardener who thought of it,' says the valet. 'I don't think Clive knows anything about it.'

Little did the gardener realise, as he planted his fabulous bushes, that he was caught up in the paradox of creating a pathetic fallacy – making the world look different for England players who had just been taught to view the world differently.

SECTION TWO

Chapter Six

London calling

---

*'You can't wait for inspiration. You have to go
after it with a club.'* **Jack London**

The eighteen-year-old man on the train from Liverpool sat back in his seat, sighed and allowed a huge grin to spread across his face. He was happy. He was free at last. Clive found his time at HMS *Conway* Merchant Navy Cadet School unrelentingly difficult. He wove his way through the social fabric of the school with considerable ease and, assisted by his talents as a sportsman, rose to a senior position and earned the respect of his peers and his teachers. But, despite all the conspicuous successes and the high esteem in which he was held, he never enjoyed himself.

When Clive left HMS *Conway*, the school closed down, not as some bold tribute to him or as a dramatic mark of respect, but because those running the school had failed to act quickly enough when it became clear that the need for naval officers was being reduced with every passing year. The nature of military conflict and the reductions in the armed forces undermined the *raison d'être* of HMS *Conway*. There was just no point in it staying open any longer. Funding had dried up and fewer cadets were going through the system. Ensuring its survival would have necessitated a departure from the school's military traditions and a step into the modern era some twenty years previously. The school needed a different purpose, but the officials clung to their naval traditions just as the men of Twickenham, with whom Clive later came into contact, would cling to amateurism – drowning men in sodden blazers reaching out for punctured liferafts.

The school's passing was marked with a Laying Down of the Colours ceremony at Liverpool Cathedral followed by dinner on the *Royal Isis*. 'We dispersed from the quayside in Liverpool without ever returning to Llanfairpwllgwyngll,' says Lance Mitchell. 'Suddenly the whole thing was over. The school was gone.'

The boys boarded the train in Liverpool and headed for home, some misty eyed, some, like Clive, delighted beyond words and entirely unable to contain their enthusiasm. He rushed into the toilet as soon as the train pulled away and tore off his uniform, shoving the formal attire aside and slipping on his jeans. He swears that he threw the uniform out of the window, and watched as the garments that signified such a difficult period of his life fluttered down on to the track and lay there – utterly lifeless and dejected. Clive has never been back to the school. He has never looked up at the cold, dark building as a survivor. 'I just never want to see that place again,' he says.

He developed an uncomfortable relationship with Wales through his experiences at school which was carried forward into his adult life. After he joined Leicester Rugby Club in 1979, the club went on a pre-season tour to Hoylake, near Liverpool. Ian Smith, a fellow player, says, 'At the crack of dawn, Chalkie White, the coach, took us for a run on the beach. I remember Clive pointing and saying, "Over there is the enemy." We didn't know what he meant but later we found out he meant Wales.'

While Clive was at HMS *Conway*, his father had been promoted to Squadron Leader, Ronald Woodward's final promotion before he retired from the force in 1976. The family had moved to Oxfordshire, where Squadron Leader Woodward was based at Brize Norton. It was to Oxfordshire, therefore, that Clive returned in 1974, a future in the legal profession ahead of him. To his father's absolute delight, he had applied to study law at Durham University, starting in September. It seemed to Woodward Senior as if his decision to send his son away had paid off. He would become a successful lawyer. First, though, he had the whole summer to get through before he could he head up north and launch himself into student life.

Clive spent his time working shifts in the car factories of Cowley, and trying to extract as much private time as possible out of life at home. Paradoxically, the constraining school years had made him fiercely independent. The intensity had made him a stronger person, and he found being in his parents' house quite a challenge. So he threw himself into work, putting in long shifts to stay away from the stifling atmosphere at home, and building up finances to take to university.

In August 1974, a brown envelope arrived from the A Level examination board. He opened the letter to see that he had been awarded a B, C and D at A Level. He had hoped for better. Certainly, the admissions tutors at Durham had expected better. Their offer hinged on him achieving B, B, C grades at A Level, so he was a couple of grades off target. It would make getting a place at the university difficult, but Clive remained confident. He believed that the college officials would recognise that he brought other qualities, not just academic prowess. With his proven skills as a rugby player and, indeed, other sports, he thought the university would take him, but when the letter came from Durham, he had been rejected. A year later, when he had further proven himself as a rugby player, Durham changed their mind and came back with an offer. By then, though, Clive had other plans and he turned them down.

Now, with the option of going to Durham no longer available, he was faced with the choice of staying at home with his parents and continuing to work at the local car factories, or applying through clearing to another university that might be willing to take him on the combination of his grades and his rugby prowess. He decided that neither option suited him, and that he would do something different.

He spotted an advertisement for a trainee position with NatWest bank that required just two A Level passes. Clive wrote off to them and sailed through the interview process. Less than a month after first making contact, he packed his bags and headed for London, like some latter-day Dick Whittington, to walk on the gold-paved streets. He would launch himself on the banking world quietly, by starting in the back office, engaged in simple administrative tasks, but he had been told that there were plenty of opportunities to develop and to forge a career at NatWest. The bank would pay relocation expenses, which meant sending him a train ticket, and assist with housing, which meant letting him know of a local family from whom he could rent a room. So, six weeks after the long, ecstatic train journey back from HMS *Conway*, Clive made the journey from the

Midlands to London to begin his new life as a city banker.

The NatWest in Richmond is a busy bank in the centre of town. Richmond is a middle-class area, fashionable and affluent, servicing commuters to Central London as well as the local community. It is a town of theatres, bars, restaurants and fashionable clothes shops, and home to three leading rugby clubs with another one, Harlequins, just around the corner in Twickenham.

Val Bendall and her husband, Steve, worked at the bank, along with Sandra Minkey, a local girl who was Val's best friend.

'I remember Clive when he first arrived,' says Val. 'He was so full of life and great fun. He was just doing basic jobs, filing letters and papers, and clipping things together. Nothing too difficult, but he had something about him, even then. You knew he wouldn't stay there long. There was so much more to him. He wasn't arrogant or conceited – just a lovely man who was clearly bright and ambitious. He stood out.'

It's no surprise that he stood out when he arrived at the West London bank – as much for his dubious sartorial choices as for anything else. He arrived for his first day in that tweed suit – all the rage in Llanfairpwllgwyngyll, no doubt, but not so in this trendy part of London in the summer.

'Boy, did I feel like some country hillbilly when I saw everyone else in their sharp grey pinstriped suits,' said Clive. He had no idea how to dress for a smart office because the only clothing decisions he'd had to make for the previous five years had been between his number ones and his 'eights'.

'None of that mattered,' recalls Val. 'He was a real hoot, quite a prankster. I remember one incident when they'd put up a Christmas tree in the offices and he moved it. It was very funny.'

Clearly, you took your fun where you could get it at the Richmond branch of the NatWest bank in the 1970s.

The town buzzed with rugby fever. Richmond, London Scottish, London Welsh and Harlequins were all top clubs in the mid-1970s, and all resided in close proximity. Whenever an international match was played, the place heaved with fans and followers. If Clive was going to supplement his life as a trainee banker with rugby training, there was plenty of choice. The two big clubs, considering his lack of affiliation with Scotland and dislike of Wales, were Richmond and Harlequins.

The latter, nicknamed 'sequins' because of the team's rather glamorous approach to life, were a club with a difference. Their strip was coloured light blue, magenta, chocolate, French grey, black and light green – none of the common or garden blue and white stripes for them. A dashing club for dashing players, it was Clive's sort of place. The former England captain, Bob Hiller, played there and the coach was Earle Kirton, a former All Black fly-half.

Clive called the club and was told that training was on Tuesday and Thursday evenings, so one Tuesday in August, soon after starting his new job, he headed down to Stoop Memorial Ground, just over the road from the Twickenham stadium, to undertake some light early season training.

Kirton had played twelve Tests for New Zealand in the 1960s, before coming to England to do a post-graduate course in dentistry. He played for Harlequins, Middlesex and the Barbarians. He stayed long after his course finished and coached at Harlequins. One September evening, in 1974, Kirton was sitting down on the edge of the pitch, considering the season ahead, when in walked a gangly teenager - a little nervous, slightly self-conscious, but happily shot of the tweed suit. He was told to join in the general training sessions so Kirton could take a look at him.

'It was not hard to see the talent that Clive had,' says Kirton. 'Straightaway, you could see he was good.'

Still, he was unproven at club level, so he was put into the fifth team. Less than a month later, he was in the firsts. This was over a decade before leagues were invented, but the leading clubs were already established and, through Harlequins, he came head to head with the best players in England and Wales. Within three months of joining the club, he was running out for England colts.

Steve Kenney played for England colts at the same time as Clive. The two would meet again, years later, when they both played for Leicester.

'I found him very likeable, very confident, but a bit cocky, to be honest. He was very sure of his own ability and his own opinion. We bonded quite well, though. As a player he was very quick, very elusive. He was prepared to put his hand up. He was a very talented footballer with strong views on life.'

Home for Clive was a room in a house in Raynes Park, an area of London near to Wimbledon, just a few miles from Richmond. He lived near to the station, so it was an easy journey to Richmond town centre. The couple he stayed with had three young children and a very family-orientated lifestyle, which didn't quite suit the man about town enjoying his first taste of freedom in the big city. He stayed with the family in the early days, then swung completely to the other extreme, moving in with two young, single rugby players whose primary aim in life was to get drunk and have a good time.

'I know he found it hard in the house,' says Val, 'but he would still have a good time and he was really into his rugby. I have these memories of him always walking in with some bandage or another. He didn't do much work because he was always injured, coming in wearing a neck-brace or some such thing. Every Monday morning, we'd be wondering which part of him would be bandaged. I really enjoyed working with him and I regret not going down to watch him play at Harlequins.'

Clive's first game for Quins was against Leicester on 28 September 1974. Quins beat the Midlands side 32–10 – a great scalp. The local newspapers celebrated the 'exciting young Quins backs'.

'At stand-off, Clive Woodward looked impressive on his first team debut,' ran the *Surrey Comet*, but he was also described as 'a modestly sensible link' by the *Richmond and Twickenham Times*. The words 'damning', 'faint' and 'praise' spring to mind. He would go on to play twenty-six games at fly-half for the West London club before moving to the centre.

Harlequins was the most sophisticated club of its era, but it is important to remember that this was the seventies – a considerable time before professionalism or professional standards burst into the sport and cleaned up its muddy image. While Harlequins played some of the finest club rugby in England and were known as the 'gentlemen' of the sport, even they had a touch of the mud, blood, sweat and tears about them. Every time the players ran on to the field, they would have to watch out not only for marauding opposition forwards but for the furry embraces of the great Newfoundland dog belonging to a prop called Terry Claxton. Every time Claxton played, his big dog would burst free from its leash, bound on to the pitch and chase him across the field. Such antics were rewarded with the biggest applause of the day.

Roger Looker, aged twenty-three, was the youngest player at Harlequins when Clive arrived. 'I remember him turning up for training as a nineteen-year-old. Earle Kirton really took him under his wing, as did Bob Hiller,' he says. 'It was obvious right from the start that Clive was an outstanding player and that he would go on to play for England. His timing and pace were supreme, and it was hard to believe it was his first season of first-class rugby. He was clearly a guy who was going to go all the way, and he was surrounded by good players. Harlequins was a good club at the time, and one that advocated back play – he was one of a team of mavericks.'

While many clubs played the stick it up your jumper ten-man rugby that Clive loathes, Quins, thanks primarily to the influence of Kirton, were determined to run the ball and enjoy the sport. It was a backs-dominated club, led by a man who was ahead of his time. Clive grew to have an enormous amount of respect for Kirton. He became the first in a series of coaches who would greatly influence the way Clive played and the way he thought about rugby. Clive's natural devil-may-care approach to the sport – running at opposition, dazzling footwork and quick thinking – were encouraged and developed by Kirton.

'We would run it from anywhere on the field, Clive in particular,' says Looker. 'He was sociable, too. He would have a few drinks after training and after matches, but he was quite quiet. Don't forget he was the youngest bloke in the side by some way. Quite a lot of people there were in their late twenties and he was still a teenager.'

Hiller was the star of the Quins side. The former England captain and full-back had joined Quins from school in 1962 and played his last first-team game for them in 1976. His England career had ended in 1972, two years before Clive's arrival.

'The first time I noticed him as a player was at a trial. He was playing fly-half and it dawned on me that he was a player of great potential. We all thought that. He had tremendous hands and he was young and keen to learn. He was living in Raynes Park at the time and occasionally we would give him a lift home. Clive was a nice bloke, nicely balanced, very much his own man, an independent thinker in the nicest sense. He didn't dumbly take instructions but wanted to know why things were done in the way they were. He fitted in quickly. In fact, it was out-standing the way he fitted in with international players. He was very mature for his age, not overawed at all, and very popular.

'Clive liked open rugby and Earle Kirton was keen for the game to be played in that way. My career was grinding to a halt then. I wasn't playing regularly in 1974, but I played with Clive a few times. Quins was always a very friendly club. As long as you could play rugby, you were welcomed.'

Away from the field, Clive began to think about his future. He was enjoying life at NatWest bank and had been promoted from the back office to the front, where he dealt with the public, but he was starting to realise that banking life was not for him in the long-term. He sat down to talk to David Cooke, a friend at Quins and a former England player. Cooke had been to Loughborough and had enjoyed a fantastic three years at the college. He spoke to Clive about a man called Jim Greenwood, the Loughborough University coach, who was one of the best in the country. He suggested that it might be a good time for Clive to study at the Midlands-based college because the course was chang-ing from a certificate in education to a degree, and the sports college was linking up with the university.

Clive was already aware of Loughborough's reputation, having played at the university for England colts in their annual fixture against the college freshers a few weeks previously. He was aware, too, of Green-wood's extraordinary reputation as an impressive thinker on the game.

'Playing with Clive was a real eye-opener,' says Cooke. 'He had amazing ability. I remember one session when we were training in the wet. Earle was doing an All Blacks routine, which we had to do twenty times without dropping the ball. Otherwise we had to start again. On the twentieth occasion, the scrum-half threw out an awful pass. Clive slid towards the ball and managed to catch it, arms outstretched, just inches off the ground. Then he flicked it up to me. He was very unassuming and willing to listen. I thought he would really benefit from spending more time on his rugby and suggested Loughborough.'

Clive sent off his letter of application, attended an interview, and by December 1974 he had been accepted to start the following September.

Clive stayed at NatWest for nine months before deciding he'd had enough. He had planned to stay there until leaving for Loughborough, but the stuffy, formal environment of banking was not for him. He also knew that he wanted to earn money on the basis of effort and performance rather than a flat salary, which did nothing to incentivise the hardest workers. It seemed that in banking, once you had signed the contract of employment, the pressure was off. He wanted to work in a meritocracy – so he became a carpet fitter.

Now this might not strike one as the most obvious or logical move for a young capitalist, but Clive found that when he was paid by the square foot of carpet, he made around ten times what he had been earning at the bank. The blunt, achievement:rewards policy of the carpet-fitting business appealed to his mentality.

The managers at the bank were disappointed to see him go, less for the high standard of his paper clipping than for the fact that he was becoming a more high-profile player with every match, and they saw great value in linking their Richmond bank with his success on the field. He found himself being offered all manner of jobs to stay with them, none of which appealed to him. In May 1975, he resigned his trainee position and began fitting carpets in offices and houses around Richmond.

As well as changing his job, Clive had changed his living arrangements, moving in with two characters delighting under the names 'Basher' Briggs and Paddy McLoughlin. McLoughlin, a solicitor playing in the fifth team at the club, owned a flat in nearby Shepperton, which he shared with Briggs, a marketing officer for British Airways. Briggs played in the third team. Clive moved in with them, sleeping on the sofa in a rent-free arrangement that suited his pocket. Colin Herridge, secretary of Harlequins, says, 'Clive was quiet and unassuming, the sort who sat at the front of the coach and was earnest and thoughtful. When he became friends with Briggs we all raised our eyebrows a little. I guess you could say they were polar opposites.'

About McLoughlin, he says, 'I hope I'm not doing him a disservice here, but my memory is that he was rather wild. Paddy and Briggsy, eh? Did he really live with those two?'

On the field, things continued apace for Clive. He was a Harlequins regular, playing thirteen matches by the end of the year, then a further eleven in 1975, including the end-of-season tour to Bath, Swansea and Cardiff. In January 1975, he was selected for the England Under-19s representative side. His first match for them was against Wales, where he came up against those he had met at the Welsh schoolboys trials. It gave him great pleasure to run rings around them and score the try of the match. England won 9–6 in a game dominated by the forwards. It was a display of old-fashioned, ten-man rugby – not Clive's sort of rugby at all.

His England experiences, even at colts level, were hugely disappointing. He had been warned by Cooke that the philosophy of the national side was a long way from the philosophy of Kirton at Harlequins. It taught Clive the importance of a coach and how essential it was to have the right person guiding the team. He knew that he wanted to work with coaches of Kirton's calibre, men who would inspire and motivate him. Men like Jim Greenwood at Loughborough University.

Chapter Seven

Posh 'n' Becks

---

*'There is no abstract art. You must always start with something.
Afterwards you can remove all traces of reality.'* **Pablo Picasso**

For Clive, it was love at first sight – a searing, all-consuming, powerful love. They met and he fell, instantly and totally. He is still in love today, in many respects. His first meeting with Jim Greenwood, a burly, burring Scotsman, had him entranced, dazed and enlightened. Greenwood, a former Scotland captain and British Lion, was the enigmatic coach of Loughborough University, frequently described as the 'best coach Scotland never had'. Clive was a nineteen-year-old with a penchant for quick-thinking, fast-action rugby. He loved the handling game, he loved thinking rugby and he liked to be challenged. It was a match made in heaven. Greenwood would make such an impression on Woodward that even many years after leaving university, when Clive was coach of the England team and had concerns about Jonny Wilkinson's decision-making ability in the run-up to the World Cup, he turned to Greenwood for help.

'It was flattering that he asked,' says Greenwood. 'It confirmed what an impact the Loughborough years had on him.'

The Loughborough years? Those four years in which Clive was free to develop his love of sport fully and comprehensively with no carpets to be fitted and no banking duties to distract him. Clive describes his time at Loughborough as being the very antithesis of his 'dark years' at HMS *Conway* – light relief, a joy. He was able to play his beloved football, develop his growing skills as a rugby player, and learn about new sports, which would, in turn, further develop his knowledge of rugby.

He used his intellectual vigour to understand the multi-faceted nature of sport. He learnt that the simple acts of passing, catching, kicking and scoring are the result of a mesh of biomechanical, physical and psychological factors. Performing those tasks under pressure relies on a mix of personality characteristics and strength of mind. He learnt much about the complexity of sport and the tiny little details that lead to improvements in performance.

In the seventies and eighties, Loughborough played an important part in sports study. It provided an environment in which many sporting disciplines came together in one great melting pot. It was Clive's first experience of the power and influence that an élite environment can wield. Loughborough also had great leaders. Many of the country's best sports coaches were gathered on campus. When Clive became coach of the England rugby team, he identified environment and leadership as two of the key ways in which he could influence the performance of the team.

Loughborough University was the best sporting environment around, with great facilities and enthusiastic sportsmen and women determined to be the best, which created a highly competitive atmosphere and produced outstanding results. Loughborough was so strong that if, for example, the university had been a sovereign state, it would have come eleventh in the medals table for track events at the 1984 Olympics in Los Angeles. In the 1986 European athletics championship, it would have beaten West Germany in the track events. That was the level of competition in the place.

The rugby club sustained a first-class fixture list. The combination of youth and lots of spare time meant that university sides such as Loughborough were playing some of the best rugby in the country. Professor Stuart Biddle was chair of the athletics union when Clive was there. He still works at the university today. 'The first-class sides used to say, "If you come to us and beat us, we'll come to you." Loughborough didn't have a proper home ground, but the teams would come and we'd find a local ground to play them on.'

So much for the environment – in rugby, the great leadership came from a certain J. T. Greenwood.

Today, Jim Greenwood is retired and living in south-west Scotland. He is sitting in his armchair looking out across Loch Lomond. His wife, Margot, walks across the room clutching two bottles of wine, as we speak. 'Perfect woman,' he mutters, visibly lifting at the sight of the wine – and his wife, of course.

Greenwood first met Clive when the eighteen-year-old bank clerk attended an interview for a place at Loughborough.

'We met in the physical education centre – a very large gymnasium,' says Greenwood. 'We talked for a while and I was impressed enough, then I said to him, "What can't you do?" and Clive confessed that he couldn't kick with his left foot. I've told this story before, but people don't realise the significance of a student, desperate to be the main man at the college, admitting to a real weakness in front of his main lecturer. He was never afraid of exposing his weaknesses in order to try to get them corrected. He just wanted to be as good as he possibly could be. I told him to go out and learn to kick with his left foot and he did. It's impossible for me to tell you how impressed I was with the man – to stand there and admit a genuine weakness and then to learn how to correct it. I was excited just to think how much he might learn from his time at Loughborough.

'The whole aim of my coaching philosophy was to make sure students understood the principles behind what they were doing. Having them analyse their own game and confront their weaknesses was key to that. If they understood themselves and the principles of play, they could apply them under pressure. There's nothing a coach can do when the players are on the pitch – it's up to them, then. Half the time I didn't even go to matches. I'd go out with my wife for the day. I wanted them to realise that it was all down to them on match day.'

Greenwood is the author of the only rugby coaching books that Clive has read (or will admit to having read) – *Total Rugby* and *Think Rugby*. The titles sum up the man. This is the thinking man's rugby coach, a bright, adventurous and thoughtful leader. He summed up his attitude to coaching at Loughborough thus: 'The campus was a huge laboratory in which I could test out all my theories and hypotheses. I always felt that I was free to try anything and everything. I'd watch how things came together and see how I would do things differently. There were no limits. We'd just try to play the best rugby that it was possible to play. Clive loved the environment. He thrived in it. He loved to be challenged and was always seeking that edge.'

Greenwood remembers Clive as an 'intensely amiable' man. 'I liked him and we had a very good relationship. He would often turn to me for help and advice and, if I'm honest, I felt sometimes that I wasn't qualified to give it, so I'd just talk through things with him – like whether he should play for a club and what he should do with his future. I tried to give him the best advice I could but I sometimes felt I was standing in for his dad. Where most students would talk to their parents, he would talk to me. I was flattered.'

Greenwood was one of the crucial half a dozen men whose words would shape, confirm and supplement the philosophy that under-pinned England's World Cup victory.

Clive razzed up to the university in his bright yellow mini a week before the start of term in order to involve himself in pre-season rugby training. He had a room in William Morris Hall, the main hall of resi-dence on the campus, as he studied for what was known as a 'three and one' – a three-year sports science degree followed by a one-year teacher training course.

He began his career at Loughborough well, attracting the attention not only of the rugby coach but also of the women on campus. The quiet, studious-looking rugby coach of today is described as the 'main man about town' in the late seventies and early eighties.

Dave Bunker was a lecturer in sports psychology and soccer coach at Loughborough in 1979. 'Clive was a bit of a "Mr Cool" about the place,' he says. 'He was good-looking, with a lot more hair than he has now. He enjoyed parties and the social life. He was very sociable. Rugby was a status sport and he was one of the big stars. He was like a celebrity when he walked around.'

Before too long, Clive had been noticed by Helen Murray, a tall, attractive hockey player, studying for a degree in PE and geography. Helen Murray captured the imagination not just of Clive, but of most of the male staff members at Loughborough. Those who struggle to remember a thing about Clive have clear memories of his girlfriend. She played hockey for Leicestershire and the Midlands. By the time she was nineteen, she was playing for England. The couple were Loughborough's answer to 'Posh 'n' Becks'. They were the Gavin Henson and Charlotte Church of their day. 'We were all terribly envious,' says Professor Biddle.

Sue Campbell, now the chair of UK Sport, was the first female lecturer at Loughborough. She taught Clive in a variety of subjects, including dance and trampolining. Sadly, she cannot remember how he fared in these unlikely disciplines. She has no recollection of his pointy toes or seat drops.

'No, I just don't remember him trampolining, but he was much younger then, and keen to try all new sports, so he was probably better than you might think. I remember him as being good at most things he did. He was a great, fun-loving, handsome guy.'

Clive was not the greatest student to stride through the gates of Loughborough University. Others spent more time in the library, wrote more lucid essays and read more books, but in terms of really benefiting from his time – not just in perfecting his own game of rugby, but in developing his sense of what sport was about – few can have gained more from Loughborough than Clive. He threw himself into all sports. He watched other sports people and tried to learn from them as much as he did from Greenwood.

Lord Sebastian Coe was a student at the same time as Clive. 'He was very inquisitive and it was not unusual to see him watching the weight training and circuit training that athletes did. I'm not surprised by what he has achieved. There's an expression that a lot of people use about Clive and it's my experience of him too – he's always had an obsession with detail.'

One of Clive's lecturers, Rex Hazeldine, taught rugby and exercise physiology at the college. He went on to become the fitness adviser for the England team, working with Geoff Cooke and Jack Rowell from 1989–95, but leaving before Clive's arrival. 'I remember Clive as an all-rounder,' he says. 'Clive could turn his hand to most sports and play them well. He had a presence about him. He was pretty positive and knew what he wanted.'

Rod Thorpe, a sports science lecturer who taught Clive 'skills acquisition' and tennis when he was a fresher, has similar memories of Clive as 'a very capable and bright guy. As a student he was a strong character, and he already showed signs that he knew where he wanted to go, what he wanted to do. He had drive and awareness. He was very gifted across the board in sports. He arrived as a rugby player, but whereas some students found gymnastics or swimming or soccer difficult, Clive was not one of them. It was in his character to be successful.'

But it was as a rugby player that Clive shone most brightly. He slotted straight into the first team, moving from fly-half to centre under the direction of Greenwood. By October of his first year, as well as playing for England colts and Loughborough, he was invited to play for Eastern Counties in their opening county championship game against Sussex.

'Clive had clear and obvious skills. You didn't have to be a rugby expert to watch the way he ran and realise he was something special,' says Bunker. 'He could ghost past players as if they weren't there.'

His skills kept him in the first team all season but then, in May, when he headed for London to compete in the Middlesex Sevens, disaster struck. This was the end-of-season jamboree that delighted so many. Thousands of people would turn up and spend the entire day getting hopelessly drunk, catching a few of the matches between rounds. Sevens is a game that is perfect for students, given its reliance on speed. On this occasion, though, it was not such a rip-roaring occasion for Clive. He broke his leg and faced a summer of recuperation. The rest of the team went on to win while Clive was taken off to hospital.

'I felt very sorry for him,' says Greenwood. 'They brought him back in a plaster cast, so we drove him to Oxfordshire where his parents lived. We thought it would be better for him to stay there than come back to halls of residence, especially since it was almost the end of term. His parents didn't seem all that happy to see any of us, if I'm honest. I felt as though they'd have preferred it if we hadn't taken Clive there at all. It was an uncomfortable feeling and I felt a great deal of affection for Clive. I probably felt I understood him a little better after that. We escaped as soon as we could and went for an Indian meal on the way back, but I won't forget that feeling in the house. It's not hard to see why Clive's so driven – so determined to be a success.'

'I accept that no one understands someone else's parents or the relationship between a father and his son, but I know that Clive felt his father made decisions that he should have made for himself, and there was a certain resentment between the two of them because of that. I certainly felt it that day.'

Clive's broken leg repaired over the summer and he returned for his second year as a student. One of his first classes was football training with Bunker.

'We were playing a small-side game – it wasn't competitive,' says Bunker. 'Clive was involved in a tackle and went to ground. Nothing seemed untoward. "I've hurt my leg," he said. He got up and I asked, "How's it feeling?" He said, "A bit achy." I said, "I don't think anything's broken." If you break your leg, you know about it. It's fiendishly painful. I said, "Do you feel nauseous?" He said no, so I told him to go back to his hall [of residence] and go to hospital as a precaution. He went and had it X-rayed and they said it wasn't broken, but the leg didn't improve. He went back and they took X-rays from different angles, and these showed up a hairline fracture. It was a real blow to him and I felt bad for making the wrong diagnosis.'

It took Clive most of the term to recover, but when he did he went straight back into the first team and was selected to play for England Under-23s. He continued to play for the Under-23s side until 1977.

'Clive really made the most of college and his game improved a great deal,' says Coe. 'Most sportspeople stuck with their own "type" but not Clive. He wanted to learn from everyone. That's why he improved so much. That's also why he went on to make such a great coach.'

In Clive's third year at Loughborough – his final year of the degree course, before he moved on to teacher training – he began playing for England students. He was called up in October of his third year to play against Argentina at Gloucester RFC. He also played for London

Counties against the All Blacks and England B against France (his only international match at B level). At the end of his third year at Loughborough, he captained the college side to victory in the University Cup (the UAU Championship).

'He stood out at Loughborough,' says Greenwood. 'He was a talented player. There were around a dozen internationals in ten years at Loughborough – but he still stood out.'

Away from the rugby field, Clive was equally well regarded. Biddle was president of the Athletics Union and remembers an incident when non-sports fans at the university were planning to call a meeting one Thursday night to push through a change of usage for one of the sports halls, which would have prevented certain sports clubs from using it for training.

'I knew they'd organised it on Thursday evening because the rugby team were training so none of them would be there to object,' says Biddle. 'The rugby team were among the most vocal at the college, so they were the ones you would be most eager to keep from protesting.

'I told Clive I needed his help. I believed that the rugby team could stop the change of usage. Clive said, "Leave it with me." I remember that meeting so clearly. We all sat there, with the non-sports people thinking they would win without a fight. I thought they would, too. They outnumbered sportspeople because the sporty types were all at training. Then, I heard a noise, and in through the door came the entire rugby squad – one after the other. They stopped the motion going through. Clive showed real support for his fellow sports students and obviously had considerable power over the team to rally them like that.'

In Clive's final year at Loughborough, he captained the college side on a three-week tour to Canada to play in the Monterrey tournament. Hazeldine was the coach.

'We won that tour,' says Hazeldine, 'and it was because Clive was captain. He showed great qualities of leadership. He was a student and certainly enjoyed life, as you should at that age, but he was respected by the other players, not only for his rugby football but as a good leader. What was most impressive was the way he handled pressure. He wanted to learn. He was a naturally enquiring person compared with many of his mates, who were enjoying rugby but letting life drift by.'

Clive graduated with a sports science degree in 1979 after living a close to exemplary college life. Clearly, it was a long time ago, and lecturers and fellow students were being asked to cast their minds back some time to recall stories and thoughts about him, but the clear message was that Clive threw himself into college life, adored sport and was quite a superstar there. No one can recall him as being anything other than 'mature', 'responsible' and 'hard working'.

After graduating, Clive spoke to Greenwood about his future, thinking that he would probably become a teacher. 'I felt that teaching wouldn't be quite right for him,' says Greenwood. 'I felt he should be in business. I told him that Rank Xerox was an excellent local company with offices round the world. He liked that idea. We also talked about clubs and Leicester was the obvious choice. It was local, which he liked, and one of the best clubs in the country, which he also liked.'

Chapter Eight

Lions and Tigers

'That's the way things come clear. All of a sudden. And then you realise how obvious they've been all along.' **Madeleine L'Engle**

Poor Mrs Woodward. It's not hard to see how she got so confused. Any mother would. Her elder son had joined some club called the Tigers. 'Then a year later, he's called up by the Lions,' says Ian Smith, a fellow Leicester Tigers player. 'His mum just looked at us all and said, "Who are all these lions and tigers?"'

As the 1970s rolled into the 1980s, Clive was having the most successful period of his playing career. The style of game played at Leicester appealed to him enormously, and he expressed enthusiasm for the family-orientated environment of Leicester, rather than the 'beers with the boys' style of Harlequins.

He joined Leicester in the summer of 1979 and began pre-season training, winning a first-team place at the beginning of the 1979–80 season. He was the first player in the club's history to go straight into the first team. Clive felt at home immediately. The combination of a good working environment, top players and a passionate, throw-the-rule-book-out-the-window coach made it his kind of place (do you detect a pattern developing here?).

Hurling the rule book away at Leicester was Herbert Victor White, known to all and sundry as 'Chalkie'. While Greenwood was described as 'the best coach that Scotland never had', White was considered 'the best coach that England never had'. He was one of the most creative and original coaches around. His shock of snowy white hair topped one of the brightest minds in English rugby. Like an old owl, he fluttered – wise and thoughtful, measured and exact.

White passed away while this book was being written. He died after a long illness that robbed a strong and dignified man of much of his memory and capacity to think and articulate his feelings. I worked with White when we were both employed by the Rugby Football Union in the 1990s. He was the divisional technical administrator for the south west. We fought constantly. I suspect he was rather alarmed at the arrival of a woman in the RFU's technical department for the first time, and he challenged me endlessly – sometimes unfairly. Then, one day, I ran a coaching day for junior schoolteachers and White turned up. He stood on the side as I encouraged plump, middle-aged headmistresses to remove their support stockings and court shoes and have a go. By the end of it, we had over a hundred pink, sweaty teachers smiling and declaring their new-found enthusiasm for the sport. A hundred new schools would take up rugby. White sent me a note promising me any help I needed in the future, any time. I took him up on the offer many times. He always delivered.

He was a remarkable man and is missed by everyone whose life he touched – by Clive more than most, I'm sure. He was successful because he challenged players to give more than they believed they could. He provoked them into thinking about the game and insisted on high standards of dress and fitness way before others had cottoned on to such things. White would become the third in the line of influential men to touch Clive's life. The effect of their impact on him was to set the highest standards.

When England won the World Cup, RFU officers took the trophy to show to Chalkie. By then, he was quite ill and living in a nursing home. Chalkie looked confused as the magnificent gold Cup was held before him, but part of that trophy belonged to him and one hopes that, even in his weakness, he understood that.

Clive's instant selection for the Leicester first team was good news for him, but not such great news for those who had previously been vying for the position. Brian Hall and Terry Burwell (who is now the RFU's community rugby and operations director) were the incumbents at the centre of the field until Clive's arrival. Burwell insists that 'It was good to have him [Clive] at Leicester – he fitted in well and really added to the team.' But Steve Kenney recalls some early difficulties: 'In training, Brian and Terry tackled Clive harder than anybody else, but Clive came back for more. He wasn't intimidated by it, at all.'

It wasn't just in the centre that Clive had conflicts. He soon faced battles with the forwards, as well.

'Deano [Dean Richards] would have running battles with Clive,' says Kenney. 'Clive wanted to run the ball from behind the posts, Deano wanted to boot it out. Chalkie used to tell us that the best bit of ball you get may be in the first minute, and you've got to use it when it comes. That [philosophy] suited Clive, as well as a lot of other players at the club.'

But there is no question that Clive was very well liked and he formed an excellent centre partnership with Paul Dodge, who describes Clive as being 'a bit eccentric but he was a good player, very talented, there's no doubt about that. We played together for a long time so we sort of knew what each other was going to do. After a while, we could read each other.'

Dodge was the sensible, calculating, organised, dependable individual. Clive was the nutter who might score you a try or lose you the game. Even Clive wasn't sure what he was going to do when he got the ball – he relied on instinct and intuition.

Dusty Hare played full-back for Leicester and England. He says, 'Clive was the archetypal student – down at the bottom of the garden with the fairies, like we all were when we were young – but he was refreshing. He always had ideas and was always doing something different. We used to create moves with the backs during training and we had one where Les Cusworth would pass the ball to Clive and he would head it over the onrushing opposition. We called it the Tommy Lawton, after the old footballer. Clive came up with that. He was always trying to come up with something different.'

Kenney also remembers this particular idea. 'Clive came up with some really wacky moves. One Thursday training session he created a move we called Maradona [clearly the move had several names!]. I had to pass to Les [Cusworth, fly-half], who passed over the top of Paul Dodge. Clive would jump up and head the ball towards the goalposts so that Dodge could run through the inside-centre channel, catch the ball and score under the posts. Chalkie said, "It will never work, don't ever try it." But Clive said, "Chalkie, it's a guaranteed six-pointer." [A try was worth four points then.] Come Saturday and twenty minutes into the game against Coventry, Les called a Maradona. The ball skidded off the top of Clive's head into the arms of a Coventry player who ran up the other end to score. At the end of the game, Chalkie had a face like thunder, but Clive told him, "I told you it would be a six-pointer!" And the move worked the following week.'

Many of the players of the time recall how Clive would warm up for a match by standing with his back to the posts and throwing the ball back over his head, trying to hit the posts with it.

'He was quite unorthodox in his thought process, on the pitch and off it,' says Kenney. 'Sometimes he would talk very sensibly, but sometimes he was so off the wall that you wondered whether it was genius or stupidity. He wasn't restricted by conventional thinking.'

Alan King was a sales manager at Rank Xerox, who lived in the Midlands and supported Leicester. He'd developed a friendly relationship with the club and, along with Henry Spokes – a technical manager at Xerox, who was also very involved at Leicester – he had found jobs for many of the club's rugby players.

King was used to being contacted by people at the club, eager to foist some fledgling star on him. 'So it wasn't too much of a surprise when someone from the club came to me and said, "We've got this young player just joined us, called Woodward, and we need to get him a job. Can you help?" I wasn't keen, to be honest. I'd had so many requests recently and I didn't want the office full of rugby players, but I agreed to meet him to see what I thought of him.'

Clive was dispatched to meet King.

'What really impressed me about him was that he went to Loughborough – where I went. Once we got talking about that, I got to know him,' says King.'He wasn't overbearing, as I thought he might be. He was quiet and thoughtful. I decided to give him a go but I was quite concerned about whether he'd be too quiet in the brash sales environment that we'd created at Xerox.'

King offered Clive a job to start straightaway. Clive pulled out his suit (not the tweed one) and prepared to dazzle the world as Leicester's hottest photocopier salesman.

'He may have lacked a certain sales ability in those early years but he made up for it by being able to get appointments because of his status as a rugby player. That's what we used him for. He was quite introspective back then – shy, self-effacing and never pushy but, God, he could open doors,' says King.

Peter Russell ran the London offices of Rank Xerox. He has clear memories of meeting the Midlands office's new recruit. 'I remember one occasion when we all went out to a lake in Leicester. Xerox had hired some boats for us to play around in. We all had a go at steering and most of us couldn't do it, including Clive. We then went to have lunch, and while we all sat in the sun, drinking beer and eating, Clive stayed on the water, desperate to get the boat working. He didn't come to join us until he could do it. He was very single-minded.'

Xerox had a reputation for its tough business environment in the eighties. 'It was male-dominated for a start,' recalls Russell, 'which created an egotistical, win-at-all-costs approach. There was certainly no intellectual management style, like Clive's is now. This was what you might call the Nero-style of management – give them loads of money, and if they don't do the job, sack 'em.'

There were performance tables through which salesmen were measured against one another, and sales teams were pitted against other branches. It was an extremely competitive environment.

'At Xerox, we defined objectives, measured against benchmark figures and put processes in place to ensure activity levels,' confirms King.'I think it suited Clive because it was a system in which there was a clear definition of what had to be done and rewards for achievement. All the managers he worked with – including me, if I'm honest – were quite ruthless. It gave him an insight into a tough but extremely effective business world where rewards came for hard work.'

Steve Holdstock worked at Xerox with Clive and played for the club. The two became close friends. 'For seven years, I don't think a day went by when we didn't talk to one another,' he says. 'Clive would go all over the place, making deals and getting business. I didn't get the impression he was shy, although I know people talk now about how shy he was back then. He always seemed confident to me, and very able. He was good at organising, fostering team spirit and bending the rules to make us winners.

'The only thing that was frustrating about him was that he had a short attention span, which could be really annoying. We'd be doing one thing and suddenly he'd completely change his mind and want us to do something else instead. He has the balls to do things differently, but we'd be left floundering when he suddenly, without warning, totally changed course. We were all very loyal to Clive, though – he is very good at getting people to want to work for him. I liked him because away from work and rugby, he was a genuinely kind man.'

On one occasion, a friend of Steve's, Helen, was in Harlow Wood Hospital with a broken back. She was in plaster from waist to neck. Steve told Clive about her and Clive said, 'Well, why don't we go and see her?' It was an hour's drive away but Clive insisted they went.

'It was a really nice gesture,' says Holdstock. 'Clive signed Helen's cast and made her day. I'll never forget that.'

He was good fun, too. 'At one post-match reception, Clive took on Les [Cusworth] in a drinking game,' says Ian Smith. 'Clive was drinking water but Les hadn't spotted it. Les was carried out pretty soon.'

The memories and stories about Clive at this time go some way towards explaining one of the puzzles of the Woodward story. As a player, he was a maverick and an eccentric, a man who didn't like training and found any attempt to organise him constraining. Yet as a coach, he was the opposite – well organised, prepared, efficient, leaving nothing to chance.

Clearly, as a businessman, Clive was hard working – not a natural salesman, according to King, but willing to put in the time and effort to get results, his innately competitive nature driving him to achieve targets and win competitions. When it comes to coaching, Clive treats the clubs he is involved with like businesses – so Clive the businessman steps up to the plate. The maverick tendencies burst through every so often, but there is no doubt that Clive the coach has much more in common with Clive the businessman than Clive the player.

Clive's aim as a coach would be to provide an élite environment in which those with intuitive skills and flair could maximise their talent and flourish. Above all, he wanted to make playing international rugby an enjoyable experience – one step up from other rugby. Certainly one step up from the international game that he experienced.

Clive received his international call-up to sit on the bench in autumn 1979. Then, in 1980, he received his first Five Nations call-up, summoned to sit on the bench again for England's first game, against Ireland. By this stage, Clive was Leicester's top try scorer, with fourteen to his name. He had been playing first-class rugby for Leicester for around six months. He joined an England team desperate for victory. England had not won a championship since 1963, or a Triple Crown since 1960. They had not won the Grand Slam since 1957.

This was an era in which replacements were rarely used so Clive could, conceivably, have watched the entire championship dressed in an England tracksuit and sitting on the uncomfortable old bench, high up in the stand. He watched England take the lead in the first half, then halfway through the second, Tony Bond crumpled into a heap in the middle of the field. Clive was told to take off his tracksuit and make the journey down to the pitch. He had gone from new boy at Leicester to international centre in the crunch of a bone. For nineteen minutes, he ran around the field, hoping for the chance to prove himself, but he touched the ball just once in that time and was penalised for not releasing it in the tackle. The game, a forwards-driven, tiresome match, ended in victory for England by 24–9 and a cap for young Woodward.

'It wasn't the best way to start your career, but Clive showed style even when he came on to replace me,' says Bond, rather magnanimously. 'When he was playing you always had to be aware – you had to make sure you could tackle him early on, before he started running. Once he won his first cap, he progressively improved his game while I progressively put on weight – a stone and a half, if I remember. He was always very well organised, very thoughtful. He'd go out, but knew when to stop. He was very popular because he was such a nice bloke.'

Clive played for England between 1980 and 1984. In that time, he marked himself out as a player of rare ability. He was a creative and elusive centre in a team that had been dominated by forwards. Fran Cotton says, 'Playing for England back then, you didn't really get to know other players like you do today, because you were with each other for such a short space of time. We'd meet up, play, then go home. But I do remember that Clive wanted to do things differently. The rest of us had probably got into something of a rut, but this skinny little new boy wanted to change the world.'

Bill Beaumont was captain of the England team when Clive began his international career. 'He was bright and adventurous, and a nice lad. I liked him immensely and he was a very talented player. One of the girls in the backs, of course, but nice all the same.'

Clive retained his place for the next game of the Five Nations, against France in Paris, where his partnership with Nick Preston helped England to win the match 17–13. It was England's first triumph on French soil for sixteen years. Beaumont said, afterwards, 'Everybody said about how the French backs were going to rip us apart. Clive Woodward and Nick Preston in the middle were really great.' Clive's career was starting to take off.

Next, England faced Wales at Twickenham. Wales was still Clive's nemesis – memories of his desperately unhappy schooldays loomed large. He was paired with his Leicester team-mate Paul Dodge in the centre. The partnership proved to be highly effective and lasted for a further three years and fourteen matches before being curtailed when Woodward dislocated his shoulder in 1983. England were outscored by two tries to nil, but an injury-time penalty won them a 9–8 victory in a brutal match.

The final game – the one on which the Grand Slam hinged – was against Scotland and Clive was responsible for setting up two tries in the first half to break the back of Scottish resistance. England created an unassailable 16–3 half-time lead and scored three more tries to win the match and the Grand Slam. Clive was named the man of the match.

'Woodward was a classy player,' says Cotton, 'but he was also fiery. I remember him grabbing a player and punching him when we played against Scotland in that final Grand Slam game. I saw it and I know this is a terrible thing to say, but I was quite impressed – him being a back and everything. I thought then, "There's more to this guy than meets the eye." He was clearly frustrated with the way we were playing but I told him to keep his head down and not say anything or he would end up not being selected. He didn't listen of course!'

Clive was at the heart of England's biggest win for a generation. Victory had been hard earned and long in coming, so it was keenly celebrated, but Clive remembers watching his team-mates in their state of near ecstasy and wondering what on earth they were so delighted about. Yes, they had won a Grand Slam – but the manner of the victory had left a lot to be desired. Clive vowed that next time they won a Grand Slam, it would be with free-flowing, thinking rugby that they could be proud of. He had no idea, of course, that England would not win a Grand Slam again while he was a player. White had always told them to use each bit of ball they got because it may be their last. Perhaps the same applied to victories – celebrate each one because it may be your last!

Clive did not enjoy his experiences of international rugby. He felt frustrated at the lack of invention from coaches and players. The clever rugby espoused by Kirton, Greenwood and White seemed light years ahead of what was happening with England. They had won the Grand Slam but, for Clive, it was not enough. He yearned to play good, fast-running, open, thinking rugby for his country as he had for university and still did for club.

There were huge differences between club rugby and international rugby for many reasons – not least the amount of time spent with the England team. Back in the 1980s, players would meet just a couple of days before matches – and there were significantly fewer matches back then – so the impact that the England management could make on the players was minimal. Nevertheless, Clive always felt that the England coaches could have done more. The conditions could have been better, players could have been made to feel special, as if they were taking a step up. The best facilities and coaches should have been on hand. But the man heralded as the best English coach of the era, Chalkie White, was considered too controversial for the role, so he wound up as the south-west divisional technical administrator, and the job was given to Mike Davis, who was described as 'mild mannered and ineffectual' by the players. It is indicative of the era, and of the expectations of the team, that a great coach was overlooked because he might be too 'difficult' to work with.

Fran Cotton says, 'Such personnel decisions at management level were mirrored in the selection of the team, which was marked by a lack of consistency and understanding. It took until 1980 for selectors even to talk to the captain, so it wasn't until then that the best team available made it on to the pitch. Isn't it interesting that that was the year England won? The structure of the game was all wrong for the success to continue, though, because the cream couldn't rise to the top. When a lot of the older players left in 1980–81, there was nobody to replace us.

'The chairman of selectors was all-powerful. He was always a former player and he picked his mates. It was frustrating because we just couldn't play at our best. The Welsh players who went with us on Lions tours were always surprised at how good we were – you never saw the England team playing like that normally. Clive eventually suffered from the selection problems – no question about it.'

For Clive, it was all desperately frustrating. Those frustrations would linger in him and eventually fan the fires of determination that would allow him to transform the England team some twenty years later.

Mike Weston was an England selector when Clive first played for England. He says, 'I'm not sure why Clive is so critical of his time with England. The problem he had was that he was a scatterbrain. He had his head in the clouds. He was very laid back, and seemed uninterested in training and preparing – indeed, he seemed to actively dislike it and disapprove of it.'

Clive would say that the reason for his active disapproval of training was his active disapproval of the style of play. Bunker, Clive's lecturer from Loughborough, says, 'He was massively disappointed with the England set-up of that time. It was very pack-driven. He hated the way his England career developed, or rather didn't develop. I think what annoyed him more than anything was that he didn't achieve his full potential while playing for his country.'

In the summer of 1980, Leicester made it through to the Cup final once again. They had beaten Moseley to win in 1979 and now found themselves top of the tree again, with Clive in the side for his first Cup final appearance. They played London Irish, and Leicester supporters strode through the streets with banners declaring, 'Tigers Eat Leprechauns'. Peter Wheeler captained the team to a 21–9 victory. The triumph would precipitate a busy few months for Clive. He heard that he had been selected for the British and Irish Lions tour to South Africa that summer then, when he returned, he would marry Helen Murray at the parish church in Kibworth.

Chapter Nine

South Africa

---

*'How wonderful it is that nobody need wait a single moment
before starting to improve the world.'* **Anne Frank**

The British and Irish Lions – surely the most wonderful and absurd
concept in the sporting world. In what other sport would you take
the greatest players from four countries, bundle them on to a plane
when they've barely had time to shake hands, and deliver them to the
other side of the globe to play against the best teams in the world?
Madness – and joy. They sum up all that is best and most crazy about
the sport.

Lions tours have been with rugby for almost as long as the international game. The first Lions left for Australia and New Zealand in 1888,
just seventeen years after the first international match was played. That
first tour took place during the days of Queen Victoria and the British
Empire. Tchaikovsky had just finished his first symphony and, more
alarmingly than all this, Jason Leonard had yet to play his first game for
England – proof, if any were needed, that these tours are an integral
part of rugby football, embedded in the history and mythology of the
sport.

The 1888 team was away for nine months, three of which were spent
in travel. The team left on 8 March and returned on 11 November,
having played fifty-three games with just twenty-two players. What
glorious nonsense! There were reports of one player breaking his leg
on the way out and staying on tour because his leg had mended by the
time they played their first match. Happy days!

In 1980, nearly a hundred years later, Clive received a phone call to tell him he had been selected to play for the Lions in South Africa.

'By being selected, he avoided the 2p phone call,' says Peter Winterbottom, the former England and Lions back-row player. Winterbottom refers to the much-espoused 2p theory, which suggests that when selectors in the 1980s needed to call players to tell them whether they were selected for international sides, they sat in the Lensbury Club with a pile of 2p and 10p coins in front of them. For a call to a player who hadn't been selected, or had been dropped, they'd put 2p in the phone box, so that when the player asked the reason, the money would run out and the selector could shout, 'Sorry, got to go.' Those who had been selected were treated to the extravagance of a 10p call.

By the time of Clive's phone call, Lions tours had been greatly reduced in size. This would be the first of the short tours, in which eighteen matches were condensed into ten weeks. It was also a slightly controversial tour, given the political situation in South Africa. A wave of opposition grew in the days before departure. South Africa had not competed in the Olympic Games since 1960. They were barred from competing in cricket and soccer but had managed to rejoin the rugby fold when the South African Rugby Board absorbed the 'coloured South African Rugby Federation' in April 1979. Now, at first glance, this may not appear to constitute progress in any modern sense of the word but, at the time, that is precisely how it was seen. In any case, the heat was taken off the Lions by the United States boycott of the Moscow Games, and the tour would go ahead.

The team was to be managed and coached by Syd Millar and Noel Murphy. Bill Beaumont became the first Englishman to captain a tour for fifty years. It was a second Lions tour for Beaumont. On the first, in 1977, he was selected as replacement for Nigel Horton but got stuck in a traffic jam on his way to Heathrow Airport and ended up running the final two miles, carrying all his luggage. He had slightly more notice of his selection in 1980. Syd Millar rang him half an hour before the names were released to the media.

Beaumont would lead his side into the unknown. South Africa had been out of international rugby for years, so few people in Britain had a clear idea of how good they would be. The Lions had a good start, winning every provincial game leading up to the first Test and lifting the mood of everyone in the tour party.

'In 1980 the camaraderie of the Lions was brilliant,' says Ray Gravell, who roomed with Clive for some of the tour. 'Syd Millar and Noel Murphy were the perfect combination. Syd had been coach in 1974. One day, he says, "Right, in 1974, we travelled on a Sunday. We won't do that this time. We'll make Sunday a day of rest."

'Well, a few of us got together in the hotel on the rest day and said, "Let's have a drink." One drink led to another and next thing every Sunday became "Sunday School", a social day when we had lovely food and lovely wine. That wasn't what Syd's original intention had been, but he was great. As long as we produced on the field, he didn't mind the drinking. We didn't abuse it [his trust].

'The rugby was uncompromising, very physical. The grounds were so hard we were bouncing off them. In the last Test I felt like Superman because I was so fit by then. In the first Test, though, I couldn't believe the hardness of the ground.'

That first Test was held in Cape Town. Clive did not play but was forced to sit and watch as the backs let the forwards down (this, incidentally, became the theme of the whole tour). They lost 26–22.

There is a tradition on Lions tours of integration into the local community – players try to understand a little more about the country, and generally spread good will about the British Isles and the sport of rugby union. The 1980 Lions tour party upheld this tradition with vigour.

'We had to attend official functions and we spoke to schools – I had never done that before,' says Gravell. 'Publicly speaking to hundreds of children at a school assembly was part of the routine, and we benefited from that. It was a two-way thing – they enjoyed it and it gave us a different perspective as well. Experiencing different cultures was educational. We met a mix of people.

'I saw things that I hadn't seen before. To understand fully what South Africa was like, you needed to have lived or worked there, but it was clearly an unjust situation – we could see that from our visit. We went to townships, gained a brief insight and were introduced to all aspects of life.'

Clive's first Test match was the second of the tour, played at Bloem-fontein. He came on as a substitute with Ray Gravell, but his arrival did not help the Lions. They slumped to their second defeat of the tour, losing 26–19 because every error they made was turned to immediate advantage by their hosts.

John Beattie roomed with Clive for some of the tour. 'He had a very unorthodox way of playing,' said Beattie. 'My memory is of him always smiling. He was never badly behaved – never doing the rock-star bit. He enjoyed a pint, though. We trained twice a day and we worked hard. In South Africa, I remember a lot of running. I imagine Clive's modern controlled appearance is part of the act – I remember him laughing and having fun. I'm sure his side of the room was much neater than mine.' Clive says it wasn't. 'I'm the messiest person in the world. John's being kind,' he says when told of the 'tidy' slur on his character.

'As a player, Clive was very accomplished, stylish,' says Gravell. 'I was a raging bull. He was elegant and very English. He was laid-back and relaxed.'

The third Test match was played in Port Elizabeth. Once again, Clive was in the team. He started in the centre, then Dodge came on to replace him so he could move over to the wing to replace John Car-leton. They lost the match 12–10, and Clive committed one of the biggest blunders of his career. He chose a fine time to do it. This was the match that the Lions knew they had to win if they were to emerge from the tour with a semblance of credibility. They were hanging on grimly at 7–6 when a kick was put through, which Woodward rather lamely tapped into touch, just when an unsubtle blast into the stands was needed. Then he turned his back when he should have stayed alert to cover the quick throw. Gerrie Germishuys, the Springbok wing, grabbed the ball, threw inside, took a return pass and scored the try that won the match.

'Clive fucked up big time,' says Gravell, with a touch of down-to-earth honesty, 'but the beauty of rugby is that mistakes are made. Mis-takes happen and when they do you've just got to get on with it. They reacted better than us on that occasion [the quick lineout], but at other times we reacted better than they did.'

The fourth and final Test took place in Pretoria. The Lions won, becoming the first Lions team to win a fourth Test, but they had lost the series. Clive watched the match from the stand. Not only did he not play in that Test but he would never play in another Lions Test. His Lions career was effectively over, remarkable mainly for a slip-up that lost a match.

Derek Quinnell was the number 8 on the tour. He says, 'It's a shame about that because Clive was a skilful, silky runner. In my day, England had David Duckham and John Spencer. Clive Woodward was the new breed. He was one of the lads, a good lad, but he and I didn't hang out. The hairy-arse forwards were my mates. He was with the girls in the backs. He had hair in those days.'

Back with England and Leicester for the start of the 1980–81 season, things continued in much the same vein for Clive. At Leicester, he felt challenged, inspired and encouraged. With England, he turned up and played and came home again. He developed as a rugby player at Leicester, but just ran through the motions with England. It was absolutely not as he'd imagined it would be.

The first game of the 1981 Five Nations was a defeat by Wales, 21–19. The final game of the championship was a defeat by France, 16–12. Sandwiched between these were victories over Scotland (23–17) and Ireland (10–6).

The game against Wales was the one in which Clive proved beyond all doubt that he could switch from abject brilliance to abject liability at a moment's notice. The game was played at Cardiff Arms Park. England had not won in Cardiff for eighteen years and were leading 19–18 with a few seconds on the clock. The atmosphere in the stadium was electric. Wales put the ball into a scrum in the England half and Brynmor Williams, the Wales scrum-half, waited at the back for the ball to emerge. Williams dummied from the scrum (now illegal, of course), moving away on his dummy run. Fourteen England players stood onside. Woodward, in the England midfield, took the bait and ran several yards over the offside line. The penalty was given and Steve Fenwick kicked Wales to victory. As the teams left the field, Woodward was still slumped in the middle in horror, as the crowds charged on around him. He had lost England their chance of glory by being too eager, too keen.

There are worse crimes a man could be accused of than over-eagerness, but not many crimes in rugby that are greater than losing a match in the dying seconds, against Wales at Cardiff Arms Park. Especially if you haven't won there for eighteen years. Especially if you are Clive Woodward, with a particularly complex relationship with Wales and all things Welsh. It was not a good day for Clive, whichever way you dress it up. Not a good day at all.

'But you have to be fair to him,' says Dusty Hare. 'He got offside because he was ready to go up before time and went a foot over the offside line. That would have to be Clive. He is a mad professor, a bit madcap, but a great bloke.'

Tim Barnwell played alongside Clive at Leicester. 'He's a mystery,' he says. 'Clive's an incredible player. People remember the cock-ups for England and the Lions, but he was just the same for Leicester. I remember one time when he did a Devon Loch about five or ten metres from the Coventry try-line. [Devon Loch was the horse that collapsed just yards from the finish when leading the 1956 Grand National.] No one could believe it. He collapsed like a sack of spuds and the crowd just laughed. Yet you look at that try he scored against Scotland [the solo run at Twickenham that is included on a DVD of the recent Top Ten England tries]. He could do that. He could be perfect one week and mess up the next. Chalkie must have torn his hair out because Woody was so off the cuff, but he had a stroke of genius in him.'

Clive toured Argentina with England over the summer, scoring two tries in their opening game, which they drew 19–19, before beating their hosts 12–6 in the final game.

'He was doing well,' says Beaumont, 'but you knew that Clive always thought things could be so much better. He told anyone who would listen that he thought the England management had got it wrong, and that England were capable of much more.'

His outspoken criticisms of the management were not going down well. Clive was seen as something of a maverick as a player. He wasn't overly keen on training and preferred to rely on his natural skills emerging in the heat of a game. They often did but he was considered a risky player, who sometimes got it right but sometimes got it spectacularly wrong. When you added to this the fact that he was critical of the England management and their selection policy, he was not flavour of the month.

'Clive was feeling very despondent about life with England,' says Cotton. 'He didn't feel as if they wanted to play the rugby he wanted to play. He was sure that England would be a better side if they played a more expansive game. He had this dream of England playing great, fluid rugby. Then, when it came to the matches, the forwards dominated. It used to drive him nuts.'

The first match of the 1982 season brought brighter news for England – a 15–11 victory over Australia and the arrival of Erica Roe, a topless streaker, in the same afternoon. She bounced across the pitch, England won, and all was well with the world. Sadly, the feeling did not last long. By the time the Five Nations Championship came along, England's captain, Bill Beaumont, announced that he would be retiring from rugby. The first game of the championship – a 9–9 draw with Scotland would be his last match in the national colours because of a serious head injury sustained in a county game. Steve Smith took over the captaincy for the next game, against Ireland, and England lost 16–15. They won 27–15 against France in Paris in what was widely regarded as being one of the national side's best performances of the 1980s. The game featured Woodward's fourth and final international try. He exploited a hopelessly disorganised French defence to chip ahead and then play football with his own grubber kick for virtually the entire length of the field before beating one last French defender to score under the posts. They beat Wales at Twickenham by ten points in the final game of the championship (17–7).

While his rugby career was swinging between brilliance and madness, Clive's career at Rank Xerox was moving in one direction – upwards. He was proving himself to be a capable and creative manager, with a flair for thinking differently coupled with a hugely competitive streak. The qualities he showed on the rugby field were equally evident in business but more keenly rewarded. Searingly high targets were set and the reaching of them was recognised. Leicester's sales team, headed by Clive, developed a reputation for being the best and winning all the prizes.

Tim Buttimore, a colleague at Xerox and fellow rugby player, says,

'When Clive was a sales manager in Leicester and I was in Birmingham, his team were always the best. Everyone wanted to beat them. He always wanted to win the Christmas competitions or the trip abroad. Even in those days, and under that pressure, he generated a great spirit within his team. He was a good manager and you could see everyone working together, enjoying it and doing different things.'

'Clive did develop into a decent sales manager,' concedes King, Clive's immediate boss. 'He took risks and many of them paid off. He always liked to gamble, off the rugby field as well as on it. I remember one time, we bought a racehorse – Wheeler, Beaumont, a few of the other England guys and me – and called it Empeepee [to represent MPP – a marketing company of King's]. I saw it run once – Woody and I went to watch it train at Newmarket. Woody was always on the lookout for angles and opportunities. That's what made him special.'

Chapter Ten

New Zealand and a new life

***'Do not fear to be eccentric in opinion, for every opinion
now accepted was once eccentric.'* Bertrand Russell**

Is there a rugby player on earth who would turn down the chance to
play for the British and Irish Lions for a second time? Or, indeed, utter
anything that may conceivably dent his chances of playing for them? It
seems unlikely. So, when Clive was selected for the 1983 Lions to tour
New Zealand while his centre partner, Paul Dodge, was left behind, the
rugby world took a simultaneous gulp as he declared that the selectors
were 'insane' to have chosen him ahead of Dodge.

The team was managed by Willie John McBride. Over ten years
previously, McBride had played a fundamental part in the Lions
victory over the All Blacks, the only side ever to have beaten New
Zealand at home. If anyone knew what it took to win in the island of
the long white cloud, it was McBride, the tough Irishman whose side
memorably presented the world with the phrase 'get your revenge in
first'.

The coach in 1983 was Jim Telfer, and the captain, Ciaran Fitzgerald.
Ireland had finished as the top home nation for the second year
running prior to the announcement of the tour party and, with an
Irish manager and captain on board, there was an undeniable prepon-
derance of Irish players. England's championship had been a disaster.
They finished bottom of the table after drawing 13–13 against Wales
and losing the other three matches – 19–15 to France, 25–15 to Ireland
and 22–12 to Scotland. Clive had played in only one match because of
injury. Leicester then lost to Bristol in the Cup final, rounding off a

thoroughly miserable rugby year for Clive. Things would not get much better on the Lions tour.

The team arrived in New Zealand and prepared for a gruelling eleven weeks of rugby, featuring eighteen games and four Test matches in one of the toughest rugby countries on earth. This was a difficult tour for Clive. He wasn't selected in any of the Test matches and endured, with the other players, some heavy training sessions.

'Training was notoriously tough on the Lions tour of '83,' says Robert Norster, the Wales second row and Clive's room-mate on tour. 'A few of the senior players took exception to Jim Telfer's ways and failed to support his intense methods. Multiple training sessions in the ugly weather of a New Zealand winter coupled with plenty of studying videos of the opposition – a relatively new innovation in the game – did little for morale and tested resolve to the full. However, my memories of Clive are of someone who, despite his failure to crack the Test team, got on with the job and did little if any moaning.'

The tour was made infinitely worse for Norster by his having to share a room with Clive, whose domestic standards had clearly slipped since he was described as being tidy on the 1980 Lions tour.

'I remember an amiable but very untidy room-mate,' Norster continued, 'whose first action on entering the room was to empty the entire contents of his suitcase into the space between the bed and the bedroom wall! Being an obsessively tidy individual myself, it was not long before I had to draw a line between his and my half of the room and police the situation!'

Clive and Norster knew each other before heading off to New Zealand, because they shared an employer. Norster also worked for Xerox. (Can there have been a photocopier in the whole of England and Wales that was not being sold by an international player in the 1980s?)

'As fellow international players, albeit from either side of the Severn, we were sometimes treated to formal occasions together with our senior management from Xerox. Clive was a relatively quiet but confident man. On the Lions tour, he did not make the Test side and was probably frustrated and on occasions as depressed as the rest of the tour party by the very tough itinerary, poor accommodation, indifferent weather and occasional lack of unity among the team party and officials. However, I got to know him as a good rugby man who enjoyed and thrived on the banter and camaraderie. He had a good sense of humour but was always in control and focused.'

Peter Winterbottom was on tour with Clive in 1983. He went back to New Zealand on the 1993 Lions tour, and is the only player to have gone on both tours. He played in every Test on both.

'That tour was quite hard. We trained bloody hard,' he says. 'I think I had two days off in eleven weeks. There were a few characters on that tour – one of them was John O'Driscoll, who is a diamond of a bloke. When he had a beer he'd go a bit mad. We were in Whangerei, where the Lions were playing North Auckland. On the night of the game, O'Driscoll was charging round the hotel, breaking into people's rooms, throwing TVs out of the window, but he could never remember what he'd done [when he'd had a few beers], and the next day he had no idea what had happened. Willie John McBride addressed the squad. He said, "Lads, we have trouble. Last night someone here threw TVs and a bed over the balcony."

'"Oh God," we thought, because we all knew who it was.

'"Lads, you can't do that," continued Willie John. "So, come on, who was it?"

'"But you did it when you played," someone protested.

'"I know, but things have changed now. So, own up, who did it?"

'John O'Driscoll was looking round the room, wondering who the culprit was.

'We said, "Come off it, it was you!"

'He said, "No, it couldn't have been. Not me."

'"Well, he sure looked like you. It must have been your brother!" And from then on, whenever we had a roll call, we always had John O'Driscoll followed by John O'Driscoll's brother.

'But the tour was serious. There was so much competition among the thirty guys who were there. It was completely amateur, though. We had a manager, coach, doctor and physio, and a New Zealand bagman. It wasn't high-tech. You got one training shirt, one tracksuit and one pair of shorts and off you went.'

The 1983 Lions tour was not one that Clive enjoyed. Consider the evidence – he was not selected for the Test team, the itinerary, accommodation and food were 'poor' and none of the players felt 'looked after'. That's not really the Clive Woodward method of management. Experiencing what doesn't work, though, is useful for someone wishing to get it absolutely right. 'I look back on the time I spent with the Lions and realise that knowing how bad a manager can make a team feel is a good motivator to make sure you get it right,' says Clive.

McBride was not a fan of Clive's, either. 'When you go on a Lions tour you must have some players with experience of a previous Lions tour. Clive Woodward was an experienced Lion and we expected him to contribute but, as a senior Lions tourist, he really didn't do that. He obviously has management skills [because he helped England win the World Cup] – he must have had them then as well.

'We expected Clive to be contending for a Test place. We needed people to contribute. It was a very tough tour. The season before, England had won the wooden spoon. There were lots of injuries and players not on form. Maurice Colclough [England lock] was injured. Woodward himself was injured for a bit of the tour. There were a lot of difficulties. The fixtures were tough – we needed everybody to pull together. Clive had played in the Tests in 1980, and he and Paul Dodge were the stalwarts of a very good Leicester side. That's why Jim [Telfer] and I picked him. We thought, "He's the sort of guy we need, he'll be an influence," but he wasn't. It was disappointing.'

Once again, there was a 'Clive-in-the-clouds' moment on tour. During the match against West Coast at Greymouth, a lineout was awarded and the two back divisions formed, facing one another. Woodward was seen ambling around, yards upfield, as if in a dream world, nearer the West Coast backs than his own. Jim Telfer roared like an old bear at a quiet moment in the game, 'Woody!' Woodward, shaken from the reverie, trotted back into position.

The 1983 Lions tour was further confirmation to Clive that British rugby was off the pace. Something needed to happen to change it. Four years later, New Zealand would officially be crowned the greatest side in the world, having won the first World Cup. Before then, it was the frequency of the victories they achieved over every team daring to visit them that provided the proof.

On the 1983 tour, another hint of professionalism's threat to amateur rugby manifested itself. David Lord of Australia developed a grand scheme to run a professional circus, and rumours suggested that some two hundred players, including many Lions, had signed up. It proved not to be the case, but the very thought struck fear into the hearts of coaches, managers and officials.

On the field, the Lions lost the first Test 16–12 and the second 9–0, letting both slip through their fingers. The third Test, in Dunedin, was lost 15–8, then New Zealand kicked for home and, in the fourth Test, inflicted their largest Test victory ever over a British Lions team – 38–6.

When the Lions returned to Heathrow, questions were asked. Why had the southern hemisphere moved forward since the seventies, while Britain appeared to have gone back? John Burgess, an RFU official, came up with a blueprint for the future of England rugby, which made urgent suggestions for a more competitive structure, but it was turned down. Instead, the role of the Lions was questioned.

There was some good news for Clive later that year, though – he was on the winning side against New Zealand when England beat them at Twickenham, their first triumph over the All Blacks since 1973.

Back in Leicester, after the Lions tour, Clive spent the summer recuperating. His days as an international player were quietly slipping away. Few sporting careers come to a happy end. Like in politics, they tend to end in failure – non-selection is public and can be humiliating to those who were once considered so great. Injuries, age and changing trends sweep players aside. Sporting careers, like youth itself, are wasted on the young. It's not until you have worked all your life, met a hundred new people and travelled to a hundred exciting places to do a hundred exciting things that you realise how utterly fulfilling and largely irreplaceable an international sporting career is. The great foes of your playing days become great friends, the stories grow more remarkable by the day and time does nothing to diminish your brilliance. 'I become a better rugby player every day,' says John Eales.

The 'playing days' – such a short time – have a defining effect on the rest of your life, but you don't realise that. 'As you lace up your boots and run on to the pitch, you're just thinking of the game. Afterwards, you look back and see it all so differently,' says Gareth Edwards. 'What you did in those games changes everything. It changes the way everyone sees you and it might change the way you see yourself.'What you expect of yourself and for yourself in later life changes.

The Leicester players went on a start-of-season tour to Zimbabwe, while Clive, just returned from the Lions tour, stayed behind.

Kevin Williams was one of those players who headed for Zimbabwe. He was a good friend of Clive's. They had first come across one another at the Welsh schoolboys' trial, Williams playing on the wing for Monmouthshire and Clive as the North Wales fly-half. Williams remembers being aware of Clive going to Harlequins, but the next time they met properly was at Loughborough University, when they found themselves in the same hall of residence. They played and socialised together for four years, then went to Leicester at the same time, in 1979.

By this time, both men were married, Clive to Helen Murray, his Loughborough sweetheart, and Kevin to Jayne Betts, a blonde, attractive woman. Jayne and Clive had known each other for a number of years and were good friends. The couples were part of the close-knit group of players and partners who gave the club its 'family-orientated atmosphere', which Clive had declared an interest in when he first joined, but neither marriage was to last.

Jayne and Kevin split up soon after Williams returned from Zimbabwe. There were no children involved, so the two just went their separate ways. Some time later, Helen and Clive split up. Both men continued to play at Leicester. Away from their marriages, Clive and Jayne had become increasingly close. They had always felt able to talk to one another and had formed an enduring friendship, an understanding of one another that had developed into a deep and lasting relationship. After the break-up of her marriage, Jayne decided to go abroad to teach for a few years, to start again, but Clive missed her too much. 'I realised that she was my soul mate,' he says. Clive knew what he had to do – he boarded a plane, found Jayne and brought her back to England. They arrived back to start a new life together, enjoying a partnership that would last for over twenty-five years.

'It was one of those things that wasn't discussed at the club. It was a bit awkward in the changing rooms for a while. Clive sat quite close to me and it made life hard, but it all got played down at the club. Helen was also very much in the dark about it all and was quite vocal. She was very angry. She felt betrayed,' said Williams.

Helen Murray was unwilling to be interviewed for this book, even though the affair took place a quarter of a century ago when they were both in their twenties. I wanted to talk to her to allow her to have her say in a book that would inevitably mention her, albeit briefly, but her friends said that she refused to speak about it.

Williams is more sanguine about the whole thing. 'We were reasonably close friends – we even shared a flat at one stage when we had a year out of halls of residence at Loughborough. I still think it's a shame they weren't more honest with both me and Helen, but we were young. These things happen. I parted company with Jayne. Clive parted company with Helen.

'I put it down to one of those life experiences. You've just got to get on with it. It's dead and buried now. I have no ill feeling towards Clive or Jayne – they're just people I see on TV. There were no kids involved, which made it easier. We get on fine. I've seen them both once or twice since it happened. I saw them at a funeral. There were several hundred people there and we didn't have a long conversation. Jayne was a very forceful character. She had a very strong will. She could be a driving force behind Clive.'

Although players at Leicester say that life continued as normal after the incident, clearly some tensions created difficulties in such a close team environment. One Leicester colleague concedes, 'There were far more silences after that, moments when no one knew what to say.'

As Clive played out his final years of English rugby at Leicester, his international career was winding to a premature end. A dislocated shoulder in 1983 had prevented him from playing for much of the championship and he had not shone on the Lions tour. Clive played his last international match against Wales in 1984, when they lost 24–15. He was twenty-eight. Thereafter, he was overlooked by the national selectors. When the 1984 Wallabies touring side came over, led by the colourful and charismatic Alan Jones, Clive played against them as a member of the Leicester side after he was not picked to play for England.

'That was absurd, looking back,' says Jones, who went on to coach the Australian national side and is now a leading journalist and radio presenter. 'Clive was among a group of talented players who were simply overlooked by the England selectors. When we arrived in Britain, I think we were more worried about that Leicester game than the England one because the Leicester side was full of talented men who had not been selected for the national team. I thought Clive was a very talented player. I'd have played him in the England side for many more years after he was dropped. He was clearly not their cup of tea because he speaks his mind and won't do as he's told without expressing an opinion. You need to be a strong personality to deal with having a player like that on your team. I guess the selectors and team management just weren't that strong.'

Clive never formally retired – they just stopped selecting him. 'He was disappointed,' recalls Cotton. 'I don't think he felt he'd fulfilled his potential and I think he was right. He played in the wrong era for the sort of rugby he wanted to play.'

Clive spent most of his international career wishing that the England set-up was as advanced as his club environment. He yearned for forward-looking coaches such as Chalkie White, and aspired to the sort of fitness levels attained by those who trained under Greenwood at Loughborough.

'He never thought that what England were doing was right,' says Cotton. 'He'd tell anyone who'd listen where he thought the selectors were going wrong.'

Instead of bemoaning his situation, Clive threw his energies into Rank Xerox. He was promoted from salesman to sales manager and his real skills began to shine through. 'He is outstanding at creating a winning environment and inspiring those who work for, and with, him,' said Tim Buttimore. 'He was great to work for. People wanted to be in his team because Clive's team was a winning team. That's just the way it was. Is. Always has been. That's his gift.' Clive's team topped the performance charts every week – won holidays, cash incentives and the prospect of promotion and felt further inspired to more success. Clive developed a strong reputation for his work and was seen very much as a man who would lead from the front. 'He was willing to go anywhere and talk to anyone,' recalls Steve Holdstock. 'He was a hard worker. He'd drive backwards and forwards across the county to get the smallest of deals.'

While Clive's career at Xerox was on an upward trend, so the company was expanding like never before. Peter Russell, from the London office, moved to Australia to manage the Australasian territory. King was moved out soon afterwards to look after the Sydney offices, based in Manly.

Clive was facing a difficult period in his life. Should he stay in England and keep playing the best club rugby he could, in the hope that the national selectors would see the error of their ways and pick him for England again? Or should he cut his losses and do something different? It was not all fun and games at Leicester either after he began his relationship with Jayne. It was time to make some changes. He picked up the phone one night and called his old manager in Sydney.

'Clive told me he needed to get away,' says King. 'He had to have a change. I told him I'd see what I could do. I called him back and told him to come out here on a visit. He did that, liked it, and we arranged a job for him.'

Woodward's recall is that King phoned him with a job offer. Jayne and Clive discussed the prospect of moving to Australia and decided that it was too good an opportunity to miss, so Clive headed off on a recce trip, to work out where the couple would live and to have a look at the local rugby clubs. While in Australia, he established that he would like to play for Manly, the club where Alan Jones had coached prior to starting work with the Wallabies. At Leicester, there was a certain amount of surprise at his decision.

'It was certainly an unusual thing to do,' recalls Burwell. 'At the time, people didn't go off and play for club sides on the other side of the world, so no one could quite imagine how it would work out for him. He took a gamble, as always – and, as always, it paid off.'

Before leaving, Clive attended a stag night for Nick Youngs, an England and Tigers team-mate. The evening doubled, to some extent, as a leaving do for Clive. He enjoyed a few beers and a curry and told them about the new life that lay ahead. So raucous were they that the police were called. They chastised the group and asked them to respect other diners by keeping the noise down. Later, Clive drove home and was stopped by the same police who had earlier appeared in the restaurant. He was banned from driving for twelve months and fined £120.

This incident seems out of character for Clive. Certainly, in the research for this book, it stood out as the only blemish on his reputation, and it is something that he deeply regrets.

'The really strange thing was that he didn't tell people what had happened,' says Holdstock. 'I don't mean that I think he should shout about it all over town, but there was this very funny moment when Clive sat in front of the television with Jayne and her parents, the night after he'd been in court. He was due to be driving Jayne's parents to the airport the next day so they could go on holiday. As they all sat round the television, Central News came on and announced, "England rugby star Clive Woodward was banned from driving for twelve months at Leicester Magistrates' Court this morning." "Ah," said Jayne's dad. "I guess I'll be driving to the airport, then."'

A week later, Jayne and Clive boarded a plane for the other side of the world.

SECTION THREE

Chapter Eleven

A land down under

---

*'Ideals are like stars: you will not succeed in touching them with
your hands, but like the seafaring man on the ocean desert of waters,
you choose them as your guides, and following them, you reach
your destiny.'* **Carl Schurz**

Three pretty girls run along the Manly seafront, all tanned, toned and
skimpily clad in brightly coloured Lycra. Long, slim legs emerge from
the shortest of shorts and hair like sunshine floats down their backs.
They are listening to their personal stereos, oblivious to the catcalls
from the cluster of men standing just inside the seafront bar.

The girls pass and the men divert their attention to the large screen.
Rugby games are shown back to back. The sound is cranked up. There
is cold beer on tap. Roars of approval accompany every score, and still
louder roars as the procession of girls continues along this beautiful
sun-drenched beach on the fringes of the Pacific Ocean. Few young
men would deny the delights of Manly. Fewer still would fail to see the
attractions it had to offer a former international rugby player, eager to
get away and enjoy a few years in the sun.

The central point of this captivating stretch is the Manly Pacific
Hotel. A large, impressive building with a marble reception area, it
takes pride of place on the seafront. The hotel has a gym, a swimming
pool and some of the most spectacular beach views anywhere in the
world. From the balconies adjoining the suites at the front of the hotel,
you can see and hear the sea crashing below. It's the brightest blue.
Waves roll on to the shore, surfers dancing across the largest of them.
Suntanned skins and sun-bleached hair are everywhere. This is a hotel

straight out of central casting. 'Hey, Junior – we need the most perfect hotel in the world.' 'Sure, Bob. Try the Manly Pacific.'

Clive and Jayne arrived at Sydney Airport in September 1985 ready for their adventure down under. Leaving had not been unduly hard for Clive. He had enjoyed his leaving party, bid his parents goodbye and gone. For Jayne, it was a more difficult decision. Much closer to her family, particularly her parents, Barry and Sylvia, she was worried about leaving them for so long. She had never been to Australia before. In fact, Clive had only been once – on his recce trip a few months earlier. The couple flew out of Heathrow Airport, Jayne's ears ringing with Clive's promises that they would come back straightaway if she missed her family too much.

This might be an appropriate point at which to flesh out Jayne Betts, the future Mrs Woodward. She is regarded by many as the 'power behind the throne', a woman who is confident, articulate and as fiercely supportive of Clive as it is possible to be. A teacher by training, since meeting Clive she has worked alongside him – first building up a company in Australia (named Bettswood Business Systems, to reflect both their surnames), then working with him at Sales Finance and Leasing when they returned to England. Clive regards her as 'one of the best business people that I have ever come across because she just gets on so well with everyone.' She is Clive's closest ally and his 'root'. While he flies off into the clouds in a battle to make the sporting world a better place, she provides the base and the family support, but also acts as his manager and agent, deciding best business policy and most appropriate projects for Clive to be involved in. 'I don't get to see the requests half the time,' says Clive. 'Jayne just deals with everything – all the negotiating and planning. She researches, meets up with people on my behalf and makes everything work.'

Over the years this has become a full-time job, enabling her to raise a family of three children and run their home while also working alongside her husband. Jayne once joked that at a conference she attended with Clive, a speaker was extolling the virtues of work-life balance. 'What's that?' Clive whispered. 'Don't worry,' she replied. 'We don't do work–life balance.' Clearly, as a sports coach or business manager, there is no start time or end time – you just do what needs to be done, when it needs doing. Having your wife working with you makes it easier to excel in work while spending time with loved ones.

Jayne is more down to earth than Clive, the realist to his maverick, the practical force to counter his creative tendencies. It would be unfair to paint her as a woman without creativity, though.

When England won the World Cup, she bought Clive a flagpole from which to fly the cross of St George. Clive, a very patriotic man, had hankered after one since going on holiday to Sweden and seeing Swedish flags flying outside private houses. It stands on a small circle of grass outside the front door of their house. It's huge, like the flagpoles that grace stately homes. I have no idea whether they lower the flag on appropriate state occasions.

She also bought him a Hobi Cat sailing boat after the World Cup, and named it 20–17. The boat is kept at the Saunton Sands Sailing Club in Devon, and children learn to sail on it for most of the year.

Jayne is an equal shareholder in Clive's business and, as his manager, is often with him at press conferences and dinners where other partners are not to be found. The most memorable pictures of her were taken during the World Cup when she was hugged by Prince Harry in a very non-English way. Jayne is different from Clive in this respect. Brought up in a loving, 'touchy-feely' house, she is an immediately engaging person, and touches people as she speaks to them. Clive is more stand-offish. He's harder to get to know. They complement each other well. She hasn't tried to launch a sideline career in designing rugby shirts or written a book about Desperate Rugby Wives. She doesn't go on TV shows or appear on chat shows, despite numerous offers. If Clive is taking part, she is there, sitting in the audience and talking to everyone in the green room before and after. She never gives interviews. She is eager not to be in the spotlight herself but supports Clive and realises that it's a necessary part of Clive's job.

Many of Clive's colleagues talk about the massive input that Jayne has into Clive's work. They say that she is the naturally sociable one, the one who will walk into a room and know everyone in it by the time she leaves, because she is just very interested in people. She enjoys company. He's happier being private. Jayne has had the effect of making

Clive more sociable. Some of his biggest meetings have taken place in their home. He integrates home and work life, and feels comfortable inviting players round to the house for the evening with their families. Jayne is a crucial part of this, and she became very close to the players and their families during Clive's time with England.

Jayne says that life is never boring with Clive and she considers herself very lucky to have been able to live her life with him. Undoubtedly, his maverick tendencies have made life interesting and their successes have brought them a fantastic standard of living, but Clive's been lucky, too. The blonde woman at his side, always explaining to everyone how great Clive Woodward is, has been a powerful asset.

At Sydney Airport, Clive and Jayne were expecting to be met by Alan King, the man who had shown Clive round on his recce trip a few months previously. The plan was for King to meet the couple and take them to the Manly Pacific Hotel to stay for four weeks before they moved into an apartment on the seafront nearby. However, by the time Clive and Jayne touched down on Australian soil, King was no longer working at Rank Xerox. A difference of opinion with Russell had led to his dismissal. He had moved on to set up a recruitment business in another part of Sydney, so it was Russell and his wife, Lynette, who met the couple from their flight.

Clive settled quietly into life in Australia, spending more time outdoors than he ever had in England. On one of his first days, he went to the beach with Alan King. 'He took his shirt off,' recalls King, with a shiver, 'and he was this fat guy. He had a beer belly. I couldn't believe it. He got fit pretty quickly and I never saw him with one again – but I remember that tummy very clearly.'

Away from beach trips and the morning runs and surfing to get rid of the jelly belly, Clive went to work at Xerox's office on Kent Street, a short ferry journey from Manly harbour to Circular Quay, possibly the loveliest way ever to travel to work. The ferry journey takes you past the Sydney Opera House and Harbour Bridge – no cold, grey mornings, no trying to start the car in the damp and the rain, no sitting in endless traffic.

Jayne resumed her teaching career at a local school. Clive had been warned by Alan King that the working environment in the Sydney office would be very different from anything he had experienced in England. The Australian teams were less motivated to hit targets – less motivated to work, to be honest. Australia has changed immensely in the two decades since Clive worked there, but back then there was certainly a reluctance to do anything but the basics. Clive arrived at Xerox full of plans to transform it, to hit challenging targets and make the environment in Sydney as vibrant and aggressive as it had been in Leicester. That, however, proved not to be possible.

'He wasn't alone,' says King. 'When I first arrived, I was shocked by the Australian way of doing things. It really took some getting used to. I put a whole load of transformations of the business into operation immediately – nothing clever, I just got the basics right and we were up 258 per cent on plan after a year. They trebled my target and we hit that, too – so can you imagine how dreadful it had been before.

'The work ethic in Xerox Australia was different from in the UK, which was a ruthless culture. Your biggest competitor would be the bloke sitting next to you, not the opposing company. You wanted to be the best in the team, and you wanted your team to be the best in the country. I knew Clive would find it difficult to adjust because he was brought up on winning league tables, getting the accolades and making loads of money. People here weren't as competitive. For example, most Australians would take three or four weeks off every January. Some people would just take the whole of January off for summer holidays.'

Clive turned up for his first day in the office dressed in a smart suit and tie. His salesmen wore shorts and sandals. He would talk about tough targets and topping the league tables. They had no interest. They had an active dislike of the salesmen who topped the tables. It was just not cool to go around topping tables. He tried to bring in the 8 a.m. daily meetings they had had in Leicester but had to settle for two 9 a.m. meetings, for which people would turn up late.

'He really struggled in that environment to start with,' says King. 'I would say that he struggled more than I'd imagined he would. I'm a lot more outgoing than Clive and I could just bop people over the head to manage them. He wasn't like that – he tried to encourage them to change, but the truth is that they wanted different things. They wanted to get the work done and go home, while he wanted to be the best sales manager ever. It would have been a steep learning curve for him to manage a group in that sort of environment.'

Australia was in a period of great change when Clive arrived, two years after Bob Hawke became Labour Prime Minister in 1983. By the end of that year, Hawke had floated the dollar. The year that Clive went there, the Medicare Health scheme (equivalent of the NHS) began operating and 'Advance Australia Fair' was proclaimed the national anthem. Green and gold were declared the Australian national colours.

The social make-up of the country was also changing. In the census of 1901 – the year in which the Commonwealth of Australia was created – 18 per cent of those in Australia had been born in United Kingdom and Ireland. By the 2001 census, this had dropped to just 5.5 per cent. Clive was not alone in struggling to adapt. Statistics suggest that over 40 per cent of people who go abroad to work return because of the cultural differences in the working environment.

While life at Xerox wasn't everything Clive had hoped it would be, Manly Rugby Club provided light relief and he slotted in with ease, enjoying the expansive game, the warm weather and the fun. He and Jayne were made to feel at home straightaway, the players showing particular delight that he did not wish to spend all his time kicking away possession. Clive moved from centre to fly-half and went on to captain the side.

'It was unusual to have a former England international and British Lion at the club in those days,' says Phil Cox, a former Wallaby, who was at Manly when Clive joined. 'These were the days before professionalism and most players stayed and played in their own districts. Clive was something of a celebrity.'

Soon after arriving in Australia, Clive arranged for Steve Holdstock to come out and play. Holdstock arrived just a few days before Clive's first game at Manly, and slotted into the A team, before joining Clive in the first team.

Manly was one of the premier clubs in Sydney at the time. There were twelve teams in the league, playing home and away. Then there were semi-finals, the final and a grand final at the end of the season.

Manly was always involved in the end-of-season finals. Warringah, a club that Clive had considered joining, was the other top club in the area, coached by Rod Macqueen, who would go on to become the Australia coach.

Clive's first game was against Randwick, coached by Bob Dwyer, also a former coach of Australia. It was this game that taught him one of his biggest rugby lessons in Australia. What he witnessed would inform his coaching philosophy and change his attitude.

'I remember how the scrum went down. It was their put in,' said Clive. 'I went round in outside centre defence and came face to face with their outside centre. I couldn't do anything. For eighty minutes, people were running all over me.'

The reason for his problems was the flat back line. It afforded him no space whatsoever. This was the tactic first used by Alan Jones in the 1984 Australia tour of the UK.

'In the whole time I played rugby in England, I never had to make a head-on tackle. Suddenly, I was over in Australia playing against Randwick and rugby became a nightmare. I was thirty years old and had to tackle people head-on. They scored forty points against us and never broke sweat. You couldn't get your hands on them because it was so quick and flat.'

The flat back line is a high-risk strategy, relying on 25 per cent technique and 75 per cent attitude. It involves thinking differently about rugby, really committing yourself. Clive was in love. It was 'total rugby' as he'd always envisaged it being played.

'I remember him being bowled over by it,' says Thomas Dooner, another former Manly player, who would later work for Clive. 'He probably celebrated with a cup of tea. Most things were celebrated with a cup of tea.'

Dooner, Cox and I are sitting in the Manly clubhouse, looking at pictures of Clive from his days there.

'I'd forgotten about the tea,' says Cox with a broad smile. 'We'd all pull out cigarettes and beers after games, but all he wanted was tea.'

'You got into the tea thing,' says Dooner.

'No I didn't. I just had beers and smokes,' replies Cox, like a man who has just had his very masculinity challenged.

The two men argue about tea drinking with Clive. 'But I didn't call him Clive,' says Dooner. 'I called him Royston because his middle name is Ronald. He used to laugh whenever I said it – so I kept doing it.'

After the game against Randwick, Manly played St George, then came the toughest fixture – against Warringah.

'There was always friction between Manly and Warringah and Clive got clobbered,' recalls Cox. 'One of their players caught him with his elbow. Warringah had taken exception to the fact that he chose Manly over them and it was a chance to have a go at an international player. Clive did a sidestep back inside from a lineout and this elbow smashed into him.'

Clive's jaw was broken and he had a fully depressed cheekbone.

The injury took Clive out of action for the rest of the season (which, in Australia, runs from April to October), but he continued to go down to the club to meet the players.

'He was particularly close to Holdstock,' says Cox.

'Yeah,' echoes Dooner. 'Let's be honest – they were like a couple of old poofs. You couldn't get them apart.'

'We did spend a lot of time together,' says Holdstock. 'Our wives became friends and the families knew each other. There was one time when Clive and I went down to The Stain, a pub in Manly. It was after his injury had cleared up and he was back in the first team. Someone in there spotted us drinking with a big game the next day. These were the days in which rugby players didn't take fitness and preparation too seriously, and we would have gone out for a few beers in England, so we didn't think anything of doing it in Manly. But alcohol passing your lips on the night before a big game was a complete no-no in Australia, so we were told off the next day and Clive didn't like that at all. Nobody tells Clive off.'

'There's only one thing we can do,' said Clive.

'Never go drinking the night before a game again?' suggested Holdstock.

'No – find somewhere else to drink.'

He would go out frequently with the players. 'But he always had a handbrake in Jayne,' says Cox.

One story, well known in Sydney, was told to me by most of the people I interviewed. It's about a time when Clive stayed too long in the bar after a match. Jayne was at home with Steve Holdstock's wife, also called Jane, preparing for a dinner party later in the evening. Clive was expected back to help prepare everything but he was enjoying himself too much.

'The phone in the bar rang,' recalls Cox. 'John the barman picked up the phone and Jayne said, "Is Clive there?" The barman mouthed over to Clive that his girlfriend was on the phone, and Clive mouthed back, "Tell her I've already left."

'The same thing happened a couple more times. Jayne would leave it half an hour, then ring back. It was all very amusing for the rest of us. When the phone rang for the fourth time, Clive was waving his arms at the barman, saying, "No, no. Tell her I'm not here."

'The barman relayed the message to Jayne, and Jayne replied, "Tell him I know he's there – I can see him. Look out of the window." '

Outside the huge windows sat Jayne, in the car, on Clive's car phone – watching everything that was going on. Aside from being an amusing ditty which illustrates that there is a far more carefree side to Clive than is usually revealed, an interesting thing about this story is that Clive had a car phone in the 1980s. In the days when only yuppies with red braces and huge expense accounts had them, he had one.

Clive and Jayne moved out of the Manly Pacific and into an apartment just along the seafront, overlooking the sea. It was in one of the best locations in Sydney. But, Clive had a problem – the sound of the waves crashing against the rocks was so loud that it used to keep him awake at night, so Clive went to see Bernie Berglin – the local estate agent, and former Manly captain, who had arranged for him to move into the property – and asked whether there was anything quieter available. Berglin looked at him as if he was a complete and utter lemon and reminded him that he was in one of the most exclusive apartments in Manly. Clive and Jayne adjusted to the sound of the waves on the beach and the spray on the balcony for a while, then moved into a house in Manly. Six months before heading back to England, they rented a house in Terry Hills, belonging to one of the Xerox directors, Phil Chambers. Clive and Jayne lived there while Chambers was away in New Zealand.

They made a lot of friends in Australia and settled in extremely well. Most of the people he met were baffled by Clive's modesty. People would find out he was a former international player after knowing him for a few months and be amazed that he'd never said anything. 'In

Australia, that's just about the first thing you'd tell someone,' says Russell. 'He didn't. I think people found that quite endearing.'

Clive had two sets of friends, those from Xerox and those from the rugby club. Manly was a very friendly club. Most people lived near enough to walk there, so didn't have to drive back. Even training evenings would turn into social events, as the players would stay for a few drinks. Much of the socialising centred on the house of John Broadfoot.

'At John's parties, Clive would let his hair down,' said Holdstock. 'He was in a safe environment and with people he knew, so he'd relax and be extraordinarily good company. We spent one New Year's Eve at John's place, which was a spectacular house with a pool outside. I remember Clive leaping off the balcony, dressed in his tuxedo and black tie, and landing with an almighty splash in the swimming pool. Come to think of it, Clive was always more of a party animal when he was dressed up. Put him in a black tie, give him a bottle of champagne and he'll party all night.'

One of the reasons that Clive had originally been attracted to Manly Rugby Club was that Alan Jones had coached there for a year before Clive arrived. He had gone on to become the coach of the Australia team. Jones had a reputation for being one of the most successful rugby coaches in the world – a man who led Australia to twenty-three Test victories out of thirty games in a four-year period, with little experience of playing the game himself. One of his greatest achievements was his 1984 Grand Slam of victories over England, Ireland, Wales and Scotland and the Barbarians, with that beguiling flat back line.

Jones defies categorisation, and there is no doubt that this added to his allure for Clive. He is a former political speechwriter and senior adviser to Prime Minister Malcolm Fraser, and after his vastly successful coaching career, he became Australia's number one radio and television presenter and a man of extraordinary influence. 'His brain is an industry,' declare his supporters. 'He's an absolute menace,' declare his opponents.

Soon after Clive arrived in Australia, once he had recovered from his facial injuries, he went to the Sydney Sevens tournament, in February 1986, and bumped into Jones. They exchanged pleasantries. A week later, Clive received an unusual phone call from the Australia coach.

'Clive, it's Alan Jones. Do you fancy coming to play for Australia?'

'Uh?' said Clive.

'Good. Well, come down to training then,' replied Jones.

The door to Alan Jones's apartment in the heart of Sydney is opened by a smartly dressed employee, who is courteous, kind and welcoming. He shows me up the stairs to a bright, airy room. Modern art hangs on plain walls and a fabulously laid table sits tantalisingly in the corner, the cutlery and glassware sparkling in the sunshine. Another member of staff comes to tell me that Jones has been delayed. He has clipped vowels and neatly clipped hair. Champagne is offered and another employee approaches with a silver tray loaded with light appetisers while the others disappear into the kitchen, from which aromas emerge.

On the far wall hangs a photo of Jones with his old mucker, Sir Donald Bradman. Another wall features the 1984 Wallabies side that he managed with such distinction. Look around and there are dozens of photographs of famous people. Look more closely and you see that Jones is in them all.

The man is so well connected that he can get anyone on to his morning radio show – his ability to do so is part of his cachet – but during the 2003 World Cup, Jones tried in vain to get Clive on. He just couldn't get an audience with him. Jones successfully attracted former United States president Bill Clinton but not Clive, leading him to report to his listeners, 'I can get Bill Clinton on my radio show but not Clive Woodward, and Clive nearly played in my rugby team.'

It transpired later that the reason Clive had turned down Jones's requests was because David Campese, the Australian loud-mouthed former international player, was to be on the show at the same time as him. Clive discovered the plans just before they were due to go on air and refused to be interviewed. Campese's ill-judged, headline-seeking comments about English rugby and England generally have been a source of annoyance to many England managers in the past. Clive decided that further unwanted headlines at a delicate time in a World Cup campaign were unnecessary.

In his large roof garden, which offers a panoramic view over the finest and most expensive rooftops in Sydney and out to the sea beyond, Jones talks animatedly while chefs and waiters move silently inside, preparing a light lunch. Jones likes to cause a stir – not for him the subtle, laid-back approach to life. He is happiest when in the headlines, courting confrontation and challenging perceptions.

'Yeah. I invited him to play for Australia. That's right,' he says with a deep chuckle. 'I had just reshaped the Australian side because we had had some injuries and there were lots of players unavailable to me. We had a one-off game against New Zealand coming up [the Bledisloe Cup match, 1986]. No one had ever beaten New Zealand in New Zealand except the British Lions so, naturally enough, I wanted Australia to do it.

'It was a great challenge but we needed thirty good, international standard players. I wasn't sure that our depth went to that. I bumped into Clive and it got me thinking, so I said to him, "Will you become Australian?" He sort of half-considered it, which was great, but in the end it didn't work out. He felt awkward coming to Australia training sessions. He said it just wouldn't have worked for him.'

As a matter of interest, Jones did coach the Wallabies to Bledisloe Cup victory in New Zealand – the first time such a victory had been achieved in thirty-nine years. The Wallabies became only the second team in rugby history, and the first national side, to win a series against New Zealand on their home ground.

'I've watched Clive since he returned from playing in Manly and, like everyone, I've been enormously impressed by his achievements. If he learnt anything from me, I'm flattered. I was the first person in world rugby to have an assistant coach. People thought it was an extravagance at the time – look at Clive now, with his bus full of helpers.

'Clive changed a lot while he was in Australia. He was always a very shy and decent sort of person and he remained decent, but I think he grew in confidence. He has been criticised for his arrogance and his aloofness but basically he is still quite a shy person underneath. He had a speech impediment, a sort of stutter, when I first knew him, which made things difficult for him. That was all down to nervousness, I'm sure of it.

'He learnt about the winning mentality in Australia. When he was in charge, England always thought they were going to win. They looked like they were going to win. You were always surprised when they didn't. That takes a lot of doing. Creating that winning mentality is a real achievement. I have a sneaking feeling that he learnt all about that in Australia.'

One of the great delights of studying the Clive Woodward story is that one is not forced into gross stereotypes or bland clichés. One is spared over-simplification and enticed into more meaningful debate. In Australia, Clive discovered that it wasn't a case of Australians simply being better than the British at everything. He didn't find magical answers to life's problems and transport them back to England. He established that at some things Australians were better and at some things they were not so good. It was just a matter of priorities. The rugby was good – fast and played on hard grounds, with some innovative ideas, such as the flat back line, which he appropriated and exported. On the whole, though, the coaching wasn't great and the players weren't that special. It was their attitude that was different. They believed they were better and didn't like to be beaten.

It is significant that Clive found the Australians to be fundamentally no better than the English players he'd known. Why, then, did they win so frequently? The answer, he would discover, was multi-layered. Belief in themselves and this ephemeral 'winning attitude' were vital, but the nation's collective consciousness of sport was a great deal to do with it, too, as exemplified by the Australia Institute of Sport, which Clive visited during his stay. In Australia, a feeling existed that success in sport was important and worth striving for.

In business, this was not the case. Clive found that the Sydney office of Xerox was decidedly not full of winners. They were a long way behind their English counterparts. Again, the reason for this was attitude. In Australia in the 1980s, most people worked to afford a certain lifestyle. For a huge proportion of Australians, this involved playing sport. In England, work itself was a means of self-expression, something to be striven for and to be good at for its own sake, which brought its own rewards.

Clive made a real success of his time in Australia by changing tack when he realised a new approach was needed. One of Clive's strengths is his ability to self-analyse. He continually assesses what he's doing and what impact his actions are having. He was the same with England years later, reining himself in and taking a more rational approach to the game when his early 'throw the ball around and stuff the consequences' approach failed to achieve.

In Sydney, he made coming to work and achieving targets fun, so that his subordinates wanted to come, instead of feeling they were being told to.

'I remember him turning his office into an Hawaiian hut to make it different and to lighten the mood,' said Russell. 'That was the sort of thing that people were doing in Europe but not in Australia at the time. Once he'd found his feet, he did very well, and brought a fresh approach to New South Wales. He struggled at first because they didn't understand him.'

Chapter Twelve

A life down under

'The toughest thing about success is that you've got to keep on being a success. Talent is only a starting point in this business. You've got to keep on working that talent. Someday I'll reach for it and it won't be there.' **Irving Berlin**

Alan King sits in Harry's Fish Café in Sydney. Through the large windows next to him you can look out over a courtyard below where other diners are eating. A chilled bottle of white wine stands on the table and fresh seafood is on order.

'Cheers,' he says, raising his glass. King never left Australia. He stayed in the country after Clive and Jayne returned to England. Peter Russell stayed, too, working in the distribution outlet that he set up after leaving Xerox in 1986.

It was only six months after Russell had left Xerox that Clive began to get itchy feet. He had learnt much about management in the Manly branch of the company and had improved the situation a great deal, and he was beginning to feel that there was little more he could do there.

'I think you tend to learn more when you're under pressure like that,' said Russell. 'There's no doubt that Clive did. It was his first big management job and it was in difficult circumstances – you saw him really blossom in that role.'

'The other thing that happened after he got started in the job was that he loosened up a little bit,' said King. 'He stopped fretting about everything and relaxed. I think that made him better company in the office, and the guys started responding to him more positively.'

One of the key reasons for the change in Clive's approach – this 'loosening up' – was the arrival of Jess, his first child. She was born at Manly Cottage Hospital in November 1986, and her arrival was a huge distraction for Clive. She put life into perspective for him and he spent more time at home than he ever had before. He describes this as his 'transitional period'.

The baby's arrival also made him realise that he had responsibilities. He was nearly thirty-one when she was born. His days as a rugby player were limited. He felt largely dissatisfied with work at Xerox, albeit he had come a long way. It was time for a change, but to do what?

At the time, the concept of leasing was new in Australia. Xerox was the only business equipment company with its own in-house finance department. Other businesses used dealers and left it to them to sort out financial arrangements for customers. Few did it effectively.

Clive was approached by Portfolio Leasing, the Australian office of US Leasing, which was owned by Ford. They wanted Clive to become their national sales director. Clive knew that at Xerox they made more money from leasing office equipment than they did from sales. It seemed a great idea, giving Clive the chance to organise his team in his own image and work in the way he thought best. One of the big companies without finance agreements was NEC. Clive called Graham Poulter from NEC and explained the procedure. Poulter was interested. The two men shook hands and Clive was in business. He moved out of Xerox, Jayne and Clive set up Bettswood and the company was retained by Portfolio Leasing. Clive's next task was to build the right team. Clive is big on this. It is his belief that getting one wrong person in a team can be extremely damaging to the morale and efficiency of the whole unit. One of his greatest skills when he came to coach England was not only getting the right people into the team, but getting them into the right place and fully cognisant of their role in that team.

Steve Bull, business and sports psychologist and the man credited with turning around the mental attitude of the England cricket team, establishing a winning mindset, says, 'It's what, in business, they describe as "getting the right people on the bus". Once you've done that, the crucial thing is to get the people in the right seats. Clive was very good at that. He found what you might call "cultural architects" very quickly – people who would understand and implement his vision.'

Jim Collins, a business analyst, claims in his book *Good To Great* that having the right people in a business team is more important than anything. The best American companies become great because they have the right people – working out what to do with them, and the vision, philosophy and *raison d'être* of the company, is fundamentally less important than getting those crucial right people on board.

Clive would go on to do this when he gathered a group of almost twenty experts and turned around the England rugby team. His skill was not only in recruiting great talent, but in giving precise instructions to make it clear how everyone's role worked. Having a large team demands acute management skills – think of the 2001 Lions tour when every coach was demanding time with the players and they wound up exhausted before the first game. If you employ people to work for you, you have to manage them effectively, making them feel they have a real contribution to make in the specific role for which they were employed. The bigger the team and the more passionate the experts, the more key the leadership role is.

Clive has extraordinary management and communication skills, which were undoubtedly revealed and honed at Portfolio Leasing. Indeed, when you look back at the Clive Woodward story and interpret how events shaped the man who would lead England to World Cup glory, this particular stage of his Australian adventure was crucial. In terms of overt learning experiences, Portfolio Leasing and all that he did with them was a huge springboard.

One of the interesting things about Clive's management of Portfolio Leasing was that he did it entirely his own way. He used the management skills he'd learnt at Xerox and his personal observations of the cultural differences between the UK and Australia, and he ran the team in the way he thought most effective.

'Working with Clive was fun,' says Thomas Dooner, who joined Portfolio Leasing soon after Clive. 'The philosophy was "work hard but have fun". We'd set ourselves very achievable sales targets and on the last Friday of every month, if we hit them, we'd go out drinking and work would pay the bills.

'Clive was a brilliant salesman, always on the car phone. When I think back to Clive at that time, he was just always doing business,' said Holdstock.

Dooner said, 'Clive developed a huge network. He was an expert at developing relationships with people. He rewarded success. He didn't micro-manage. We all felt part of the big picture and shared in its success. He'd be on the phone, talking to people and encouraging them. The numbers he was doing were enormous. Portfolio Leasing were so amazed with what he achieved that he could do whatever he wanted. Whatever he asked for he got because he was producing the goods.'

Clive brought Tim Buttimore to Australia in 1987. Buttimore had worked with Clive at Xerox in England, albeit at a rival office – Clive in Leicester, Buttimore in Birmingham. Buttimore played for Coventry, but when Clive moved to Australia, he took Clive's place in the team at Leicester. He met up with Clive in Australia after Clive arranged for Leicester to come out on tour to Manly. His arrival took the team to twelve people.

'That's when his rugby started to move slowly to the backburner,' said Dooner. 'He recognised that the job represented the future. He also absolutely hated training. He would strategically turn up late to miss the fitness training at the beginning of sessions. This made it difficult for me because I was working with him. "Come on," I'd say. "Let's get down to training," but there would always be some crucial reason why he couldn't go in time to join in with the fitness work.'

Buttimore and his wife stayed with Clive and Jayne in the early days, until they could find a place of their own.

'He was great,' says Tim. 'He sorted out the job, had no problems with us staying with him and found us a flat. He was also great to work for. It was all very team oriented, very supportive. He knew exactly what he wanted and he explained that clearly to everyone. He developed a new team from scratch, built it up and made a great success of it.'

Buttimore cites Clive's 'fierce will to win' as the defining characteristic that has helped him. 'He also works unbelievably hard and he's innovative – always looking to see how he can do things differently. Even when he was a sales manager, he was always looking for different ways, and I think that refreshes people and keeps them interested and motivated.

'He always stuck to his principles. If he believed in something, he'd do it, regardless of someone else saying it was wrong. I'm not saying he didn't take advice, but he'd always back his abilities and his beliefs.'

Buttimore describes a life at Portfolio Leasing in which they would go out every Friday after work, in the sunshine.

'The thing I always remember,' says Dooner, 'was that he was more than happy for us all to go out and have a good time but it couldn't interfere with work. So you could go out on a Tuesday night and get home at four in the morning, and he'd come to the bar, too, but even as he was buying the drinks he'd be saying, "You've all got to be back in the office at eight o'clock."'

Clive was keen for the sales force to be out winning business rather than sitting around the office. He encouraged them to 'go out and hit a few golf balls' rather than languish in the office all day.

'He has this ability to make you want to work for him. Even when I was really fed up with him, I'd still want him to be pleased with what I was doing – like a child with his father. It's a very peculiar skill that he has. People want to please him,' says Holdstock.

Under Clive, Porfolio Leasing grew from a minor to a major player.

Early in 1987, Clive and Jayne married in a small, romantic wedding in the Manly sunshine surrounded by friends. Alan Jones and most of the Manly team joined them on the beach as they said their vows. It was an extremely special day for the couple who had been through so much to be together. A few weeks later, they held a second celebration – a marriage blessing in England, with both families present – but before there could be a wedding, in the great tradition of these things, there had to be a stag night.

'We just drank and drank,' recalls Holdstock. 'I ended up having to take Clive home in a shopping trolley because he couldn't walk. I pushed that trolley all the way back to my apartment – then we sat up all night, talking, drinking brandy and eating fried-egg sandwiches.'

Although Clive's interest in playing rugby subsided, he retained a great interest in the game and in sport generally. He went to Canberra to the Australian Institute of Sport, the large, multi-sport organisation that has been credited with turning round so many of Australia's sports. The AIS was opened in 1981, the chief motivation being Australia's dismal performance in the 1976 Montreal Olympics in which they won just one silver and four bronze medals. Rugby union was incorporated into the Institute in 1988, while Clive was living in Australia.

The aim of the AIS rugby programme was to take players aged sixteen to nineteen and prepare them for representative schools and club rugby, as well as the Super 12s and the national youth sides. Players live at home and continue to go to school and play for their local clubs in the usual way, but have additional élite training squad sessions, organised through the auspices of AIS.

Clive was immediately impressed with the set-up, in particular the way in which 'best practices' were shared across sports. It is important to remember the time at which this was going on. In the late 1980s, rugby was not only an amateur sport but also fairly amateurish.

I went to work for the RFU in 1991, just four years before the arrival of professionalism, having come from a background of gymnastics and dance. While watching an English lineout session one day, I mentioned the work I had done on plyometrics, and the way in which gymnasts elevate themselves way beyond their normal height to perform aerial moves.

'What are you suggesting? That we get a bunch of ballet dancers in here? The players would never take them seriously,' came the rather mocking response.

'Yes,' I said. 'That's exactly what you should do,' but of course, they didn't, not then. It was an overtly masculine culture in those days, and defining yourself as a big tough man was far more important than winning. Interestingly, I think the players would have responded very well to instruction from someone outside their comfort zone. The problem was not with them. The problem was with those surrounding them, people who felt instantly threatened, challenged and confused by change.

Eventually, rugby did open its doors and ballet dancers did work on plyometric techniques with second rows, just as darts players worked on throwing with hookers, athletes worked with the players on their running skills, and aerobics and yoga teachers worked on conditioning. This took a long time to happen, and until it did, rugby union wallowed in a mire of arrogance that prevented the sport from moving forward. There was an absolute, unchallenged belief that the only people who could advise rugby players were rugby players.

While other sports became glamorous, multi-million-pound entertainment industries, rugby union tightened its old school tie and became the sport that time forgot. Coaches were considered an unnecessary extravagance, training was cheating and diets consisted of deep-fried small farm animals and enough beer to float a large ship. It's easy to see the fun in this, but equally easy to see why players didn't improve and the sport failed to move forward.

Proof of this, if any were needed, came in 1986, when Dr Craig Sharp, then a sports scientist working at Loughborough University, conducted an analysis of British sportsmen to establish how their fitness levels compared. He found rugby union forwards to be the least fit of all sportsmen in the country. They came fiftieth, behind bowls players and archers. Rugby union backs fared better, coming in fortieth place. No one in the sport cared. Indeed, there was a secret pride in the fact that the sport had not succumbed to this new overly competitive spirit that seemed to be enveloping other sports. Their attitude was strangely similar to that of Australian Xerox salesmen to league tables in the eighties.

Once the results of Dr Sharp's study were published, rugby became defensive, saying that gymnasts and stage dancers, who topped the list, wouldn't last a minute in the physical contact of a rugby match. This response was indicative of the beliefs at the time, as if, somehow, the fact that rugby was a physical contact sport meant it couldn't be understood or helped by any other sport. Rugby players wouldn't have lasted a minute on the beam, either, as it happens, but that wasn't the point. Their double somersaults off the bars would have been laughed out of town, but that wasn't the point. No one was suggesting that a fourteen-year-old female gymnast could have slotted into the England front row and taught them how to scrummage. The point was that, although the sports were very different and the fitness required for them was very different, when the fitness components were broken down and compared, rugby players were considerably less fit, in the broadest sense. Perhaps rugby players could have taught gymnasts about strength, and gymnasts could have taught rugby players about flexibility, balance and coordination.

Clive saw the cross-fertilisation of ideas at the AIS and realised that this was exactly what rugby needed. He'd felt it at Loughborough, and he felt it even more profoundly now. He was impressed by the fact that every athlete at the AIS was carefully selected and given everything he or she needed to become the best they could. What interested Clive was that each person was chosen on his or her abilities in a certain sport. In the UK, getting access to the best facilities, coaches and training opportunities depended on academic achievement – sporting prowess was secondary.

Coaches and staff at the AIS were full-time professionals. They learnt about sports science and they learnt from each other. That was the way academia worked in England. Professors and PhD students would work alongside one another in an élite academic environment. Significantly, this did not happen in sport.

At the AIS, they had the right competitive environment and it had produced great results. Phil Kearns, John Eales, Tim Horan, Jason Little, Matt Burke, George Gregan, Ben Tune and Joe Roff were among the graduates.

This was what separated England and Australia in sport, this seriousness of approach and determination to succeed – the environment rather than the people. Talented people existed in England as much as they did in Australia – it was just the winning mindset and facilities that separated them. There was too much reverence to the southern hemisphere. Clive had felt it himself and yet, in his time working in Australia, he'd found nothing to suggest that Australians were inherently better. It was time to stop the mindless copying, but by the time he returned to England, the All Blacks having won the first Rugby World Cup, the dependency on and excitement about all New Zealand-related rugby had reached fever pitch.

Clive and Jayne flew back to England late in 1989, now with two children in tow – Jess and Joe – primarily because they missed the country. The trip to Australia had been planned as a visit – it was never intended to be for more than a few years. As Clive sat on the plane bound for Heathrow, he felt renewed optimism about the possibilities for rugby and work back at home. He was going to work for the London branch of US Leasing and he planned to make the same success of that as he had of Portfolio Leasing in Australia.

The family settled just outside London in Pinkney's Green, near Maidenhead, and he got down to work, but by the middle of February, he'd had enough of working for someone else. By April, he had set up his own company, Sales Finance and Leasing, with headquarters in a converted garage at his new home. It was a huge risk. He had a young family to support and had been away from England since the mid-1980s. He knew that if he didn't make a success of it, life would become very difficult indeed.

Chapter Thirteen

Out of the box

---

*'Wisdom is knowing what to do next;
virtue is doing it.'* **David Starr Jordan**

Jayne Woodward was not the only woman in Clive's life at the beginning of the 1990s. As managing director of the newly formed Sales Finance and Leasing Company, Clive filled his offices with so many women that Steve Holdstock was once moved to complain, 'If I hang around this office any longer, I'm going to start having periods.'

Ann Heaver was the first employee to join Jayne and Clive. A slim blonde with a background in retailing and fashion, she might have been seen as an odd choice for a small finance and leasing company, but Clive is interested in skills, ability, personality – your heritage is not your destiny, and all that. Clive needed someone bright and personable. Ann was bright and personable. She was also a good organiser, which Mr Disorganised desperately needed. She turned out to be an absolute star – a self-deprecating woman who has been behind so many of Clive's successful moves. She and Jayne became his biggest allies and greatest supporters. She still works for Clive today, fifteen years later, having learnt considerably more about finance and business than she knew on that first day.

Ann first met Clive in Australia where she was posted with her husband, Paul, for a few years. Paul and Clive had known each other at HMS *Conway*. (Clive had been his fag for a term.)

'When we arrived in Manly, Paul decided to wander down to the local rugby club, and he saw Clive's name on the team-sheet so went along to talk to him,' explains Ann. 'He wanted to see whether Clive remembered him. Jayne and Clive had just got married and the four of us became friends. I came back to England in 1988, before Clive and Jayne. I settled into life here, but my kids were at school all day and I wanted to do something with my time. I was working at lots of part-time jobs to keep busy. Then Clive arrived with great plans to set up his own company, and he asked me to come and work for him.'

Originally, Sales Finance and Leasing was set up to sell financial software. Clive had found a product in Australia that he strongly believed would sell in the UK. From the Woodward family's converted garage in Pinkney's Green, Clive went out to sell the software, while Ann fixed up the appointments, did the secretarial work, answered the phone and helped to hunt for new business. Jayne did the books, submitted VAT returns and looked after the couple's two young children. Before Ann arrived, Jayne had been doing everything.

'It was a happy time. We all enjoyed coming to work. Clive was great to work for — always full of ideas and longing to be part of the fun. There was one time when he had a separate office for a while, but it didn't last long because he couldn't hear the gossip and had to keep running round to find out what was going on. I did enjoy that time. He'd be the first up to make the tea and really muck in.'

Since this is Clive's new business we're talking about, inevitably things changed. They moved on.

'Even though it was good fun, it was hard work. Clive made it clear that he was keen to develop and grow the business. One of the people I was talking to, and trying to sell the software to, was a business manager in the NHS,' says Heaver. 'They had just opened up the whole leasing business and changed the rules, so a lot of hospitals were getting involved in leasing to obtain the expensive equipment they needed. They didn't have a clue how to analyse the contracts they were signing and were being totally stitched up. The product that Clive had brought back from Australia was a lease-evaluation programme and I was trying to sell it to my contact in the NHS.

'This chap phoned me almost on a daily basis to ask me questions about the software. I was just thinking, "I'm getting close to selling this guy a big package," when Clive asked, "Who is this guy that you keep speaking to?" When I explained, Clive said, "Oh my God, I've got to get to see him. The software is not the issue here. If we can act as advisers to him, we'll write our own leases." '

Clive's willingness to change the business's direction so quickly and become whatever was needed by the burgeoning market at that moment would lead to huge growth. The company would change from being a three-man band run from a garage to a major player with multi-million-pound contracts.

'I arranged for Clive to meet this consultant, and Clive said to him, "Let me see what you've done recently." The chap got his contracts out and Clive said, "Do you realise how much interest you're paying?" He didn't, nor did he know how to get a better deal. Clive said, "Next time you're going to do a deal, call me first and I'll sort it out for you." Overnight, we went from a company selling a software product to a leasing company.'

Then, while Clive was making a rare foray back into rugby at the Bermuda Classics Golden Oldies rugby tournament, Ann took the call that would transform the business. The NHS consultant whom Clive visited was on the phone. He said that he was just about to take on a huge lease and did Clive want to bid for it. The lease was for equipment valued at over £1 million. It was crucial that Clive got the contract. He jumped straight on the next flight back and won the business. It was the first step in a whole new, much more lucrative, direction for the company.

Once Clive had put the leasing package together, he discovered that lots of companies were waiting to be paid by the NHS. Several had waited up to a year because the NHS simply didn't have the finances to meet their bills. Clive spotted another opportunity. He set up a series of lease agreements that meant the companies could be paid the money owing to them. It was all making quite an impact on Clive's bottom line. One of the companies owed money was a very large computer corporation. They had installed a huge amount of equipment but hadn't been paid a penny. Clive suggested to them that he become their leasing company.

'We started off selling software and suddenly we were a leasing company and lease advisers, and Clive was involved in the NHS, and then he's off working for a computer company. Clive was able to see the opportunities that other people couldn't,' says Ann. 'He could always see the bigger picture. We all worked really hard but what changed the company overnight was not the hours and hours of phone calling, but Clive's quick thinking.'

Holdstock, Clive's old friend from Leicester and Australia, had joined as a salesman. The work started to pour in and the company moved to proper offices.

'It was difficult at first because we were building a business from scratch,' said Holdstock. 'We all worked very hard. Then things started to turn around after the big deals and we made a lot of money. I'd worked very hard and pulled in lots of deals, so Clive took me to a hotel in Saunton Sands, in Devon, to celebrate. We ordered dinner, then Clive called the waiter over and ordered champagne. The waiter asked what champagne he wanted and Clive said 'the best' very confidently. It would have sounded arrogant, but he looked at me and said, "I've always wanted to say that," and suddenly he looked like an excited little boy whose dreams had just come true.'

Holdstock remembers how generous Clive was as soon as the business picked up.

'He bought Jayne a Jeep Cherokee and said, "Do you want one?" They were new at the time, hardly any of them around, so I said I'd love one. It was great. I felt I was appreciated. The business was going from strength to strength and life was good.'

Mike Poulson sat at Henley Rugby Club and looked at the slip of paper in his hand. It bore the telephone number of his old college mate. He hadn't seen Clive for years, not since the guy upped and left for Australia five years previously. They'd lost touch but now Woody was back, living in the area. Poulson had heard that Clive was helping out with the coaching at Oxford University. He would call him to see if he fancied a beer. Clive might even fancy coming down to Henley RFC to help him out. You never knew. He could certainly do with some assistance.

Poulson was player, captain, chief executive, coach, kit washer and general dogsbody at Henley Rugby Club when he picked up the phone to call Clive. He had moved to the area to take a job in London and had been attracted to the local side because Nick Joyce, an old friend, had started playing for them. He then persuaded Mark Duffelin, also of Loughborough, to come down, creating an East Midlands mafia in the Thames Valley.

Poulson worked hard at the club, but always felt that Henley could be a better side. The standard of rugby played wouldn't have mattered in the past. Winning was about as important to the players as regular fitness training and low-fat diets. Rugby at Henley's level was more to do with meeting a group of mates, going on liver-wrecking tours and scaring the locals. However, leagues had come in for the first time in 1987, forcing the sport on to an instantly more organised level. Winning matches suddenly had a purpose. Teams would get the chance to work their way up to the national leagues and earn more money from the RFU, sponsors and television. This, in turn, meant they could improve the facilities at the club to attract more supporters. Even if they had no aspirations to become the greatest club in the country, they could become a better local side with better facilities for the community. These early days of the leagues, before professionalism, were a particular moment in rugby history.

Players could not be overtly paid – although clubs handing out jobs, cars, accommodation and 'bungs' were all part of this era of shamateurism – but much was suddenly being asked of them. The only reward for the players' increased hard work was success, so achieving it became vital as a way of keeping good players. As soon as clubs rose up the tables, better players would be attracted to them, thus continuing their upward trajectory. The converse was true, too, of course. Clubs who couldn't make it to the top leagues lost their star players. They were sent into a downward spiral. There was no 'legal' way of buying in a couple of big names to help stem the tide.

Clive took Mike's call when he was working late in his garage-cum-office one night. He was tired but pleased to hear from his old friend. By the end of their conversation, Clive had agreed to go down to Henley RFC to talk to the players about what he had learnt in Australia. He wasn't going to bloody coach them – he made that very clear to Mike. He wouldn't even take his boots in case they tried to persuade him. He'd wear a business suit and just talk.

'He came down and clearly liked the warm response he received. The players were genuinely interested in what he had to say. He didn't do any coaching – he just told them about Australia and how they played there. I knew he liked what he saw at the club because he came down to watch our games soon after that with Jayne and the children.

When I suggested it would be great if he could come to a few more training sessions to help out, he said he would.'

Clive remained involved with Henley in a very casual way, using it more as light relief from the stresses of running a leasing business than anything else. Then, at an end-of-season barbecue, Poulson sidled up to him.

'I told him that Henley really needed a coach and asked him if he'd be interested. I knew he was enjoying the club and was fairly confident he'd say yes and he did.'

So, with his business on full throttle, Clive took up another challenge – coaching a south-west division two side. In traditional Clive-style, he was not content just to coach the side – he wanted to coach them to promotion. He wanted to recreate the 1984 Wallabies style of flat-back-line rugby at this small club in rural Oxfordshire.

'Clive called me to say that if he was going to do this coaching thing, he would do it properly – he couldn't do any half measures. He wanted to be the sole coach. I thought that sounded perfect. I was chief executive and captain as well as player and coach. I was thrilled at the thought of him taking over.'

One of Clive's overriding concerns was to make the sessions as much fun as possible. He wanted to build on the strengths that the team already had, while figuring out new ways to ensure that Henley stood apart from the other teams in its league. Fundamentally, though, he knew that he had to take the players with him every step of the way. He didn't want a repeat of his Australian experience and was keen to understand the culture of the organisation and the needs and wants of the players before starting.

Clive sat down and wrote a plan. As well as making sure the players were with him mentally, he also had to ensure that they would put in the physical work needed to improve the basics of their games. Henley were an inconsistent side at the time and Clive was sure this was because they hadn't properly mastered the basics. Tackling, scrummaging and passing were identified as particular weak spots.

Nigel Dudding was a player/coach at the club when Clive arrived. He is still involved at Henley today – as an administrator – having just retired after thirteen years as club coach.

'He held meetings with players that summer to explain what his plans were,' says Dudding. 'I don't think the players had experienced anything like that before.' Clive liked to hold non-playing meetings, whereas the players were used to getting out on the pitch and getting on with it.

'Clive would spend an hour saying where the players lost the game. He had a great analytical brain. One time, we went to a restaurant just to talk about rugby, how they'd played and what areas they could have improved.'

Clive wanted them to understand, intellectually, what he was trying to do. Bringing the philosophy of Alan Jones, Bob Dwyer and the Ella brothers to the club would not work if they didn't understand what they were supposed to be doing and why they were doing it – no point in demanding strict business-like behaviour from a bunch of blokes who just wanted to go out surfing, was there? He'd been there before.

Clive had plans for the team to adopt the flat back line – the simple-sounding, but infinitely harder to execute, process of lining up backs in a line straight across the pitch, rather than diagonal to the opposing team. Obviously, if players are staggered back in a diagonal line, they are farther away from the opposing side and farther away from the gain line. The diagonal line-up affords a team more time but, logically, that is something you want to deny to your opponents. If your players are skilled enough to adapt to this approach, then denying time and space – the two fundamentals for success in rugby – to the opposition side presents your team with a clear advantage. The crucial thing, of course, is the 'if your players are skilled enough' bit! That's why Clive was keen to go back to basics over the summer before launching his new style.

'Classic English thinking is to go wide and create an overlap,' explained Clive, 'but even if you have the fastest man in the world and the opposition stand a man on the touchline, you can't do it. That's how the Aussies defend. They're in your way.'

'It was a style of play that he'd learnt in Australia,' said Peter Wheeler, a fellow England and Leicester player, 'with the backs sitting up flat, in their opponents' faces, rather than lying back in the comfort zone. The handling had to be slicker and quicker because they didn't have so much space, and they were closer to the gain line.'

Henley were not promoted in that first season, but there were significant improvements in their game. They won their last eight games and the Oxfordshire Cup, but that pesky flat back line was still troubling them.

'To be honest, I think the players thought he was barking mad,' says Dudding. 'He'd introduced this flat ball game that he'd seen down in Manly with the Australians, and for some time the players found it very difficult to get to grips with. They were scoring quite a lot of tries, but defensively we were very naïve and making a lot of mistakes – dropped balls everywhere because they had to react so quickly.'

So, the players were struggling a little in the brave new world. They had won the Oxfordshire Cup, but not promotion. Perhaps it would be best to forget all these grand ambitions? Better to cut his losses and surrender gracefully, saying that at least he'd done his best? Yes?

Er, no.

Chapter Fourteen

Fame and glory

'You sort of start thinking anything's possible if you've got enough nerve.'
J.K. Rowling, Harry Potter and the Order of the Phoenix

On a warm evening, early in September 1991, while the rugby world was preparing for the arrival of the second World Cup, two Australians touched down at Heathrow Airport for a six-month sabbatical in Henley. Rob Gallacher ('Gals') and James Perrignon ('Junior') arrived from Manly with instructions to bring the flat-ball game to England. The two had been approached a few weeks previously by Bob 'Moose' Lane, the Manly club coach, who had received an odd phone call from a guy called Clive Woodward, who'd played for Manly three years previously.

Gals had been working in finance and Junior was studying for an agriculture degree when Moose called them with the suggestion that they might go to England for a season. Gals handed in his notice and Junior was given special time out from his studies. They packed their bags and headed for the airport. For them, it was to be an adventure – playing rugby on the other side of the world. For Clive, it was to be an experiment with spectacular results. The Australians were the latest stage in his plan to turn Henley round. They would slot into the first team and encourage the other players to raise their games and think differently about how to play rugby.

'From the start, we found Clive a great bloke for whom nothing was insurmountable. He really looked after us,' says Perrignon.

Gals worked for Clive at Sales Finance and Leasing, while Junior helped out with rugby coaching at nearby Shiplake College. In addition to the money they earned, they were given spending money each week and fuel vouchers.

'He welcomed Gals and me into his family and life unequivocally,' adds Perrignon. 'He used to pick us up on Friday nights prior to a game and take us for a couple of pints at a different pub each time. We used to have some great laughs on these little trips. I know that Clive put a lot of his personal money into making sure we were OK.'

'They had a house and cars,' says Dudding, 'both of which were trashed, but none of that mattered – they were great for the club, in terms of setting standards. All of a sudden, Henley was getting noticed.'

The gentle folk of Henley had never seen anything like it.

'When we first started at the club, it was like we were from another planet,' says Perrignon. 'The grounds were really soft and wet and the Henley boys were wondering who the hell we were. The rugby was slower but by no means less confrontational. Gals and I would not take any crap from opposition and we let them know this early via the odd fist or two and soon the Henley boys also started playing like they "could".

'Clive was a great person to work for – easygoing and ready for a beer and a laugh as well as working hard to achieve success. We adopted a bar in the town called Hanks, an American-style place, taking Clive with us occasionally. We would try our hardest to get him "full as a tick" and get him into trouble with Jayne.'

'As well as bringing in the Australians, I noticed Clive discreetly weeding out the people who couldn't play the new-style rugby, particularly those who didn't seem interested in trying,' said Dudding. 'He got hold of the individuals whom he thought could do it, and worked on them intensely. He recognised that he had to have numbers ten, twelve and thirteen really keen on the new philosophy and he worked incessantly with those guys, really boosting their confidence and skills.'

'Clive was at the stage where he was determined that this wasn't going to fail. I remember one occasion when Mike Poulson couldn't get a penalty move that Clive wanted him to do. He just kept dropping the ball. Clive threw down his clipboard and whistle, and walked to the fly-half position. "This is how I want you to do it," he said.'

In the 1991–92 season, everything came together. Henley were promoted to south-west division one after not losing a game. It was the

beginning of a phenomenal run for the club. They won the Oxfordshire Cup every year and, in 1994, they made it into the national
leagues. It was a spectacular achievement and the whole world wanted
to know how they'd done it. The press descended on Henley after that
first successful season, eager to discover their secret.

First to arrive was the BBC's *Rugby Special* with their camera crews
set to record and their reporters primed to report. Clive, dressed in a
grey V-neck pullover decorated with the diamond pattern so popular
in that era, stood before a flipchart, pen in hand, and treated *Rugby
Special* viewers to five minutes of fascinating insight into the contents
of his head, his world and his manner.

Looking back at that programme now, I'm inclined to wonder why
we didn't see what was coming. There were insights at this stage into
the Woodward who would become the coach of England – the turn-
around leader who wasn't afraid of failure, the bolshie individual who
dismissed all other coaching philosophies while espousing his own. He
condemned the tactics of the current England team, to the dismay of
Dick Best who was sitting in the London studio at the time. Clive
didn't care. He was in his element as he preached to the world from the
rather unlikely setting of a small side room at Henley Rugby Club.

'This is how you should be playing the game,' he said. 'Forget everything you've heard before – listen to me.'

From the head-on, balls-out, critical approach, to the shoes (shiny and
tan-coloured with grey trousers – a look that would curse the bodies of
England's finest rugby players in 2003), he was the same man who would
so confidently and dominantly take on the England rugby team nearly
six years later. What he lacked in sartorial judgement he made up for in
outstanding coaching sense – and that's saying something!

'Most people thought he was talking absolute nonsense,' says John
Inverdale, who later became the presenter of *Rugby Special*. 'They
thought he was nuts with his talk of short pop passes and a whole new
idea of back play, but the man has such self-belief that, in the end, he
could convince you of anything. He absolutely knew that it worked.'

Clive changed everything he could at Henley – the culture, the style
of play, the attitude and then the results. He brought in a glamorous
aerobics instructor to take fitness classes and, seeing how the players
responded – not only to the sight of a female form in Lycra, but also

to the loud music – he set about incorporating music into training sessions. He blasted uplifting pop across the pitch when they were training.

'He didn't try to do everything at once, though,' says Dudding. 'He just phased in things. He would drop in something new, then, when the players had got that, something else new would come along. It meant the players stayed alert and fresh. He had reasonably skilful players and he got the best out of them, made them more skilful.'

He tried to raise standards in all areas. 'I can remember when we went away once and he just thought we looked like a load of Canadian lumberjacks because everybody was dressed up in checked shirts and jeans. From that point, he insisted on everyone wearing polo shirts so they felt part of the team.'

When Dudding injured his hand, he stopped playing and joined the coaching team.

'Clive never liked to take whole sessions on his own – he liked lots of people to be involved. I think he was pleased when I stepped in to help with the forwards. They'd always had a joke at the club about when Clive worked with the forwards – they said they should get a seat made on the side of the scrummage machine for him to sit down and watch!'

When it came to selection, though, Clive was clear that it was he, and no one else, who was in charge. 'He wasn't a great one for having a ten-man selection panel or anything,' says Dudding. 'It was always his decision. I can remember once, we had a cup game on Sunday and the fly-half got injured on Saturday. I couldn't get hold of Clive to ask him what to do, so I made a decision to bring up the reserve in that position. Woody was livid. He said he wanted to change things round. He wanted to play people all over the place. I don't think he would have done, he was just showing his anger at me for making a decision. Fortunately, we won the game by a mile so it didn't matter, but he was grumpy the whole afternoon because he felt he hadn't been fully consulted.'

This need to assume overall control of crucial elements of management, such as selection, is something that would become clear when Clive moved on to his next coaching appointment and, in turn, coloured his tenure of the England team. While he was always prepared to have a big coaching team under him, he was always in charge.

Clive was generous with praise when the team played well, but made his dissatisfaction clear when they didn't. When Henley won a game against Banbury by the scruffs of their necks, the chairman and the president brought in boxes of beer to congratulate the team on their victory. Clive sent them away, saying, 'Give those to the supporters out there, this lot don't deserve any.'

'Clive would never socialise with the team and he didn't come on tour. It meant he was able to step back when making decisions, and do things for the right reasons,' says Dudding.

Clive's tenure at Henley was an out-and-out success. It proved that he had real skills as a coach. Perrignon says, 'I can remember telling Clive that he would coach England one day. He instantly dismissed the idea. I bet him the black BMW he was driving at the time that he would. Where's my black beamer, Clive?'

Chapter Fifteen

Paddy power

'There can be no happiness if the things we believe in are different from the things we do.' **Freya Madeline Stark**

Ann Heaver bustled into the offices of Sales Finance and Leasing, threw her bag down and sat at her desk in disgust. It was April 1994. Clive looked at her.

'OK?'

Ann reported that no, she was not OK. She was far from OK. Her beloved London Irish were falling apart. First, they'd been relegated, now Hika Reid, the coach, had left and taken Dean Shelford, the assistant coach (and younger brother of All Black legend Wayne Shelford), with him. So, just to repeat, in the interests of absolute clarity, she was not OK.

Talk of the weekend's rugby was a regular Monday morning occurrence between Ann and Clive. The two would come into the office and compare notes on how their respective teams had fared.

Clive was in a much better mood than Ann. He was having a storming time at Henley. Everything he touched turned to gold – promotion, promotion, promotion, Cup win, Cup win, Cup win. Why, he was setting himself up as one of the best coaches in the area. Ann looked at him.

'Clive,' she said, peeping out from beneath a blonde fringe. 'You know I said that the London Irish coach had gone?'

'Yes.'

'Well, I was just wondering whether maybe you'd be interested.'

Ann noted the look in his eye. He had achieved massive success with

Henley, but London Irish was a further step up.

' "Interested in what?" he asked, but I knew I had him,' said Ann. ' "Would you do it?" I asked. I could tell he would. "I might," he replied. That's all the encouragement I needed. I phoned Mike Gibson, the former Ireland international who ran London Irish at the time, and set up a meeting. Next thing Clive knew, he was down at Sunbury, meeting Mike.'

London Irish players trooped off the field, shoulders hunched, feet shuffling – the last game of the season and they'd just lost it. This was becoming quite a habit. At least they were consistent! Next year, they'd be playing down in division two. Colin Hall, the team's number 8, remembers looking up as they trudged off. Clive Woodward, the former England centre who would be their new coach, was sitting there. 'He's not going to like that,' thought Hall. Still, it was the end of the season. They'd have a few beers and enjoy the summer.

On the first day of pre-season training, the players of London Irish Rugby Football Club lumbered into their Sunbury ground like schoolboys being called to detention. A sense of despondency hung over the team.

'No one knew all that much about Clive when we arrived,' says Hall. 'We obviously knew about him as a player but not really as a coach. We'd seen what he'd done at Henley but – and I know this sounds silly now – we all thought the step up from Henley to London Irish was massive and we wondered whether he'd be up to it.'

Clive walked into the clubhouse bar where the players sat waiting for him. It was a small room that stank of stale smoke and beer.

'He looked around and said, "This is no good," ' recalls Hall. 'He took us out into the fresh air, which was immediately pleasanter for everyone. We headed for the school pitch at the back of London Irish. He stopped and looked at us. Most of us were wearing trainers. "You will always wear boots for training from now on," he said.

'I remember thinking how interesting that was – we all thought we'd be punished pre-season with loads of fitness work, so we didn't even bring boots. After that first session, you could sense a shift in people's attitudes. We actually had fun in that session – and that hadn't happened in a while.'

Clive didn't waste much time before explaining to the players what he expected of them.

'We'd guessed,' said Hall, 'after everything he'd done at Henley, but it was still quite a shock when he explained what he wanted.'

Clive brought in videos of Australian rugby matches to show to the players.

'There were gasps,' remembers Hall, 'when Clive showed how close the backs were. He pointed out players who were offloading the ball and running at short angles. He was quite clear about what he wanted. He said, "This is the way we're going to play." If people said, "I don't want to play like that," he'd repeat, "Well, this is the way we're going to play. If you don't like it, go to another club."'

Clive was always in control. There was one occasion when Clive looked over at Jim Staples, who was playing full-back, and told him to move over a bit. Staples refused. 'I stand here,' he said.

'Well, I want you to stand there,' said Woodward.

'I won't stand there.'

'If you don't stand there, you won't play.'

'You won't drop me.'

'Go to the changing rooms, now. You're dropped.'

He would sometimes call impromptu sessions on a Sunday morning, with very little notice. If players told him they were too busy to attend, he'd say 'your choice' and walk away. Players were never sure what he meant. Would they be dropped? Was it really their choice? Few would miss the sessions if they could possibly avoid it.

Such confidence in his designated style of play, his management skills and his abilities to turn the club round did not have the effect of alienating the players, as you might imagine it would – quite the reverse. What London Irish lacked at that time, more than anything, was someone with a big vision – an answer to their problems and the guts to force it through. When Clive walked in with a huge vision, and the absolute determination to see the project through, he created a feeling of genuine belief. His determination to do things 'his way' spilled over into everything. Once again, it was on the issue of selection that he was most determined to have his own way.

Hall recalls a strange incident when he was captaining the team. Clive had brought Mike Duffelin over from Henley to work with the forwards. Duffelin, Hall and a couple of other people met Clive to discuss the team for the weekend's match. Clive went round the room and asked everyone whom they thought should be in the team. They all gave their thoughts and Clive nodded and made notes. Everyone thought they'd contributed to the debate and that Clive would go away and consider their thoughts.

'But it wasn't like that,' says Hall. 'He walked up to the flipchart, lifted up the page and said, "That's the team I'm having."' There was no further debate on the subject. Clive had already decided on the team but chose to ask us, only to make it clear that our views were of no consequence.

'Sometimes I'd play golf with him in the morning and he'd be great, we'd chat and have fun, then in the afternoon we'd have rugby training and he'd say, "I haven't selected you for Saturday."

'"Why didn't you tell me when we were playing golf this morning?" I'd ask. He'd say, "Because we were having a good time this morning – that wasn't work. This is work, now." At the time, I'd be furious and think it was an appalling thing to do. Now, I think it was probably a good idea. He had a healthy separation between work and play.

'Sometimes you'd come off the pitch after a game and say, "Where's Clive?" and someone would say, "He's gone home." He'd got the train rather than sit in the coach because he was so unhappy.'

Hall remains a huge fan of Clive's despite these testing times.

'I'd think it was awful when he read the team out and I was forced to sit there. He'd say, "Obviously, some people are disappointed because they haven't been selected. I don't want to discuss that now – come and see me afterwards." I can remember storming into his office, demanding to know why I'd been dropped. He'd hand over a tape with all the things I'd done wrong on it and say, "When you get all those right, you'll be back in the team." What more, as a player, could you ask for?

'He's also a tremendous motivator. One time he brought Steve

Redgrave in with his gold medals. Steve handed the medals round – there were four at the time and he got three back.'

Don Rutherford, technical director of the Rugby Football Union, sat back and considered his options. He needed a coach for the Under-21s but he wanted someone different, someone who would really shake things up. Whom should he choose? He thought that Clive Woodward would be a good bet. The man was so persuasive, such a good salesman and an accomplished coach who really made things happen. Clive had been to Twickenham a few weeks previously to talk to a group of coaches. He'd shown great enthusiasm and the coaches had genuinely engaged with him, but was he experienced enough? Was he too much of a maverick?

'He struck me as a man who could make a difference, a man who could change things. I decided he was the right person for this role,' said Rutherford.

Clive was driving along in his company car with Holdstock in the passenger seat, on their way to a business meeting, when the car phone rang.

'Clive answered the phone and kept saying yes, yes, yes,' said Holdstock. 'I thought a big deal had come in. When he put the phone down his whole face had lit up. "They've made me England Under-21s coach," he said, banging the steering wheel and nearly driving us off the road. "Yes!"'

Clive combined his new responsibilities as national Under-21s coach with coaching at London Irish. He invited Andy Robinson to be his assistant coach, and Jeff Probyn was the forwards coach, after Clive blocked requests for him to become team manager. That honour went to Mike Poulson. The new team manager witnessed the same sweeping changes and creative thinking with the Under-21s that he'd seen at Henley and, more recently, on the pitches of Sunbury.

'For his first selection, he had every one of the backs playing in a different position. He thought, first of all, that some of them weren't necessarily in the best positions for their particular skills, and second, there was the typical Clive thing of wanting to challenge and force them to think differently about their role on the pitch.'

David Rees, who would go on to win eleven senior caps under Clive, describes the coach's arrival at England Under-21s as 'a breath of fresh air'. He continues, 'He put the emphasis on changing styles. He had a style he wanted to impose and he told you clearly how he wanted you to play. He was very ambitious. He'd say, "Let's go out and play, let's play a wide game." I felt very confident and I liked the way he talked, his philosophy and the way we trained. He wanted a quick, fluid, wide game, using the wings. The way he encouraged us to change positions [on the pitch] gave a new dimension to how I thought about my game.

'I remember the time I arrived late before a game against France at Bath [in 1996]. I'd been playing for my club [Sale] against Leicester and they [Sale] held me back. It was going to be my first cap, but Woody told me I was dropped [for arriving late]. They flew someone else in, a winger from West Hartlepool. Woody was testing me out to see if I'd stick with it. I was very down – it was going to be my first Under-21s cap – but I stayed and watched the game and at the end Clive said, "Well done for sticking it out. You'll be involved in the next game." That was a lesson in punctuality for me.'

Matt Perry remembers being moved around the pitch by Clive – outside-centre on tour after schoolboy rugby at fly-half and centre, then a move to full-back. 'I was open to the changes,' he said. 'I'd have played anywhere to be in the team.'

With London Irish, and with the Under-21s, Clive was eager for players not to look when they passed the ball. The only way to do this effectively, without dropping the ball every five minutes, was to stand close to the player next to you – in other words, not to lie deep but to flatten the lines and make passing easier.

On 20 August 1994, Clive and Jayne's third child, Freddie, was born. Jayne continued to go to matches with friends and the players' wives and girlfriends, to show support for her husband, taking the baby and his siblings with her. At this time, Clive was running a business all week and coaching a club in the evenings and weekends, so this was special family time.

At London Irish, Clive needed to move things on to the next level, as he had at Henley by flying over the two Australian players. This time, he would turn to Ireland in search of back-up.

Ann Heaver reports, 'We were chatting one day and Clive said to me, "I can't understand it. This is an Irish club – why aren't there more Irish people?" I said I had no idea, so Clive took himself off to Ireland. He just said, "Who are the best players?" and he found them and brought them over to England.'

Ann was welfare officer for the club and organised accommodation, travel and food for the new arrivals. She excelled in providing Sunday lunches.

'They were famous,' she admits. 'The players would come over at the weekend – Rob Henderson, David Humphreys, Conor O'Shea and Justin Fitzpatrick and many more. Gabriel Fulcher, Victor Costello and Jeremy Davidson came over. At one stage, thirteen players in the Ireland squad were with London Irish. Clive brought them over, one by one.'

O'Shea was Clive's first signing. He had been a budding Ireland international living in Dublin and studying – rather reluctantly – for a Bachelors degree in banking, when he received Clive's call.

'Banking just wasn't me,' he says, 'so I started to think about other things that I could do – maybe sports science. Then I got a letter from Clive. He wanted to meet me and we agreed to get together at the Gresham Hotel in Dublin. I told him about my interest in doing a sports science degree, probably in the USA. He listened and then he told me all about his plans for London Irish. He went away and I got another letter from him. It was the most amazing letter ever. In it, he convinced me that what I really wanted to do was play for London Irish. He could sell anything to anyone, that man.

'He invited me over, I went to dinner at his house, he showed me the club and I just thought it sounded like a great idea. I loved all his plans.

The way we played back home, at that time, was turgid, stale – focused on training hard and running yourself into the ground doing fitness training and weights.'

O'Shea joined the club.

'It was different,' he said. 'I used to play Gaelic football and Clive thought it would be a great idea for me to punch a ball. I was supposed to stand with David Humphreys on my left and as I dropped the ball to my foot, smash it with my hand. I tried it once and the opposition scored, but Clive didn't care – he was so happy that I'd tried something new. We had normal old bog-standard things that everyone else does but, in a match, Clive liked us to do something a little bit different, whether it was making me stand with the forwards and chase all the kicks because of my Gaelic football background, or something else. He just liked things to be different.'

Chapter Sixteen

Wrong shirts

'Creativity is a drug I cannot live without.'
Cecil B. DeMille (1881–1959)

Brendan Quirke liked to have a couple of drinks at London Irish on a Saturday lunchtime. Why not? He'd had a busy week in his solicitor's office and Saturdays were for relaxing with his dear friends at London Irish. He'd been involved with the team for longer than he could remember, heading down to Sunbury, man and boy, to cheer them on. They'd been good to him over the years. They'd made him the announcer on match days, which was great fun. He knew the players well, so it wasn't too much of a challenge. He could easily have a couple of drinks and get out there and do the job. In fact, having a couple of drinks was part of the fun. As long as he was sober enough to see the numbers on the backs of their shirts, he was fine.

So, as kick-off time approached, Quirke thought he'd have just one more pint of Guinness. Lovely. He sat and supped it in the directors' room. If he hadn't had that extra drink, if he'd gone down to his commentary position just five minutes earlier, he would have heard them announce that there were fifteen changes in the London Irish team. All the players had changed shirts. Quirke didn't hear the announcement.

I'm sure there have been funnier commentaries in the history of this great sport, but it's hard to imagine how.

'It was when someone wearing the number three shirt stepped up to take a kick that he knew something was up,' says Ann.

Then began a sequence in which the venerable, highly respected commentator reported to his bewildered audience that, 'Your number seven is scoring a try, but it's not seven it's – now then, let me see. That try was scored by – oh, never mind. We'll get back to that. Now the conversion has been taken by ... by ... by yer man, there. Oh, look. Yer man there's scored. We'll be back to you later with the names.'

Clive chose to send his players out in the 'wrong shirts' in order to persuade them that the numbers on their backs should not define the way they play or inform their game in any way. Total rugby, thinking rugby – that's what he hoped for. If the prop found himself in front of the try-line with the ball at his feet, he should pick it up and score. It mattered less what was written on the shirts and more what the situation demanded. Clive's clever, theatrical way of making this point was to send his players out in the wrong shirts. For some, though, clever and theatrical was just one stop short of barking mad.

The players very quickly found a new name for Clive – Dr Jekyll and Mr Woodward, because some days he would be polite, mannerly and understanding but, in a flash, apparently unprovoked, he'd flair up and be astonishingly cross with everyone.

'I remember the first night we were drawn against Leeds in a Cup game,' said Kieran McCarthy, rugby manager of London Irish. 'Halfway there, a snowstorm started. We knew that the match would never take place in those conditions, but when we rang, the Leeds committee insisted that it would be OK. "We'll put straw on the pitch," they kept saying. By the time we checked into our hotel, the snow was heavier. Leeds were insisting they were going to clear the pitch and everything would be OK. We weren't convinced, so we decided at dinner that night to let our hair down. We had a few jars and Clive duly got involved until the early hours. It was the first time in ten years that he'd sung. We managed to twist his arm to sing some little ditty from the navy. It was a great night and I remember thinking how much more relaxed he appeared than I'd ever seen him in the past.

'Next morning, he went completely batty. He was screaming and shouting because Leeds called off the match. He was really cross that his time had been wasted. I sat there and thought, "Eight hours ago, Clive was on great form singing a song and having a drink and now he's getting at everyone about Leeds." He was shouting that we would write letters to complain to the Union. What was astonishing was the dramatic switch – nice guy, nasty guy.'

He was once so cross with the way the team trained that he threw a tape of their match out of his BMW while driving along a country lane near his home. When the other coaches asked to see the tape later, he was forced to admit, "It's stuck in a tree somewhere in Buckinghamshire." '

His passion was equally evident when the team did well. Ian Smith of Leicester recalls one time when London Irish played Leicester in the Cup.

'During the game, Clive was on the touchline. London Irish had an attacking chance in the left-hand corner and we noticed Woody was on the pitch! We couldn't believe it. His enthusiasm was all-consuming. I said, "If you go on the pitch again, I'm going to tackle you!" '

On the training field, Clive continued in his own sweet way, having his moments of madness that, it transpired, were closer to genius. He bought a slip-catching machine to speed up the players' reactions and their hand/eye coordination.

'It proved to be great in the end, but at the start he almost killed me,' said O'Shea. 'He set this thing up and the ball came whizzing past my head, just missing me. I soon got the hang of it, though, and we definitely speeded up through using it. You know, at the time, everyone thought Clive was a bit bonkers, bringing this thing, but look around now and lots of clubs are using them.

'We also did this thing where we split the kick-offs. I wore the number six jersey and stood with the forwards. We were one of the first teams to split and actually have a back chasing rather than the forward chasing as a catcher.'

'Clive always wanted the best for the players,' recalls Hall. 'Whatever we wanted, we got. If the players wanted to travel by train, we travelled by train. If we wanted to go the night before, we went the night before. He'd always be asking when we wanted to train, did we want to stay on longer, when did we want to eat. He always wanted things done properly.'

Of course, there was a cost for such extravagances, and it was here at London Irish in the pre-professional era that Clive's penchant for 'the best' and his tendency to demand larger budgets first became apparent. At one stage, he said he wanted a team room, so that was provided. Then he wanted a coaches' room so the coaches had somewhere to go, away from the players. The club supplied a Portakabin. Next, he wanted showers put in so the coaches wouldn't have to shower with players. Then he wanted a power shower. None of these is an unreasonable request, but each was new to a club operating in the amateur era.

'He brought in first-class rail travel to away games,' says Hall. 'He didn't want players worrying about driving themselves or sitting in coaches in traffic. He wanted everything sorted. He didn't want players worrying about anything except playing.'

'Clive just didn't understand that there was no money in the club,' says McCarthy. 'Everyone was giving their help for free. The players received a little boot money and he was being paid – through his business, not direct. There was no more money. He'd say, "I don't give a toss where the money comes from, I need it." He took the team down to Saunton Sands Hotel in Devon, where he used to go on holiday, for a bonding weekend. Oh God, I remember the expense of the thing. I remember saying, "Is this really the cheapest way you can do this?" Instead of booking a dormitory room or school lodgings, he booked them into a bloody five-star country club and it cost us about £4,000 just for a three-day jolly.'

The point is, though, that Clive was successful as a result of all that he did – isn't that what really counts? The other point is that the £4,000 did manage to buy a trip to a five-star hotel for thirty players for three nights. 'I got an incredible deal,' says Clive. 'I got to know Peter Brent, the guy who runs the hotel, and he did the thing at cost for us. I was pleased with it. It was a great few days in which we did lots of training and the team really bonded.' As a result of all his work, London Irish was buzzing. The ground sold out for Cup matches, the social side of the sport grew, sponsors were attracted and Clive worked hard to integrate them into the club. He took London Irish back up into the first division in the season that professionalism came to the sport. If he hadn't, they might never have clawed their way up.

During Clive's period at London Irish, rugby union changed forever. In August 1995, at a summit meeting in Paris, the sport went professional. For clubs, it meant that more money had to be found quickly. The RFU declared a moratorium year during which no players were to be paid, while they worked out how to handle the fundamental changes in the sport. The trouble was it was extremely difficult to police a sport turning professional, and many clubs simply flouted the moratorium and paid players. Once one did it, they all had to or the players would have left for the paying clubs. As such, the year was a disaster in which the RFU lost all control over the sport and its most valuable assets – the players.

The immediate concern for London Irish was the raising of revenue to fund player payment. Michael Watt, head of the TV rights company CSI Ltd, gave them a donation to start them off, but while the donation was extremely helpful, it was never going to be enough to sustain the club in the professional era. They needed, somehow, to create a system to raise money regularly, year after year, to cover the players' salaries.

Early signs of how big the salary bill would be came quickly, when John Hall stepped in and bought Newcastle Rugby Club. He immediately signed Rob Andrew as a player/coach, paying him £250,000 per annum. The entire profit of London Irish in the year ending 1995 had been £60,000. How would they compete?

The club signed up the players they wanted for season 1995–96, resulting in a wage bill of £1 million. They would have to write it off as a loss – but what about next year? They needed to find a way of generating revenue. Inspired by the system at the RFU whereby Twickenham became a mutual and provident society, London Irish became a limited company during the 1995–96 season. A consortium of investors, London Irish Holdings, put up around £1.6 million and no single member of it owned more than 12.5 per cent of the club. It meant that London Irish was in a far better position than most clubs to tackle the problems inherent in a new professional sport.

At the end of the 1995–96 season, after two seasons of the Woodward touch, London Irish were promoted. Suddenly, the club looked extremely well placed to thrive in the professional era. The club was on a sound financial footing (certainly compared with other clubs), in the top flight and ready to embrace the demands and delights of the new professional era.

An AGM was held at the end of the season and Clive attended with Ann Heaver. He says he expected 'a hero's welcome' for all he had achieved, but that was not quite what he got.

'Clive feels that, at the AGM, we were trying to impose a rule to prevent non-Irish people from being involved in the club,' said McCarthy. 'He spoke out when he thought this was what was being said, and stormed out of the meeting, but that wasn't what was going on. He was too rash. He lashed out without listening properly. I said, "Clive, you've misunderstood again." What happened was that we incorporated the business from an unincorporated entity at that meeting because we were warned about liability. If you're unincorporated, the officers are open to being sued personally, so to protect them and to limit liability, we needed to become incorporated.

'Of course, what incorporation does is stop discrimination, so we were aware that we would have to change the line in our handbook that read, "You must be of Irish birth or descent to be an officer of the club." In discussing this change to the handbook, which we all agreed was a good idea, there was a feeling from some of the older members that we ought to try to have a note in the Memorandum of Understanding of the company and Articles of Association for the club to do all it could to maintain the Irish ethos. All it meant was things such as the green shirts, the Irish music, the association with Guinness and the celebration of St Patrick's Day. Nothing heavy.

'Then Clive leapt up and said, "Hang on, I'm in charge of coaching." It was a case of not engaging brain before mouth.'

Clive recalls it differently. He remembers an angry old man in a brown suit pointing at him and crying, 'We know what you're trying to do. You're trying to turn this into a whole team full of English players. You're trying to make this an English club!'

Clive felt blatant discrimination was going on, so he walked out. A few weeks later, he agreed to come back and coach for the 1996–97 season but, before he got too far into it, everything would change again.

First, though, he had the summer ahead of him – a chance to focus on his business a little, and go on an Under-21s tour to Australia. It was also when he would meet a crazy dentist whose views and philosophies would profoundly affect him.

Chapter Seventeen

Paddi power

'You don't have to assert your status by being rude and brusque to people. Behaving politely and giving consideration to others will improve your position far more effectively.' **Dr Paddi Lund, 2005**

It was the middle of the night when a self-confessed crazy Brisbane man strode into a dental surgery clutching a chainsaw, intent on causing massive destruction. He stood before the reception desk and swung the saw, sinking the jagged metal teeth into the wood and carving it to pieces. He worked until the entire reception desk was in pieces, then this quiet, polite man smiled to himself, tidied up a little, and left, closing the door behind him.

Welcome, dear readers, to Dr Paddi Lund, the man whose determination to be happy at work, create a happy working environment for himself, those he works with and those he treats, led to an evolutionary new business philosophy called the happiness-centred business. From that simple premise of *let's be happy* grew a new approach to work – a nice environment plus nice employees equals nice clients equals a nice life. Easy!

Part of Lund's approach was that the waiting room should look good. He wanted people to sit and sip tea in small lounges rather than hover around the reception desk like they did in most dental surgeries. How could he stop people congregating at the reception desk out of habit? 'I know,' he thought one evening, 'I'll go and smash the reception desk to pieces!'

Clive first heard about Dr Lund in 1996 when he was at a three-day Jay Abraham marketing conference in London. One of the things that Clive is very keen on is making sure that he is aware of all other good business ideas and talking to anyone who can add clarity or a new dimension to his own thoughts. Clive can often be seen scribbling notes on a yellow A4 notepad, whenever he hears something that strikes a chord, or makes him think differently.

This particular conference had cost him £2,000 per person for the three days – an expensive outlay back then. He was determined that he and Ann should sit through all the speakers, however boring some of them may be.

'I had other ideas,' says Ann. 'I was totally fed up. There were thousands of people in the room and lots of people talking – I was bored, so I went for a walk and picked up this little book called *Building The Happiness-Centred Business*.'

Ann came back, sat down with her new book and began reading it from cover to cover. Clive was not impressed.

'What are you doing?' he asked, upset at her lack of concentration. 'We paid a fortune to come here and you're not listening to a word anyone's saying.'

'This book is brilliant,' said Ann, handing it to Clive.

'He looked through it, flicking faster and faster through the pages and nodding his head. He loved it.' It was a book about the philosophies of Dr Paddi Lund.

Later, they attended a talk by Mike Basch, one of the co-founders of Fed-Ex in America and a devotee of the Lund philosophy. Basch said that to be a successful business, you do not have to be an all-striving, nasty organisation full of pressure, stress and misery. In fact, if you strive to create a happy working environment, then people will be drawn to you and business will improve. Great in theory, but in practice? Lund was stressed and miserable. Now he works three days a week and earns three times the salary of the average dentist. He has turned his life around and companies around the world are copying his example. Clive wanted to know more.

After the conference, Ann sent a letter to Dr Lund telling him how impressed she was with his book and how much she had enjoyed Mike Basch's talk. She received an immediate fax back from Fletcher Potanin, Lund's publisher and business adviser, who thanked her for the note.

'Clive picked up the fax and said, "What's this?" I explained that I'd sent a letter and he was very interested. Clive was working with the Under-21s at the time, and was going out to Australia that summer, so he decided to go and meet with Potanin and Lund in Brisbane, to find out more about them.'

What he discovered was immediately incorporated into his own business and later affected his decisions in laying down the ground rules for the England team.

Dr Lund's dental practice is located on Old Cleveland Road, a vast highway sweeping through Capalaba, a suburb south of Brisbane. The end of the road closest to the airport features large, well-maintained houses, diminishing in size as the road stretches out towards the ocean. In short, there's a wide mix of social and professional classes based along it. Lund's practice is situated beside an American-style row of shops, next door to, and indeed integrated into, a beauty salon.

Lund's surgery is distinct precisely for its lack of any distinguishing features. Outside the practice grows a cluster of lollipop-shaped trees. There is no indication whatsoever that herein lies a dental surgery. This is no accident. Indeed, the culmination of a lifetime's experience has led Dr Lund to present his practice in this way. People don't much like going to the dentist, so why not have a dental practice that looks nothing like one? Why not do things differently?

A large cappuccino machine is visible through the windows – the place looks like a bistro inside, the sort of place where everyone knows your name, as if the cast of *Friends* might come and sit down at any moment. They won't, though, not unless they've been specifically invited. A sign on the wooden doors lets you know that attendance is 'by invitation only'. Not only does everyone know your name in this place, but they have to know a great deal more about you as well before access to the inner sanctum is permitted.

People come from far and wide for the Lund treatment. To get to Capalaba, they must pass over the Gateway Bridge, which spans the River Brisbane. Below, the indigo waters are still and dark. If you have ever heard anything about Paddi Lund before, it will be that he once tried to commit suicide by throwing himself into this river. This, like many things about Lund, is untrue.

'I couldn't have,' he says. 'There's a big fence around the top of the bridge – I'd never be able to get over it. Anyway, I haven't got the guts. I heard once about a guy who jumped and got stuck in the mud and broke both his legs. A very inelegant way to die.'

What actually happened was that he was on board a ship, on holiday with his daughters and dreading having to go back to work.

Lund was depressed about his job. Dentists have the highest suicide rate among all professions in Australia.

'As human beings, we have an aversion to causing people discomfort,' says Lund. 'Most of us have a need to be loved. Dentistry tends not to engender those positive feelings in customers unless you do it a very different way, which I decided to do.'

Once Lund returned from his holiday, having pulled himself back from the brink, he realised he needed to make changes and got cracking. He discovered that 20 per cent of his customers were bringing him profit, and 80 per cent were costing him money to serve. He eliminated the losers straightaway. He wrote to them all, explaining that they had driven him close to suicide by seeing too many patients for too little satisfaction and would they mind going somewhere else for their future treatment. He enclosed a list of other surgeries nearby that they might go to instead.

Then he wrote to the remaining 20 per cent, thanking them for their custom and explaining that because of them, he had not committed suicide. He welcomed them to keep coming to him and asked some of them to refer friends. After that, he set about creating a lovely working environment at his practice, with classical music, kindness, sophistication. Lund was soon inundated with nice, new customers.

Clive was entranced. Dr Lund was the fourth man, after Kirton, Greenwood and White, to exert a huge influence on him.

Lund found it much easier to create the working life he desired once he became very clear about his primary objective – he wanted to be happy. All his decisions in relation to the practice had this as the primary motive. Would a particular acquisition or change make him happier? If it did, he considered doing it.

This was a tactic that Clive used with England. He had a fundamental goal when he took over the national squad. He wanted 'to inspire the nation'. Once that became clear in his mind, he no longer craved victories in the Six Nations or one-off Tests against Argentina. He wanted to do the most inspirational thing in rugby – he wanted to win the World Cup.

Lund's first step in creating the happiness-centred business was to talk to his staff and ask them whether they were happy. They were not. A lack of courtesy was robbing the working environment of happiness, so Lund instituted the courtesy system. He insisted that staff would say please and thank you, help each other and be courteous at all times. This applied to Lund, too. He could no longer shout for equipment without even looking up at the dental nurse – he had to be courteous. He also vowed to stop himself worrying about things needlessly and relaying that stress to the team.

'It's important to recognise how much environment affects us,' said Lund. 'When I read about concentration camps, I found that almost everybody associated with them, guards, administrators and inmates, behaves badly towards each other. Very few people seem to be able to keep their morality in that situation – most act like animals. Our environment really does have an effect on us. It also affects people's perceptions of each other. It's very hard to feel happy and valued in an unpleasant workplace atmosphere.'

Lund sent out a welcome book to all his hand-picked clients, detailing the way in which he wished them to behave. 'We expect you to say please and thank you and speak politely, and if you have a problem with someone, to talk with them about it,' he wrote.

After Lund had created the right environment, he devised the 'critical non-essentials' theory. CNEs are those things that are outside the core of the business but add such value to it that they are critical to the business's success. 'Most people don't understand dentistry,' said Lund. 'So they will make judgements on peripheral things that are not essential to good dental work but help them to enjoy the experience.

'It's my job to get the dentistry right,' he says, 'but other things matter, too.' He serves tea and coffee to his customers in Royal Doulton china. 'If I serve you nicely, with a silver tea service, then you think, "This dentist must be a cut above average." As a matter of fact, you have no idea whether, as a dentist, I am or not.'

We unwittingly make judgements on service in an emotional way rather than an intellectual one, assessing the overall experience. So, if Lund were to present his Royal Doulton china cups chipped and covered in lipstick, we would assume that the dentistry was ropey, too.

'If you find a different shade of lipstick on your cup from the one you're wearing, you start to question the way I sterilise my instruments, and no amount of science in the world will convince you otherwise,' says Lund. 'We don't have any signs on the wall saying we sterilise our instruments to 180° centigrade and seven or eight hours of gamma radiation, which is meaningless to most people. They will assume we are doing whatever's necessary because we take care of things that we don't have to.

'People assume that Clive's players play rugby really well because they are treated in other aspects of their life as if they do. It is intimidating to the opposing team – "Jeez they must be good if they spend all this time on the non-essentials. How much time must they spend on their training? We've got no chance." '

It gives a team the psychological edge, the winning mentality.

One of the other interesting things about critical non-essentials is that they allow you to engineer stories and create myths around your work, which help to define you and raise you in people's estimation. Lund deliberately goes overboard with some of the non-essentials, such as the cappuccino machine with the big eagle on top.

'I could have a much smaller coffee machine, but the point is to generate a story. The point is that people go away and say, "He's got this incredible coffee machine worth thousands and imported from Italy." '

The point is to get people talking, and people are never going to exclaim with quite the same degree of excitement, 'Oooohh, he has a lovely X-ray machine.'

Clive would use this principle with England and on the Lions tour to New Zealand, where he brought Prince William on board, commissioned a Lions anthem and provided the team with wristbands to celebrate the 'Power of Four' theme of the tour.

Clive took the 'welcome book' concept and made similar books for his customers. He created a pleasanter atmosphere at the firm's offices, offering a range of teas and coffees on a customer's arrival, and tried to make his business into a more convivial company. His business was growing. At London Irish, though, things were not going quite so well.

It was the first year of professionalism, 'but Clive wasn't acting like a professional coach,' says McCarthy. 'The players were full-time but only trained in the evening on Tuesdays and Thursdays because Clive was working during the day.'

McCarthy says the officials at London Irish sat down with Clive and told him that they needed more of a management/administration input plus daytime training for the players. They struck a deal that Clive would come in three days a week. To begin with, these would be half days when Clive would attend to administrative matters, and evening training would continue.

McCarthy recalls that Clive struggled to do this, so 'around November time we talked to him about it and he said he was too busy to come in during the day. He told us we should get him an assistant, so we employed Willie Anderson.'

Anderson came from Dungannon, where he had been director of rugby. One of his primary concerns was to change the training to daytime.

'We had all these professionals lying in bed until three o'clock,' said McCarthy. 'Victor Costello loved it – staying in bed all day and getting paid for it – but it was no good for the team. Willie said he needed to change the training, and he and Clive had their first big row.'

A subsidiary company, London Irish Trading, ran the professional arm of the club. The chief executive was Duncan Leopold. He and several key members of the management met and decided things weren't working. They agreed that it was unfair for Anderson to be full-time at the club while Clive made all the key decisions.

'They thought that what was needed was to switch the roles and make Willie the director of rugby and Clive the head coach,' said McCarthy.

Clive, of course, thought this was an absurd idea and told the management that he couldn't accept working as assistant to Anderson. There is no surprise in Clive's reluctance to work as a second-in-command. He's an all-or-nothing sort of guy and does not believe in compromise or sharing decision-making. What is interesting, though, is that Clive would come up against the same problem a few years later, when working for the England team. Roger Uttley was manager of the national side on a part-time basis and Clive was the coach, working full-time. Clive found that situation totally unacceptable.

The London Irish experience ended bitterly after Clive failed to attend a number of meetings designed to fathom a way for him and Anderson to work together. When Clive did turn up at the ground, a meeting was taking place – Clive walked into it and was told to wait outside. He refused, jumped in his car and drove off. It was the end of the London Irish adventure. Clive decided to focus on his business, and leave rugby coaching for a while. Certainly, he had no plans to coach full time – something that was increasingly being demanded in the professional era. Then, a few weeks after he had left London Irish, he received an offer that he couldn't refuse – a part-time role as coach of Bath – one of the country's leading clubs.

Clive joined Bath and was able to bring in bright new ideas without any of the commitments of a full-time coach. He enjoyed the experience immensely, even though it was short-lived. He stayed just six months and worked with Andy Robinson, the club's first full-time professional coach. They knew each other through England Under-21s so Clive slotted in easily. The part-time position suited the demands of his business and meant he had no dealings with committees, committee men or the politics of the club. Clive describes this as a 'magical' time. He worked with world-class players on Tuesday and Thursday nights, then went back to his business.

The relationship with Robinson worked brilliantly. Their skills are complementary – Robinson the tactician, the practical coach, and Clive, the overseer, the leader.

'He hasn't changed at all over the years,' says Robinson. 'He was always quirky, looking for new ideas, but he was always enormously good fun, the sort of guy you like to have around. I remember when we coached the Under-21s and they had practice games against the England team – Clive and I would stand on the side trying to wind them up all the time. We tried to goad the Under-21s into having a real go at the England players. Jack Rowell [England coach at the time] would keep telling us to stop it. It was a fun time.'

Clive did not stay long because the offer of a job as England coach came through. While the debates were raging in the paper about who would be appointed, Clive kept his counsel and tried to calm down all the speculation.

At a Monday meeting at the club, soon after Rowell had resigned from the England job and rumours about who would take over were rife, Clive assured the Bath players that he would stay at the club until the end of the season. A few days later, he went back to the club to say he was leaving to coach England. Richard Webster said, 'Oh, I get it, Clive. So you will be coaching us to the end of the strawberry season, then?'

Clive laughed. He left Bath on good terms and continued his friendship with Robinson, which would result in the latter being called in to work alongside Clive with the England team. However, as Clive drove out of the recreation ground for the last time, he had no idea just how much the world he was entering as national coach was embittered by the stinging effects of professionalism, shrouded in secrecy and unprofessional behaviour, and one in which he would have to fight – gloves off – for every inch of progress.

SECTION FOUR

Chapter Eighteen

Growing dissatisfaction

'A chain is no stronger than its weakest link.' **C. Kingsley**

It was early evening on a cold winter's day in December 1996. Cliff Brittle, chairman of the RFU Management Board, wrapped himself up in his coat and wandered through the empty Twickenham ground, past the discarded cans and fast-food wrappers and towards the committee box, lost in thought. Two hours previously, England had beaten Argentina 20–18 – by just two points. The narrow margin of victory against a team some way down the world order, a team that England should expect to defeat with comfort, had caused derision among the fans.

'Our own fans were booing the England team,' recalls Brittle. 'I'd never heard anything like it before, and I realised that we couldn't go on. We had to do something.'

He sat in the committee box, looking out over the Twickenham pitch as the floodlights faded before him. 'I started to think about everything. Just a year into professionalism and England had gone backwards. That hadn't been a good performance. There was more to professionalism than paying players. They needed to conduct themselves like professionals. We needed to see the playing standards increasing, not just the wage bills,' said Brittle.

He thought about the situation. England had full-time professional players and a part-time coach. This had never seemed like too much of a problem before, but perhaps it was. Jack Rowell, a supremely successful businessman, was the perfect coach in the amateur era, but once the sport went professional, he didn't have the time to dedicate to it. When you think of professionalism, you think of players being paid, but turning an amateur sport into a professional one involves much more than that – the whole landscape had shifted. As Brittle left the committee box and walked alone in the darkness back to the Rose Room, it was clear to him that if England were to play like professionals, rather than well-paid amateurs, they needed a full-time coach.

A week later, he called a meeting of senior RFU officials, in order to discuss professionalism in the game. They all knew that the success of the England team was vital – yet there were stirrings of concern about how the national team was performing. On the agenda was a discussion about the part-time nature of the England coaching role. They debated whether Jack Rowell would be willing to work full-time and thought it most unlikely. They did agree, though, that a full-time coach was essential. It was December. The Five Nations tournament was just around the corner so nothing would be done immediately. They decided simply to go away and think about the discussions that had taken place, with a view to meeting again after the Five Nations. Nothing should distract from the preparation of England. The meeting was strictly confidential. No one should reveal that the discussions had even taken place.

The next morning, Jack Rowell flicked open his newspaper to discover that he was all over the front and back pages – 'Jack Rowell to be sacked', 'England coach will be replaced' ran the headlines. He picked up the phone and called Cliff Brittle. 'Morning,' he said. 'Have you seen the newspapers?'

Jack Rowell was an Oxford-educated, multi-millionaire businessman with an impeccable track record in coaching. He had been plucked from Bath in 1994 to become the coach of England when Geoff Cooke retired after conspicuous success, including back-to-back Grand Slams and a place in the 1991 World Cup final. Rowell was the obvious successor. He had begun his career managing Gosforth Rugby Club. When he moved to the south-west on business, he took over as manager of Bath and oversaw the club's rise to glory, including a succession of Cup victories between 1984 and 1992, and five league titles in seven years. In his three years with England, he steered the national side to a Grand Slam in 1995, a championship victory, two Triple Crowns and the semi-finals of the 1995 World Cup, including the memorable quarter-final against Australia. Under him, twenty-one of twenty-nine matches were won – not bad for a part-timer.

Brittle was furious that private discussions had been leaked to the press. When the group met again to talk about a future England coach, he reduced the discussion group, inviting three other people whom he could trust – Don Rutherford, Fran Cotton and Bill Beaumont. He felt sure that between the four of them, they had enough expertise to solve the coaching dilemma, and do it privately without involving the British media. Meanwhile, he had to see Rowell to explain the situation.

'I went along to talk to Jack, thinking he was going to be an extremely angry man. In actual fact, he just wanted to know what was going on,' said Brittle. 'Was he going to be sacked? What were we planning to do? We hadn't any concrete plans at the time but I told him that we were concerned about the fact that he was part-time. Jack made it clear that he wanted to stay part-time and that he would leave rather than become a full-time coach. Now we knew that we had to find someone else.'

In the summer of 1997, the British and Irish Lions undertook their hugely successful tour to South Africa with Fran Cotton as manager and Ian McGeechan ('Geech') as coach. The England Under-21s, guided by Clive, were in Australia and those England players not on the Lions tour were in Argentina with Rowell.

'The undercurrents were that the England players weren't happy with Jack,' recalls Rutherford. 'They had no idea that we were talking about replacing Jack with a full-time coach – there was just a general feeling of dissatisfaction. A lot of them were saying they wanted a change after seeing how good Geech was on the Lions tour. Jason Leonard and Lawrence Dallaglio called me and said they wanted to talk to me formally about it. We met at their hotel in South Africa [the one, incidentally, that Clive refused to allow the England players to stay in a year later, because it had been downgraded]. They said they wanted me to employ Geech as the coach of England.'

'Geech was in a class of his own,' says Martin Johnson, captain of that victorious Lions trip. 'Anyone who has coached the Lions to two winning series has proved himself to be a legend and he's now a massive part of British Isles folklore and history. I thought Geech was a great bloke and worked superbly with both Fran and Jim [Telfer].'

Before flying home to England, Rutherford made a detour to Australia to watch the Under-21s, and had a chat with Clive about the team and how everything was going. In the course of their conversation, he asked Clive who did he think should be the next England coach.

'We just chatted through the options over a cup of tea,' recalls Don. 'I don't think he came up with any name in particular – he was probably thinking he should do it.'

'When Don asked me who the next England coach should be, I thought, "Ah – you obviously don't think it should be me, then," ' says Clive.

In July 1997, Brittle had to fight an election as chairman of the management board, so the appointment of a new coach was delayed. Once re-elected, he made immediate recommendations to the RFU council that Cotton, who had come on to the council as Lancashire's representative, should be on the management board as deputy chairman, responsible for all international playing matters. Cotton had developed a close relationship with McGeechan on the Lions tour to South Africa, so it was agreed that he should travel to Northampton to 'sound him out' about the England coaching job. The first point of call was Keith Barwell, the owner of Northampton, who had McGeechan under contract.

'Geech was earning between £80,000 and £100,000 at Northampton at the time, and the RFU could have done a deal with him for around £100,000 – an amount they were eminently capable of paying,' says Rutherford. 'Problems arose when Barwell wanted too much compensation for McGeechan.' Don recalls it as being £150,000, but Cliff Brittle recalls it as being much higher – around half a million pounds. Geech never had the chance to consider whether he would or would not accept the job – Barwell's demands were too high and the group decided to think again. It is worth mentioning, though, that Cotton was left with the feeling that McGeechan would not have taken the job even if he had been able to do so.

'We went to talk to Richard Hill at Gloucester after that, and offered him the job,' says Rutherford, 'but he said he wasn't experienced enough, and declined.' Brittle says that he is unaware of such an offer being made. From his point of view, they were not looking for a 'coach' in the traditional understanding of the word – but a manager, a professional facilitator with a wider vision of business. He says that only one person was approached before Clive – Ian McGeechan.

The summer was drawing to a close. By July, the national press were speculating wildly about who the next coach should be. It had become clear that Rowell was on his way out, and considerable space was given to debates about who his replacement should be. I was the editor of *Rugby World* magazine at the time, and we received numerous calls over that summer, offering 'tip offs' about who would get the job. Needless to say, they were all wrong!

While the debates continued in the papers, the discussions behind closed doors developed. The name Clive Woodward was thrown into the mix.

'He was on our initial shortlist,' says Brittle. 'When people say he was a complete wild-card, that's not true. We had considered him from the start and only McGeechan was approached before we came to him.' Fran Cotton was dispatched to meet him.

Meanwhile, the RFU was being pounded in the press for their apparent inability to appoint a new coach. Stories appeared on the sports pages suggesting that Rutherford had travelled to New Zealand and offered the job to Graham Henry.

'That's just not true,' says Rutherford. 'I spoke to Graham Henry and Maurice Trapp. I wanted Henry for the England A team because I thought it would be useful to get a New Zealand influence between England Under-21s and the main England team. We could have used him without making him full-time responsible for England. The trouble was, he wanted between £200,000 and £300,000. Maurice Trapp was an old friend. He was ex-Loughborough and had advised me on a number of occasions. I just wanted to sound him out, have a chat with him. Of course, the papers were full of claims that I was out there offering them the England job.'

The meeting that led to the transformation of English rugby took place near the NEC in Birmingham, halfway between Fran Cotton's and Clive Woodward's homes. Fran outlined his vision for England. He wanted to implement a blueprint for Club England, and accelerate the development of the England team. Cotton also mentioned his interest in bringing in certain rugby league players. He had taken them on the Lions tour and advocated fast-tracking them into the national team.

Clive wanted the job immediately. 'You could see it in his eyes,' recalls Cotton. 'I knew he would give it his all when I saw the look on his face as we talked about it.' Clive confirmed that, yes, subject to contract negotiations, he would take the England job.

'I was asked to sort out all the details with him,' says Rutherford. 'It was then that the demands began. He wanted a £160,000 salary, we had to pay for his current lease car and he wanted a 15 per cent contribution to his pension scheme. His wife's travel had to be free to all functions and matches. It seemed a lot – more than we expected to pay – but Clive had us over something of a barrel by this stage because the press were screaming to know who the new coach would be. Bill and Fran said yes to it all. They just wanted the whole thing finished and done with. They were worried about how silly we all looked in the eyes of the press.'

Brittle refutes this interpretation of events entirely, claiming that 'the appointment of the next England coach was a massive undertaking, the first full-time professional coach in a new professional era for the business of the RFU was very important. We were determined to get it absolutely right. We took our time to do just that and never reacted to any pressure from the press or anyone else.'

Cotton recommended to Brittle that Clive be appointed as England coach. The two men discussed the appointment in great detail. 'It's up to you, now, Cliff,' said Cotton. The final decision had to rest with the chairman. Brittle recommended the appointment to the management board, subject to negotiation with Bath and negotiating Clive's personal terms.

Brittle then met with the Bath directors in the international boardroom at the East India Club to negotiate Clive's release. In Brittle's view, the amount being paid to Bath for the release of Woodward was 'very small in relation to the potential enhanced value of RFU income over the years if we had the right man'.

Rutherford, though, was incensed that anything needed to be paid to Bath. 'Clive had assured us, up to this point, that he had no contract with Bath. It was purely a verbal arrangement that he could leave at a moment's notice. Then, when I went to see him that final time to shake hands on the whole arrangement and confirm that he would be the new England coach, he presented me with a piece of paper indicating that he was being paid as a coach at Bath and it would cost us £75,000 to buy him out of his contract. It turned out he'd been leading us all on. For the eventual amount we paid him and Bath, we could have afforded to employ Ian McGeechan after all.'

'That is simply not the case,' insists Brittle. 'Clive did not lead us on. We entered into formal negotiations with Bath as we would expect to with any club for the release of one of their coaches.'

It is interesting to add at this point that Clive never had a formal contract with Bath. He had a letter from them offering him a weekly retainer for two nights' coaching a week. He was on no contract, so any money paid to Bath by the RFU was paid without his knowledge or understanding.

Clive was offered the job. He would become the first full-time professional coach in English rugby history, but while the country's leading administrators had been battling to secure a coach for the national team under the unrelenting gaze of the media, there was bedlam within the organisation. Rugby was never going to move seamlessly from amateurism to professionalism overnight, but few expected the level of backstabbing and conflict that the change incited. No one anticipated the situation of utter crisis and confusion at Twickenham, or that it would develop into a power struggle at the heart of the sport, for the heart of the sport – the players.

The extraordinarily chaotic way in which the change to professionalism was 'managed' by the RFU created tensions in the sport that still resonate. The complicated set-up whereby the coach is a full-time employee of the Union, accountable for the performances of the players and judged by their results, while the players are part-time, temporary employees of the Union and full-time club players, is at the root of all the major problems in the sport.

It is worth reiterating the events of August 1995 just to see what the troubles were when rugby went professional, why they occurred and their immediate aftermath.

Chapter Nineteen

Professionalism

---

*'There is very real concern over whether the game will
change its fundamental character and lose its special ethos.'*
Vernon Pugh, August 1995

The moment of rugby union's complete transformation from an amateur to a professional sport is simple to mark. After the tortuous decades that preceded it, and the complicated years that were to follow, the moment itself has a breathless simplicity. In late August 1995, Vernon Pugh, the chairman of the International Rugby Board and a distinguished, well-spoken barrister, rose in the colonnaded splendour of the Hotel Ambassador in Paris. He had just chaired a conference on the subject of amateurism in rugby union. The assembled journalists clicked on their tape-recorders. The announcement was that the sport would be 'open' and that 'amateur' would be deleted from the game's rules and regulations. In reality, from the precise second that the announcement was made, rugby union became a fully fledged professional sport.

❦

Sir John Hall, the sixty-two-year-old multi-millionaire creator of the MetroCentre, and the saviour of Newcastle United Football Club, was sitting alone in his office when his advisers informed him that rugby union had become a professional sport. Fewer than seventy-two hours later, he had bought Newcastle Gosforth Rugby Club. In return for the club's eleven-acre site, Newcastle United Sporting Club Ltd agreed to wipe out all existing debts and pump in at least £3 million over three years. The plan was formally announced on 5 September, nine days after the Paris announcement.

Never, in the history of rugby union, had there been a time when quick action was more desperately required from the RFU than when the sport went professional, but while millionaires and big businesses clambered over each other to buy a share of the sport – purchasing the clubs and shifting the power base of rugby forever – most officials at the RFU stared at the prospect of professionalism like startled rabbits stunned by the headlights of an oncoming vehicle.

It was as if they hadn't countenanced the idea before – as if it were an absurd, ludicrous, abstract proposition that no one expected. Yet half the world was already professional. England took a year in which to adjust while the club game exploded. While men in blazers called meetings, men in boardrooms bought players and took rugby to a new level. The officers of the RFU had worn amateurism like some sort of snug and comfortable woollen shawl against the cold winds of modernity and the fearsome prospect of change. Now it was being taken from them and the vast majority felt naked and vulnerable.

It is important to remember that rugby union had not been 'amateur' in any meaningful sense of the word for twenty years prior to the announcement in Paris. Since the 1980s, certainly, it hadn't stuck to the amateur ethos, except that it refused to offer financial compensation to its prime assets – the players. Officials and executives would travel business class and players in economy. That's what amateurism was – deceitful and improper. It had to change. The question concerned the form it would take when it became professional. The lack of haste from the RFU, and poor leadership, threw that momentous decision into the hands of the commercial world. Ironically, the rugby establishment lost a significant amount of control by exhibiting the kind of inertia that had kept them in control for so long. The old, slow ways that had served them so well now served them badly.

The woolly shawl of amateurism was no protection against the machine-gunfire of the corporate world, but still the men at Twickenham wrapped it around themselves in the hope that the bullets wouldn't penetrate. The millionaires continued to arrive and the men of the RFU decided to prevaricate – they announced a year-long moratorium.

'The moratorium was a mistake,' says Brittle. 'It was introduced in September 1995 [six months before Brittle became chairman] and it took the RFU's eyes off the ball, allowing others, with different agendas, to stake their claim for changes within the new professional game. The members of the RFU council were well meaning as a collective body, but no business can be run by sixty-five people, however good their intentions. There were rumours that the moratorium was circumvented and it was obvious that it would be.'

Brittle's old adversary, Tony Hallett, who was secretary of the RFU when the sport went professional, argues that they had no choice.

'The RFU was a very amateur organisation. I don't mean that in any derogatory sense, but merely to say that it was an amateur organisation, and when the sport went professional, not everyone could react with lightning speed and become professional overnight.

'Even though, to the outside world, it appeared that rugby union was professional in all but name, there proved to be a big difference between the prospect and the reality of what happened when it went professional. I think the moratorium was a good idea. It seemed such a sensible thing to do at the time. Only England players could be paid during the moratorium year, and because the clubs had no money, this was designed to protect them, and allow them to think about developing funds and organising themselves.

'I had no idea that the big backers would come into the sport so quickly. I was genuinely shocked when men such as Sir John Hall got involved with the clubs and started appearing at Twickenham with demands. I just hadn't seen it. I couldn't see where the business was for them. I thought that people would wait and watch with interest. I was amazed when they arrived within weeks of the Paris announcement. The speed with which the club owners came in took everyone's breath away.'

'My memories of amateurism are of being invited to a meeting with Don Rutherford in his office at the RFU,' says Jason Leonard. 'Don was the technical director at the time, and he gathered together some of the more experienced England players to discuss the way forward for the sport. "This professionalism," said Don, "we'll give it six months and it'll fold. There's not the finance in the game. It won't last, so we're not going to sign you up and put you on contracts because it will just go belly up. Any fool can see that." It was so bloody frustrating.'

The RFU's stance was rigid and they refused to believe what was happening, let alone believe that it would grow much further. Matt Dawson adds, 'I had no problem supporting Northampton in the ensuing club-versus-country wrangles. By then I had a mortgage and day-to-day security, all of which had come from Keith [Barwell – Northampton's owner].The RFU had assumed they would get control of the players, but they faffed about with different contracts and how best to move forward. I preferred to be paid by someone I trusted and felt loyalty towards. The Union was not, at that time, a body I felt I could trust.'

Frightening stuff.The truth is that if the RFU had put the players on central contracts and asserted primacy of control over the key England players, the national sport might be in a different position. Instead, players signed for the clubs. So, a decade later, the clubs have the predominant pull on the players' time.

Tony Dorman, an executive of Richmond Rugby Club, was at home with his family in October 1995 when a call came through that would transform, and ultimately wound, the club. Vinnie Codrington, the club's president, called Dorman to report a most unusual conversation – a thirty-five-year-old Monte Carlo-based millionaire, Ashley Levett, had just rung to say he was interested in investing in the club. A week later, Dorman and Codrington found themselves *en route* to Battersea Heliport to wait for a helicopter to take them to Monte Carlo.

'It was like something out of a Hollywood movie,' recalls Dorman. 'We thought it might be some sort of wind-up, but this big black helicopter appeared. We were at the top of the third division at the time and virtually guaranteed promotion.The members were very keen for the club to develop, and once we met him, it was clear that Ashley Levett was a serious guy.'

After an EGM, Levett bought 76 per cent of the club and Richmond was changed from a members' club to a friendly society and then to a limited company.

On 6 November 1995, a Special General Meeting was called at Saracens Rugby Club. More than three hundred and fifty people attended as Nigel Wray, one of the 400 richest men in Britain, was introduced and it was explained that Wray had offered to invest £2 million in the club, and pay an additional £500,000 to underwrite shares for the members. The club would be changed into a public limited company, Wray would join the board as a non-executive director, and Saracens would retain 20 per cent of the equity and hold a 51 per cent veto. The average turnover of Saracens in the amateur days was around £150,000 a year. They knew that things had to change if they were to thrive in the professional era. The motion was carried.

It's not hard to see where the club-versus-country conflicts came from. Just ten days after the RFU's moratorium year was declared, the ten Courage League One clubs issued a vote of no confidence in the RFU's seven-man commission set up to establish guidelines for the new open era. England's leading clubs issued a manifesto for the administration of professional rugby union, seeking an annual income of £1 million each. The clubs formed themselves into their own organisation, English Professional Rugby Union Clubs Ltd (EPRUC), and threatened to split from the RFU. It took until May 1996 for a peace deal to be thrashed out whereby players were contracted to their clubs, but competed in RFU competitions.

The public battles between the RFU and the clubs reached an all-time low a year before Clive started his job. In September 1996, the clubs called on England players to miss England training and they did. Only Rob Hardwick, the Coventry prop, turned up for a training session. The newspapers featured a miserable-looking Rutherford standing amid rugby balls and cones waiting for the players. Rutherford described it as the worst day of his rugby life.

While the clubs and the Union fought, so the Union simultaneously battled with the rest of the world. It seemed they could do nothing right. Scared into raising as much money as they could in order to satisfy the demands of the clubs and the players, and to prevent more dreadful incidents like the training no-show, England signed an independent TV rights deal with BSKYB and found themselves expelled from the Five Nations because of it. They were allowed to rejoin when they offered to put a percentage of their £87.5 million windfall into a communal pot, but this meant they wouldn't have the income they needed to meet the clubs' demands.

Clive, a football-mad young boy.

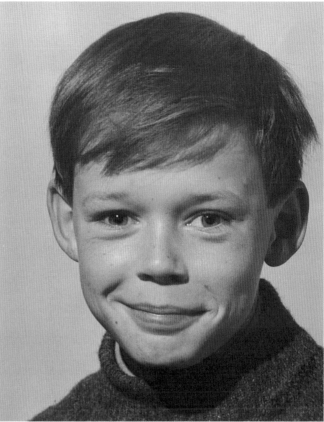

Ex-Scotland international Jim Greenwood was one of the first men to have a huge influence on Woodward's career when Clive went to Loughborough University. (*Scottish Rugby Union Library*)

Clive Woodward touches down on his debut for Harlequins in 1974. (*Colorsport*)

Earle Kirton, the coach at Quins, was another of the early influences on Clive's career. (*Colorsport*)

ABOVE Supported by fellow centre Paul Dodge, Clive makes a break. (*Colorsport*)

LEFT Thanks to the free-flowing style espoused by coach 'Chalky' White, Clive Woodward always felt happier playing for Leicester than for England, whose approach was much more cautious. (*Colorsport*)

BELOW After a disastrous Lions tour to New Zealand, six Leicester players lined up against the All Blacks in November 1983: Peter Wheeler, Nick Youngs, Peter Winterbottom, Les Cusworth, Paul Dodge and Clive. Together they helped secure a momentous 15–9 victory. (*Colorsport*)

TOP Clive Woodward in action during his debut season for England in 1980 in the game that secured their first Grand Slam since 1957. (*Colorsport*) **ABOVE** A year later and the Scots are on the receiving end again, as Clive scores his first try for England. (*Empics*)

Gary Player provides Clive and some of the Lions squad with helpful golfing tips.

LEFT Waiting in the airport ahead of the controversial Lions tour to South Africa in 1980. (*Colorsport*)

BELOW Clive powers through midfield in the second Test, hotly pursued by legendary fly half Naas Botha. (*Colorsport*)

Ann Heaver was Clive's first recruit when he set up his business on returning to England after his time in Australia, and she has continued to work with him ever since. Here she and Clive celebrate at her daughter Alex's wedding to Conor O'Shea.

The crazy dentist Paddi Lund, whose ideas on Critical Non Essentials were to have such an influence on Clive. (*Solutions Press* – www.PaddiLund.com)

The press conference in 1997 to announce that Clive Woodward would be England's first full-time head coach, as the RFU realised that it needed to move with the professional times. It was never an easy relationship. (*Colorsport*)

An early England training session for Clive at Bisham Abbey in September 1997. Roger Uttley is in the background. Soon the England squad would have superb new training facilities at Pennyhill Park. (*Empics*)

Roger Uttley, Clive Woodward and John Mitchell can hardly look as England are humiliated by Australia 76–0 on the 'Tour from Hell'. (*Colorsport*)

The beginning of a pattern: England lose 32–31 to Wales as Scott Gibbs scores to rob them of a Grand Slam in 1999. (*Colorsport*)

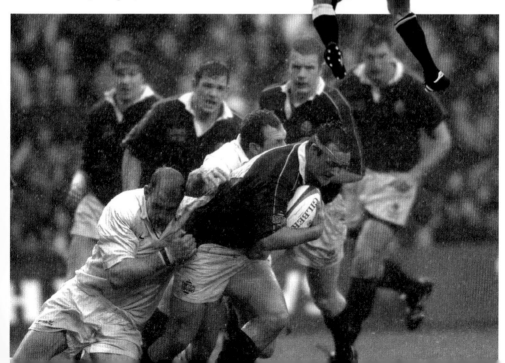

ABOVE 'Judge me on the World Cup.' England lose their crucial group game against New Zealand, where Jonah Lomu was once again a nemesis. (*Colorsport*) **RIGHT** Jannie de Beer drops another goal in the quarter-final of the 1999 World Cup – and England were out. From that defeat was formed the spirit that would see England through four years later. (*Empics*) **BELOW** Another Grand Slam for the taking – another defeat: this time Scotland win through in the rain in 2000. (*Colorsport*)

LEFT Don Rutherford, the RFU technical director whose methods clashed with Woodward's. (*Colorsport*)

BELOW Sherylle Calder was part of Clive's revolution. Her role was to help players develop their peripheral vision – if other muscles could be trained, why not eye muscles? (*Colorsport*)

BOTTOM Martin Johnson calls the team together during a training session at Sandhurst when the players almost went on strike in November 2000. Clive was furious with them. (*Empics*)

ABOVE At last! The England team celebrate winning the Grand Slam in 2003 after a comprehensive 42–6 victory over Ireland in the title show-down. (*Empics*) **LEFT** Clive was already setting the next challenge: could this team go from good to great and win the World Cup later that year? (*Colorsport*) **BELOW** Fifteen people celebrate winning rugby's Grand Slam, but this is just the management team. As the RFU would complain, Clive was never knowingly understaffed. (*Getty Images*)

England's massively influential captain Martin Johnson in action during England's comprehensive victory over France in the 2003 World Cup semi-final. (*Colorsport*)

Clive's attention to detail ahead of the final was a crucial element in England's success, and he made sure no one could spy on their training. (*Getty Images*)

The end result: Jonny Wilkinson drops the goal to win the World Cup in the last minute of extra time. Australia are beaten 20–17. (*Empics*)

OPPOSITE PAGE:
Clive celebrates his greatest triumph with his family. (*Colorsport*)

Clive had set out to make a nation proud again, and on 8 December, as they paraded the Webb Ellis Trophy round London, he had achieved what he set out to do. (*Getty Images*)

In the aftermath of England's success Clive wanted to move things forward, but the RFU's annual appraisal felt there was room for improvement. The frustration shows. (*Getty Images*)

With Francis Baron, the RFU chief executive, looking on, Clive Woodward resigns on 3 September 2004. (*Getty Images*)

TOP LEFT The nation at least showed its gratitude as Clive went to Buckingham Palace with his wife Jayne to collect his knighthood. (*AFP/Getty Images*)

TOP RIGHT Clive Woodward and Brian O'Driscoll prepare for the Lions tour of 2005: the warning signs were there. (*Colorsport*) **ABOVE** The controversial appointment of Alastair Campbell to the Lions tour party was to be widely criticised. (*AFP/Getty Images*)

LEFT The haka at the start of the first Lions Test against New Zealand – it was almost the last time the two sides were on an equal footing. (*Empics*)

Clive Woodward joins Southampton chairman Rupert Lowe ahead of his resignation from the England job. The idea of moving into football hugely appealed to him. (*Empics*)

Clive joins the crowd for the first game in Southampton's season after relegation from the Premiership. (*Getty Images*)

Simon Clifford, whose innovative ideas at Garforth Town and successful coaching schools led Clive to suggest a role for him at Southampton.

Meanwhile, the clubs continued to spend money. Vaiga Tuigamala became rugby's first million-pound signing when he joined Newcastle RFC. England Rugby Partnership (ERP) was developed to oversee the professional game. The in-fighting at headquarters continued as Fran Cotton was voted president of the RFU reform group and promptly called for the resignation of Tony Hallett over the BSKYB fiasco. Hallett resigned.

An extraordinary level of confusion reigned at Twickenham because (and this is important to remember) some of the officers at the RFU also had strong associations with clubs. It was not even a straightforward them 'n' us situation. There was conflict within the Union as well as between the Union and the clubs. Officials would accuse other officials of wrong-doing and, at a time when they should have come together to fight for the sport's assets, show a united front and some authority in the new professional age, they showed themselves to be full of cliques and far from united.

Those clubs without millionaire backers were revealing the extent of their difficulties in the new era. Bristol, for instance, announced losses of almost £500,000 for the year to April 1996. It was chaos and the whole thing was starting to turn very nasty. At *Rugby World*, I received dozens of anonymous phone calls from people telling me that club representatives had bugged the phones of the RFU men. 'They're being followed wherever they go,' said one caller.

One man asked to meet me at a pub near the magazine's Central London offices. He said he would tell me about death threats that had been made to RFU committee men. Thinking that it might be unwise to go alone, I took the biggest photographer I could find. He entered the pub separately and by a different door. I waited for half an hour but the phone caller didn't show, so I went back to the office. When I got there, I had a call from the man saying he didn't talk to me in the pub because I'd gone with someone and he had asked me to come alone. He said he had followed me from the *Rugby World* offices and saw me with someone. He would not talk to me unless I was alone. It was all becoming increasingly sinister.

There were allegations, counter-allegations and rumours that RFU officials had had their phones and faxes bugged and had employed security guards. Rugby union was suddenly worth money and everyone wanted to get their hands on it. No one knew what would happen next, and into this maelstrom, on 16 September 1997, stepped Clive Woodward, England's first-ever fully professional coach. Good luck, mate!

Chapter Twenty

Enthusiastic, full of ideas, but ever so slightly nuts

'A truth ceases to be true when more than one person believes in it.' Oscar Wilde

So began Woodward's England story – the greatest theatrical production in modern sport. His time with the England rugby team has the narrative and overarching concept of an American soap, from the moment of his arrival at Twickenham, when he burst unexpectedly on to the scene like Bobby Ewing re-emerging from the shower in *Dallas*, until his departure seven years later, like J.R. Ewing – battle-hardened, angry and frustrated.

Take one:
Interior shot of reception area at the RFU – a plain white room with a desk and two uncomfortable chairs for visitors. A wilting pot plant stands next to the chairs with an array of dated newspapers and rugby magazines on a low table. The room has the feel of an NHS dentist's waiting room from the 1970s (where's Dr Lund when you need him?) – stark and colourless.

Scene one:
Day one. Morning. Emily, the receptionist, is flicking through a copy of a magazine while mentally calculating whether she can get into the centre of Richmond at lunchtime to buy some new shoes. It'll take her forty minutes to get there and forty minutes to get back with fifteen

minutes for shopping. Her lunch break is forty-five minutes. She couldn't get there if she had a helicopter waiting for her on the pitch outside. She does some quick calculations and works out that she can do it with ease. She calls her friend.

While she is on the phone, a bespectacled man, dressed smartly and clutching a briefcase, comes through the revolving doors in front of her. He's the most important man in English rugby, but the distracted receptionist doesn't realise this. She sighs. Emily hates interruptions. It's the worst thing about this bloody job – that and the phones ringing. Happily, the man doesn't look very important, so she goes back to her call.

EMILY: OK, see you outside the shoe shop at one. Bye. (Turning to the visitor) Can I help you?

BESPECTACLED MAN (breezily): Good morning. How are you today?

EMILY (examining her nails): Yeah, whatever.

BESPECTACLED MAN (realising she has no idea who he is): I'm Clive Woodward. I start work today. Could you call Don Rutherford?

RECEPTIONIST (reaching for the phone): Woodwood? Is that two woods?

CW: No. W-o-o-d-w-a-r-d.

EMILY (dismissively): Take a seat. (She picks up the phone and calls the technical director's secretary.)

(Stage left. Rutherford comes racing down the stairs, taking them three at a time, breaking the current land-speed record in the process. He looks over at Clive. His face is tinged pink and a look of alarm has spread across it like a rash. Clive stands and moves forward to shake hands with him.)

CW (breezily): Morning, Don. Could you show me to my office?

DR (more alarmed than ever): Your what?

CW (bemused): My office.

DR (laughing): You have no office. You're supposed to be out on the road – visiting rugby clubs.

CW (concerned): I need an office, a secretary and a computer.

DR (clutches his company chequebook in his top pocket and reels backwards as if Clive has just asked him for his major internal organs and permission to sleep with his wife.) You want what?

OK, so maybe it wasn't quite like that – but painfully near to it. From the moment of Clive's arrival at Twickenham to his departure seven years later, the narrative of his story reads like the overblown efforts of a first-time novelist. It all seems so unlikely. He arrived on his first morning to find no office, no secretary, no computer, no desk, no phone. He stormed out on his final day into a barrage of photographers and journalists, leaving a trail of lawyers behind him and the sports world at his feet.

'It may sound odd,' says Rutherford, 'and I know much has been made of this "no office" thing – as if I somehow didn't understand what his role would be. That's not the case. The plan all along, as Clive knew, was for him to go out to the clubs, meet everyone and work with them for England rugby. We never envisaged it as an office job.

'We had this vision of clubs being integrated and working together on training and talent identification. Clive didn't want that, though, and that's why he had so many problems with the clubs farther down the line.

'Before Clive joined, I had employed Dave Alred [kicking] and Dave Reddin [fitness] with the aim of building a coaching team who would tour the country working with clubs and representative sides and raising the whole level of English rugby. No one ever envisaged Clive being locked away in an office and using every talented coach entirely for the England team. That wasn't what we agreed.

'Also, very few people had offices at the time because we'd just moved into the new RFU building. Clive has complained that there were no posters or pictures on the walls in reception – that was also because we'd just moved in. We'd had no time to do anything.'

From Clive's point of view, it looked as if they had a naïve and out-dated interpretation of the role of England coach. All the men employed by the Union for the benefit of the England team, including Alred and Reddin, were part-time. This view was exacerbated when Rutherford asked for access to Clive's diary, so he would know where Clive was if people wanted to get hold of him.

'You can just check with my secretary,' Clive said.

'Secretary?' said Rutherford. 'What secretary?'

Rutherford confesses, 'We just didn't get off to a very good start. I'm of the old school. I didn't like the fact that we had to pay Bath in the first instance. Then he turned up at Twickenham, refusing to fulfil the role we'd discussed. I felt frustrated and let down.'

The relationship between Clive and Rutherford would get worse.

Clive planned to separate the élite part of the game from the rest of the sport. He asked what the budget was for Team England. There was none. Clive would have to ask Rutherford for anything he wanted and Rutherford would judge the request on its merits and act accordingly. Budgets, or the lack of them, would prove to be a sticky area between the two men.

Clive's approach to the RFU's budgets was simple. He knew that a great deal of money came into the Union but only a tiny percentage of it was being spent on England. He knew that the success of the national team was crucial to RFU business but not enough resources were allocated to it. Clive developed a reputation for bursting through every budget put in front of him, and there is no question that he insisted that more RFU money was spent on players than ever before. However, it would be unfair to accuse him of recklessness. Clive came to the RFU from running his own business. He understood accounts and he questioned the accountants. He wanted to understand why there was no money available for England when there was clearly money coming in to the Rugby Football Union. On what was the money being spent? How could they justify huge bills to take the committee to matches and functions and claim that there was no money for the players? Clive questioned everything. He insisted that money was spent on the players. He would not accept 'no'. If this involved going over Rutherford's head to Brittle or Cotton, he would do it. It was vital that they adopted an 'act now' approach to the England team and worked to improve every part of it.

Over the next few months, the team had to play the three biggest sides in world rugby, one after the other – Australia, New Zealand, South Africa then New Zealand again, all before Christmas. Straight after Christmas, it was the Five Nations Championship. He had just three days prior to each match in which to prepare the players. In this time, he had to assert his own ideas, change their mindset, bring them together as a unified team despite the fact that they were all off at different clubs for the vast majority of the year – and turn England into the best rugby team in the world. It was definitely an environment in which 'act now' would be vital if anything was to be achieved. He knew that the knives would be out if he did not show signs of success quickly. On his coaching team, he had Roger Uttley and John Mitchell, both working part-time, and he had the resources of Don Rutherford's department. It just wasn't enough for him. He wanted full-time, accountable members of staff.

Clive began to think of the ways in which he could remodel England rugby, as he had his own business. One of the problems was that Clive had control of neither the coaches (all part-time) nor the players (the leading clubs 'owned' the players because they paid them). Clive considered the state of the England team and thought through his priorities. To succeed consistently, England would need:

- The basic skills taught well
- Fitness and nutrition of the highest quality
- Good mental preparation
- Medical and recovery organised properly
- Analysis and IT of the highest quality
- Good leadership
- Good management.

He would take the best coaches in the country in each of these areas – including those already appointed by Rutherford – and have them working exclusively, and full-time wherever possible, with England.

Clive also had to work on the players' belief in themselves. He had to get them thinking properly. It was essential that he built a winning mindset in the team. He had to change the reverence to the southern hemisphere because he felt it was holding them back. He also knew that he had to change it quickly because from November to November in his first year, England had sixteen Test matches, ten of which were against Australia, New Zealand and South Africa. Winning these matches would necessitate doing things differently, vastly differently.

There was a particular 'fear' of everything associated with New Zealand, and an overdependence on all ideas emanating from the country. England coaches copied the All Blacks with a vigour verging on slavishness, maybe hoping that copying New Zealand training drills would make the England players as brave, fearless and, ultimately, victorious as the men in black. One of Clive's first moves was to insist that the players stop calling them 'the All Blacks' and start thinking of them as a bunch of blokes from a country in the middle of nowhere with a population the size of Birmingham.

I worked as a rugby development officer in the early 1990s. The first document we were all given was the *New Zealand Skills Drills* book. It was considered the ultimate in modern rugby thinking. So we went on our merry way, teaching New Zealand drills and practices to junior schoolchildren and delighting in the fact that we were just like the New Zealanders. There was a certain prestige, even, in copying them. Coaches would proudly announce that these drills came straight from New Zealand. They even had appropriate names, such as 'Auckland grids'. In effect, we were force-feeding children with the idea that New Zealand was an utterly superior side. Psychologically, it was a ridiculous thing to do. Why not nick the best bits of the drills package, rename them the Guscott Grid, the Carling Catching Game and so on, and mix them with the best thinking from this country? Why inanely copy everything that New Zealand did, as if English coaches had no ideas of their own? Was it any wonder that England never caught up, let alone overtook, if they were forever fighting to sit in New Zealand's slipstream?

It was as if English coaches were producing cover records of every New Zealand hit. In music, some cover records are perfectly acceptable versions of the original, but rarely are they as good. The worst cover records are those that are just direct copies of the original, with none of the artiste's personality on show. That's not producing a cover version of a record – that's karaoke. So much of the coaching that was going on in England at the time was karaoke coaching.

Clive had to break through this and make English rugby players proud of who they were, not who they were copying. England had to stop giving the southern hemisphere sides a twenty-point advantage by holding them in such high regard. Clive needed to make Team England a vibrant and challenging place to be – an organisation that every other country in the world would want to copy.

'That's something people don't always understand about rugby,' says Martin Johnson. 'It's not that you're going out there thinking, "We can't win against this team" – it's more subtle than that. It's associating the southern hemisphere countries with difficult games that puts you at a disadvantage because you don't really expect to win them.

'Getting rid of that attitude and building a winning mindset takes time. I watched a rerun of the 1999 World Cup the other day, England's game against New Zealand [which England lost and thus had a much harder route through the rest of the competition – effectively, defeat in that game wrecked their chances in the tournament]. We were much better than I remember, and I thought, "I wish we'd realised back then how good we were." We were a good side. If we'd realised that, we might have won.'

Clive began work with the England team from a point of utter frustration. They were ranked sixth in the world – the same position they had held when he played, over fifteen years earlier. Nothing had changed in that time. Why? The world of rugby had changed beyond all recognition. The game had gone through a huge transformations but the world order had not shifted one inch. Could it be that the players from the southern hemisphere were inherently more capable than those from the north? Clive knew, from his time in Australia, that was not the case. England could be the best team in the world, but they had to believe it.

Two days after Clive began work at Twickenham, Humphrey Walters sat in his office planning his next venture. Walters, a management consultant, had just returned from a 30,000-mile round-the-world yacht race. His purpose in completing the gruelling journey, in which boats travelled the 'wrong' way round the globe, was to explore the concept of 'winning'. He'd picked the toughest environment he could, one rich with stress and fear where success was dependent on leadership and team building, in order to understand what it takes to be number one under pressure.

The phone on his desk rang. 'My name is Clive Woodward,' said the voice on the other end. 'I've just been appointed full-time coach of the

England rugby union team. Can I come and see you?'

Walters asked Clive when he'd like to come, reaching for his diary to make the appointment. 'Now?' said Clive. He was in Walters' office in twenty minutes. So began one of the most important early relationships in the England team.

'Clive said, "This is the business of rugby. I want us to look at rugby as we would look at a small business,"' recalls Walters. 'I told him I thought that was a brilliant idea and that I'd love to help.' Clive had to find the £20,000 fee for Walters – but he'd sort that out somehow. The most important thing was to get going. Walters started by doing a simple, analytical research project.

'I looked at playing for England like you would look at a journey,' says Walters. He looked not just at the time on the pitch, but at the whole experience, starting when the players turned up for England training.

'To be honest, it was a bit of a joke,' he says. 'Wilkinson turned up at the hotel and there wasn't even a room for the night for him. No one knew who he was. The first step of the journey was rotten. He'd come down from Newcastle, a young kid of nineteen, playing for his country for the first time, and the hall porter didn't have Wilkinson on his list and tried to send him away again.'

This was supposed to be an élite group and they were being treated with less respect than a bank clerk on his first day at work. Walters produced a report that gave details of every aspect of 'the journey'. Since 90 per cent of the players' time is not spent on the field, he thought it vital that their time off the pitch should be comfortable, too. This tied in neatly with Clive's thoughts, and those 'critical non-essentials' that Lund had talked to him about.

'When I used to turn up at businesses such as Asda, the back room where the staff sat down to have a cup of coffee was crap,' said Walters. 'All the effort went into the front – into what people could see. It was horrible. Why treat staff like that? What are you saying about your staff if you treat them like that? You're saying we don't value you.'

It was the same with the England rugby team. For a long time, the RFU believed that playing for your country was such an honour in its own right that players would tolerate anything in order to run out in white. The RFU were giving players the ultimate treat by selecting them for the team. Walters knew it had to change. Clive vowed to change it.

In October 1997, sixty-five hopeful England players squeezed into a lecture theatre at Bisham Abbey National Sports Centre in Buckinghamshire, waiting to be addressed by their new coach.

'Nothing you've ever done before in your international careers can prepare you for what lies ahead,' Clive told them. 'From this day forth, it is vital that we all start to think differently about how we play and how we train. The difference between good teams and world champion teams is what goes on between the ears.'

Clive introduced the players to Walters, who put a slide on the screen, which read:

> Finished files are the result
> of many years of scientific
> study combined with the
> experience of many years.

'How many fs are there on that slide?' he asked, telling the players to stand up when they had their answer. They all stood up.

'Sit down if you saw three fs.' Everyone sat down. 'There are six fs in the sentence,' he said.

Clive admits that, like 98 per cent of the population, he too saw three fs when he first looked at the slide. The word 'of' is so common that the eye runs over it and the brain doesn't register the f. The detail is missed.

'But we have to see the detail,' Clive told the players. 'We have to see six fs in everything we do.'

Detail, detail, detail – if the rest of the rugby world was wrapped up in three-f thinking, England had a chance to move ahead by adopting six-f thinking.

'We walked out of there thinking, "This is amazing," ' said Jason Leonard. 'It really was a breath of fresh air. Everything about the session was different. I realised that we probably could be a hell of a lot better if we looked into the detail of everything and didn't miss a thing. It felt like a new beginning for England.'

There is a funny story to add here. A short time after introducing the players to the delights of six-f thinking, Clive and Humphrey Walters went to talk to the RFU committee. They put up the six-f slide and asked the committee members to sit down if they saw three fs. All but two sat down. One of those remaining standing was a man who had opposed Clive's appointment. Walters admits to feeling a certain disappointment that this particular man remained standing.

'Anyone who can see four fs please sit down,' said Clive. 'Now five fs.' One man sat down, leaving just the obstructive committee man on his feet.

'I thought, "Oh, not him." I really would have preferred him not to realise there were six fs,' said Walters. 'It felt like really rotten luck.'

'OK,' said Clive, with an air of resignation, 'six fs.'

'But,' recalls Walters with a smile, 'the man stayed standing. Imagine that! He thought there were seven fs. That made my day.' It's one thing not to notice the fs – quite another to see them when they're not there.

Clive's primary objective had been to encourage the players to think differently. The players left clutching a copy of Dr Paddi Lund's *Happiness-Centred Business*. Whatever they had been expecting from their first session with the new coach, it cannot have been a lecture on six-f thinking and the philosophy of a barking-mad dentist from Brisbane.

'From day one,' said Martin Johnson, 'the team changed, the way we trained changed – suddenly, everything was different. He didn't want to do anything in the same way as it had been done before. In particular, he was desperate to get rid of the staid forward-dominated English rugby of the early nineties, although, to be fair, I think we'd done that by the time he came on board. He said, "You must never use the words 'game plan' – just go out there and play it as it comes. Give everything a go." It was naïve but very refreshing.'

Clive's reputation as half madman, half genius began at this time. He had plenty of great ideas and a few that the more down-to-earth members of the squad, including Martin Johnson, thought slightly barmy.

'The years between 1997 and 2000 were very, er, interesting,' says Johnson, with a smile. 'We were a long way behind the southern hemisphere at the time and Clive was desperate for us to be the best team. He thought that if we did things that they just didn't expect us to do, we would beat them. Some of the ideas were good, some of them OK and some just plain crazy – like the computer system from Mosad. What was that all about? I guess Clive and I are just totally different sorts of people. I believe that on a rugby pitch everyone basically tries to do the same thing – it's who does it best that counts.'

The Mosad computer, incidentally, came courtesy of a man called Yehudi Shinar. Clive travelled to Israel to meet the expert in 'leadership and skills in high-performance individuals' in the summer of 2000. Shinar's background was in handwriting analysis but he went on to design a computer programme to assess an individual's ability to perform under high levels of pressure and stress.

Shinar had researched over three thousand individuals and compiled a database of common characteristics among the successful. He established that there were very clear trends. He also found that when an individual's pattern of thinking was changed, his personal performance improved. Competitors become winners. Shinar was drafted in to work with the rest of the management team. His computer programme identified the psychology of the true winner and Shinar claimed he could develop those skills in an individual.

'It all sounded great. Then when Clive turned up with this bloke and his Mosad system, it was like a computer game,' recalls Johnson. 'There was a joystick and you had to line up all these targets and fire things and line things up. The younger players were better than anyone else straightaway because they were used to using a joystick and playing games like that. The management team were hopeless at it because they hadn't played computer games.

'At one point Clive said, "The results of this exercise may determine who gets selected for the team." At that point, we thought Clive had completely lost it. There were lots of moments like that, when we thought he'd lost all sense, but I think it was just enthusiasm – he'd say these things because he was so excited by this new gadget or that new idea. From a player's point of view, though, we'd believe everything he said. In this case, we used the programme for a couple of months, then we never saw it again.'

Clive had gone to Israel to meet Shinar and his willingness to travel anywhere, any time to seek advice from anyone who might make a difference to Team England became legendary.

'I remember some bloke from Ireland writing Clive a probing, derogatory email,' says Walters. 'The next thing, Clive is on the plane on his way to talk to him and find out where he thinks they're going wrong. He's just unbelievable – he will go to any lengths.'

The players recall Clive coming back and announcing that the man from Ireland had said that he felt England weren't succeeding because they weren't financially dependent on England's success.

'So,' said Clive. 'I have decided to sell my business.'

'Oh, no,' chorused the players. 'You shouldn't have done that.'

'Don't worry,' replied Clive. 'I got a load of money for it.'

'But that means you're not financially dependent on England winning, then,' muttered the players.

'Right,' said Clive. 'Let's get out there and train.'

'There were lots of crazy moments along the way,' recalls Johnson, 'but, to be fair to Clive, there were plenty of good ideas, too.'

There were certainly plenty of decent ideas when it came to creating the right environment for the players.

'We had to make lots of changes immediately because the environment and the way coaches were working was absurd,' says Walters. The first meeting with the team was a prime example. 'I was used to doing presentations in hotels. What I didn't expect to have to do was talk to sixty-five people crammed into a hot, stuffy room with some people sitting on tables and others on the floor. I wouldn't allow any of my staff to work in such conditions and yet here was the élite England squad being treated worse than a shop-floor worker.'

England's first game under Clive was against Australia, on 15 November, just two months after he started the job. He signalled his intention to do things differently straightaway by making Lawrence Dallaglio captain when everyone expected him to appoint Johnson, the victorious Lions captain. Clive was aware of the vital relationship that had to exist between coach and captain in order for a team to function effectively and he saw Dallaglio as a man in his own mould, someone who would understand what he was aiming to do and be key to translating this vision to the players.

'In a way, you could describe Dallaglio as being like a cultural architect,' says Steve Bull. 'In any organisation, in order for the head man – whether he be a coach or CEO – to lead effectively, he does need to appoint people around him who understand what he's doing and will get on with the job of making things happen on a practical level.'

There is no question that Clive saw Dallaglio in this way. He has described the 'hunger for success' and Dallaglio's eagerness to make it in memory of his sister Francesca who died in the *Marchioness* disaster. Clive recognised something of himself in Dallaglio. The two men spent a great deal of time together – they were both big thinkers and had a great vision of the future. Jayne and Alice, Dallaglio's partner, got to know one another.

'Clive and I weren't that similar,' says Martin Johnson. 'We always got on because we both wanted to win and that's what made the relationship work when I did become captain, but it didn't surprise me when Lawrence was his first choice as captain. I suppose I've got my feet on the ground a bit more. Clive would have his barmy ideas and I'd just stand there and look at him.'

Clive selected five new caps to play in his first game. Matt Perry, David Rees – both of whom had played for the Under-21s under Clive – Will Greenwood, Andy Long and Will Green, all found themselves in the England team for the first time. Perry was at home, in the house he shared with two other Bath players, when the call came through.

'We were watching television and just messing about when Clive rang. I was gobsmacked. My mates were jumping round the room. In the early days, Clive had so many ideas coming through from his business background. He wanted to change things, to be different. I remember a backs session where the attackers had to wear black hoods. We'd be lying on the floor and then jump up and take off our hoods, and the defence would be on us straightaway. [The idea was to help reaction time and the ability to think quickly under pressure.]

'Clive had an intensity and passion. He wanted to win. He was uncompromising. He was very different from any other coach I've come across. I was 100 per cent into it. I'd have run through a brick wall if he'd asked me to.'

'We did group-bonding stuff,' said Rees. 'At Twickenham, each player had a name plaque above their station in the changing room. Woody joked about how players will know if they're not involved any more because they'll get their name plaque in the post. The players used to joke about that from time to time afterwards.'

Andy Long was one of the players to receive the metaphoric 'plaque in the post'. He won his first cap against Australia when he was just two months past his twentieth birthday. He says his mum, Gill, still has the cap at her Bournemouth home. Long's story did not have a happy ending, though. Clive replaced him with Richard Cockerill at half-time and he wasn't selected for the next game. Long fell back down to the Under-21s side with a bump, joking that 'someone forgot to pull the ripcord at A-team level'.

England drew 15–15 with Australia, then lost 8–25 to New Zealand a week later and 11–29 to South Africa the week after that.

Then came a seminal match, the fourth of the pre-Christmas matches, against New Zealand. England drew 26–26 in a display of such confident, fast-moving rugby that even those who had previously wondered about England's ability to make it, suddenly found themselves thinking that maybe, just maybe, this side had the makings of a great team. Clive learnt two crucial things from the match. First, he had to raise the public's expectations. There was such an outpouring of joy at the result because everyone just expected England to lose against New Zealand, so a draw seemed positively triumphant. Clive did not want the public to be feeling like that. He wanted them, like him, to expect England to beat everyone. He needed to convince a sceptical English public that their team could and would be the best team in the world.

His second lesson was that much more work had to be done off the field. England had drawn with an excellent New Zealand side on the pitch, and had outscored them three tries to two, but had started to wane in the closing minutes of the match, indicating that they were nowhere near the fitness levels of the All Blacks. England's mental preparation, believing they were capable of victory, had to be backed up by a serious hike in the levels of fitness.

'We just kept saying, "Right, how can we make this better?" ' says Walters. 'How can we make the meetings run better? How can we make the environment better?' They questioned everything. Why were they training at the Bank of England ground at Roehampton when Twickenham was the home of rugby? They wanted to train on the pitch at Twickenham with crowd noise blasting through the loudspeaker systems to try to simulate match days. With so many new players coming into the sides, it was essential. 'I kept thinking of examples from the army, where they sometimes train with live ammunition because it's so vital to simulate war accurately. Men may die in training-field incidents but it's considered essential. Surely, based on that, we should have been training at Twickenham.'

Clive called Don Rutherford to let him know what they planned to do. He explained the idea and Don hated it.

'In fact, he went up the wall,' says Walters. Rutherford insisted that England had an hour on the pitch and the Australians had an hour on the pitch, and that was all. 'Clive said, "Can you imagine Manchester United doing that with Arsenal? This is not on. We're trying to build a winning team here – why are we giving away every advantage?" '

When Clive insisted that he wanted to train on the pitch, Rutherford told him to ring the turf committee chairman who would have to convene a meeting to discuss it. The organisation of the meeting would take at least four weeks because people would have to travel from all over the country.

'We're going to do it anyway,' said Clive. Rutherford replied that Securicor wouldn't let them in. Clive said, 'Fine, we'll go to the South Stand, jump on the top of the bus and climb over the railings.'

As it happened, the security officers did let them in and everything was fine – they didn't have to leap off the top of the bus and hurdle the perimeter walls. 'But my God, the fuss that was created before we could do anything. It was quite astonishing,' says Walters.

Walters' perspective on the barriers that were put in Clive's way is interesting. Here is a man who has been working in business transformation for three decades – going into major international companies and offering advice. Suddenly, he came up against the RFU and was staggered by the degree of resistance.

'I have to say that I had never seen anything like it. No company I have worked with would ever, ever treat someone in Clive's position like that. A CEO would never put up with it. There was just no support coming from them. All the big institutions I deal with have boards that, when the chips are down, will back their CEO. As far as I can recall, Clive didn't get much backing. Everything he did was opposed. Things would be leaked to the press, and his every move seemed to be challenged. The RFU way was to undermine people all the time. The only people there who really supported Clive were Cliff Brittle, who got fired, and Fran Cotton, the big, understated, humble, courteous, tough guy.

'Fran was absolutely fantastic. He was rock solid. He just backed Clive all the time. I had lots of chats with Fran and he just said, "Keep going ... keep going ... keep going." Fran wasn't in it for the money, the status or anything – he wanted England to win.'

Woodward spoke to Cotton 'every day' through his seven years at the helm of the England ship. Woodward once said to him, 'You're the only person who doesn't shout at me.'

'We can't both shout,' replied Cotton.

Fran Cotton sits in an office the size of a boardroom at Cotton Traders – his eponymous shirt manufacturing company based near Altrincham. His glamorous blonde assistant brings in coffees and teas on demand. For Cotton, it's a cup of herbal tea and a pear.

'Watching the weight,' he says, patting his admittedly stocky frame. Down the road from his business headquarters lies the manufacturing plant of Cotton Traders, producing rugby shirts and leisurewear to be sold around the world. He has made a fortune from selling rugby shirts to people who don't play rugby.

Cotton developed his business after being banished from rugby union for writing a book. The measly profit that the book produced was enough to have him struck off as an amateur and unable to involve himself in rugby union in any formal capacity. With his international career behind him, and all hopes of coaching snuffed out by his new professional status, Cotton found himself out of favour and working for Bukta, a sportswear manufacturer, alongside Steve Smith, also a former international.

The company was bought by French Connection, and Cotton went along to the first meeting organised by the new owners. Also in attendance was David Jones, then the chairman of Next. Cotton and Smith had previously talked about rugby shirts being a big retail seller because they were what all their friends wore. Cotton brought this up at the meeting and Jones told them about J. Crew, an American company that sold rugby shirts by mail order. Smith and Cotton got hold of the catalogues and looked through them, thinking, 'We could do this here.' They decided to try it. They put a catalogue together, took out an advertisement in the next month's *Rugby World* magazine and spent the weeks wondering how they'd be able to cope with the demand. Cotton drove down to the post office the day the advert appeared, pondering how he'd be able to fit all the orders in the back of his car. He was handed three letters.

'It hadn't occurred to me that *Rugby World* sold just 25,000 copies a month,' says Fran.

Undaunted, they placed an advert in *You* magazine in the *Mail on Sunday*, with a circulation in the millions. This time they set up a phone line and Cotton went down to the office on the Sunday the magazine came out, saying to Steve Smith, 'I'll call you if we need you, mate, but I'm sure it'll be OK.' He got there and it was bedlam. He called Smith straightaway, saying, 'Steve, you'd better get down here quick. The phones are jumping off the desks.' Cotton Traders was born.

Woodward lost touch with Cotton while he was working in Australia, but got back in contact soon after he started with the Under-21s.

'He'd call up and text me, complaining that the sport was dominated by kickers,' said Cotton. 'Even at Under-21 level he opposed the amount of kicking going on in the game. "You win by territory and possession," he'd say. When you listened to what Clive was saying, you had to agree with him. He was very astute. Very ahead of the game.'

Cotton gave Clive tremendous support throughout his seven years as England head coach. Many people in the background of the Woodward story lent a tremendous amount of support, listening and helping but also arguing Clive's case and pushing for the changes he wanted. Cotton was one of them. Clive recognises this. In the small reception area below Cotton's large office hangs a collection of pictures – old team photographs showing Cotton and Smith in their prime. In pride of place is a framed montage of photographs taken from England's 2003 Grand Slam victory. It is dedicated to Cotton. 'Let's go from good to great,' it says, referring to the World Cup six months later. The team went on to win that, too. Fran Cotton played a large part in that victory.

Chapter Twenty-one

Inspiring thoughts

'One should always be a little improbable.' **Oscar Wilde**

Clive is not a regular pub-goer, although he admits to liking a pint or two. Readers who have flicked through these pages in chronological order will know by now that he is even inclined to the occasional bout of fun when on the wrong side of a few drinks, but it would be unfair to say that he is to be found routinely propping up the bar at his local.

However, it was in such a drinking establishment that he developed his mission in life. He picked up a beer mat and wrote down the aim that would underline, define and make purposeful everything that he did. 'We want to inspire the nation,' he wrote – clear and exact. From then on, Clive was able to identify what was important and what wasn't by the extent to which it took him closer to this stated aim. Friendly matches were less important than big tournament matches. He wanted to beat the big nations in the big games. It was as simple, and as complex, as that.

If you seek to inspire the nation, you must provide an inspirational environment for your inspirers. It makes for a rather unwieldy sentence but it lacks nothing in its logic. The players had to understand that they were part of something great – the white shirt on their backs, the rose on their chests, the national anthem in their ears and the sight of each other as they made every tackle and passed every ball. They had to know they were doing it for each other, for their dedicated management team and for all the fans glued to television sets every time England ran out on to the pitch.

How do you heighten expectation and create an environment in which the great feel greater, the strong feel stronger and the competitive feel like winners every time they pull on their shirts?

Walters' vision of playing for England being like a journey was crucial in identifying all the areas for improvement. The hotel, from the staff to the accommodation, the transport, the arrival at Twickenham, the changing rooms, the shirts – everything had to be the best. Clive spoke to the coaches about picturing the world of England rugby as a room. They had to envisage throwing everything out of the room until it was empty – then bring everything back based entirely on its merits. Everything they brought back had to be the best it could possibly be. So, the changing rooms? Do we need them? Yes. Are they the best they can be...?

When Clive began, the England dressing room had breeze-block walls and a cold stone floor. There was nothing in there to lift the players an inch. The reason for this was simple – no one considered that players needed 'lifting' before a big game. It seemed almost a ludicrous proposition. What international player needs extra help to rise to the big occasion?

But what if having an inspirational dressing room for England and a dull, uninspiring room for the visitors helped just one person 0.001 per cent? What if a couple of players felt more at home with their names on the wall, inspiring passages and photographs and their own individual area for changing? What if Clive made a tiny little difference by doing this, and did lots of things like this? The sum of the small changes would add up to an enormous difference. What if Clive set out to make everything better – even in the tiniest of ways? Wouldn't every improvement be an improvement worth having? Clive thought so.

This thinking was well founded. It would be impossible to go into an élite group and make such enormous changes that you could improve a player's performance by 10 per cent. The players were at the very pinnacle of their game. The way to take the team forward was to make every improvement that could be made. Each 0.001 per cent improvement would make the difference in the long run.

The dressing room was changed, courtesy of *Real Rooms*, the BBC programme. They brightened it up, added red roses, name plates, inspirational words and pictures, and 'Welcome to Fortress Twickenham' on the door.

Hotel rooms? Do players need hotel rooms? Yes. Are we giving them the best possible? No, they share rooms. This was changed straightaway. Players would have their own rooms, with their names on the door, and the rooms would be full of inspiring photographs. They would have the same rooms every visit to make them feel as comfortable with their surroundings as possible.

To transport the players, a coach was commissioned, with the red rose on the side, to make the players feel special. Small things, perhaps, but the overall effect was that England looked more professional. They looked like an élite organisation. If the saying 'We are all products of our environment' is true, the standard of the players' performances should rise as the standard of their environment did. 'I remember when that coach turned up in Paris,' says Walters. 'People were saying, "Where the hell did that come from? How much did it cost to bring it over here?" '

There was a fixation on the cost of all the changes, irrespective of their impact on performance. There are two reasons for this. The first is that the sport was newly professional. People weren't used to money being spent. The second is that there was no immediate, apparent benefit from the expenditure. At least when you employ a fitness coach and are shown statistics indicating how much the players have improved since his arrival, it makes sense. But a bus with a rose on the side? A changing room with paintings on the wall? Give me a break. Critical non-essentials were not high on the list of priorities for RFU officials in the 1990s.

They would have to get used to it. The name of the meeting room was changed to 'war room' and when players or management were in it, they would talk business. It would have the feel of a boardroom – no socialising or messing around in there. The team room was separate. That was where the players would mingle, play videos, pool and chat. Clive was keen for the players to use this room as much as possible, to get to know each other better and to avoid cliques forming.

The 1998 tour to Australia, New Zealand and South Africa was nick-named the 'Tour from Hell' by the press. It came in the summer after England had lost the Five Nations Championship after getting off to a very poor start against France at the new Stade de France stadium. France won 24–17, setting the French off for their second consecutive Grand Slam, and forcing England to leave the field with their tails between their legs, yet to win a match under the new Woodward regime. The first victory came against Wales. England won 60–26 – a record margin. Victories over Scotland (34–20) and Ireland (35–17) followed, giving England the Triple Crown.

The 'Tour from Hell' was an utter disaster because England suffered ferocious record defeats on it. It was also considered a triumph for precisely the same reason – like an alcoholic needs to reach rock bottom before he can find the strength to pull himself up, so the tour showed England a glimpse of rock bottom that was enough to alarm them all, Clive more than anyone else. It prompted him to make all the changes necessary to transform the England rugby team. Francis Baron, who later became the chief executive, says he decided to join the RFU when he watched that tour. He never wanted England to stoop that low again.

For Clive, the tour was a springboard. The problems, constraints and thundering defeats served only to make him more determined that nothing like this would ever happen again. He resolved to do things his way. He made a unilateral declaration of independence and, in defiance of the entire RFU, most of his management team and the South African Rugby Union, he moved the players from one hotel to another (vastly more expensive) one. That marked the beginning of the no-holds-barred, it's my way or no way philosophy that would lead to World Cup glory. 'I feel history will show us that the results from this tour will galvanise English rugby and the England team as never before,' said Clive, prophetically.

The tour hit trouble even before it started because of the structure of English rugby, which allowed the clubs to hold back their key players. Some players had niggling injuries that needed treatment, but many were simply exhausted after two big years of club and international rugby, folded round a Lions tour to South Africa. Club owners did not wish to see their precious assets pummelled to death all summer, return in pieces, then struggle through the club season with recurring injuries. This was one of the most ambitious tours ever conceived – to all the 'big three' southern hemisphere countries. So, before they even set foot on the plane, seventeen of England's leading players were not available due to 'injuries'. Clive was forced to select a third-string team in which only six players had more than ten caps to their name. Twenty out of the squad of thirty-seven were debutants.

The good news was that the tour gave Clive a chance to blood new players. He had asked Brian Ashton to join the management team before they departed, as part of his effort to try not to separate backs and forwards but to separate the coaching in terms of attack and defence. Ashton would focus on 'attack' while Larder worked on 'defence'. Clive has always resisted separating players according to perceived roles on the pitch because the 'role' of every player is to win. Taking so many new players allowed Clive to look at the strength in depth of his squad. It was also the tour on which he had the chance to see a bright new young player called Jonny Wilkinson in action. Wilkinson had made his international debut in the previous Five Nations.

'When I look back on that tour now, and think of what Clive was like, I just have this overriding impression of a man who was trying to get things absolutely right,' says Wilkinson. 'I found him very easy to get along with because I always felt that he was trying to do the right thing for me. For example, I was very nervous at first, and Clive asked me to stand up when we were in Brisbane for the first Test, and write things on the whiteboard. I was terrified of doing it, but Clive urged me to stand up there. I realise now that in those moments, I really developed. He helped me to come out of my shell and to communicate more with the other players, which, in turn, made me a better player. I think he knew exactly what he was doing and I'm very grateful that he took the time to work out what each player, individually, needed in order to play better rugby.'

The result of the Test against Australia was dismal – the worst result against Australia of all time – 76–0. One glimmer of hope was the excellent play of Wilkinson. He missed two early kicks, but his style shone through. The Wallabies mounted wave after wave of physical attacks, which emanated from their ability to keep possession. Without any possession, England were reduced to trying to limit the damage, which they significantly failed to do.

'I remember sitting in my hotel room in Brisbane after England lost and crying my eyes out,' says Wilkinson. 'I was on the phone to my dad, telling him what a nightmare the whole experience had been. My first game at fly-half for my country and a record Test defeat.'

One of the key things that Clive had been espousing was that 'To make a team perform to its maximum, it is better to try to do 100 things 1 per cent better than one thing 100 per cent better.' So he looked at some of the smaller things that were going wrong. On the pitch, one statistic that gave him great cause for concern was that there were thirty-seven missed tackles. Clive knew that to beat the southern hemisphere sides, those misses had to be whittled down to single figures. It was, as he said, 'a suicidal number'. That became a crucial area for the defence coach to work on. The value of having specialist coaches was becoming clearer to him as the tour progressed. Next, England suffered their worst ever defeat in New Zealand – 64–22.

The cracks in the relationship between Uttley and Clive were growing more and more visible. Clive wanted everything to run perfectly and Uttley thought this simply impossible to achieve. Graeme Cattermole, the RFU officer on tour, found himself caught in the middle.

'We had a number of clashes during that tour,' says Cattermole, 'many of them administrative problems where, say, the coach that was transporting the squad to the training ground arrived fifteen minutes late at the hotel to collect them. This became a major bone of contention between Clive and Roger, with the former blaming the latter for incompetence. Clive considered that if the coach was late on a match day, Roger should sack the coach company and find a more reliable one. I took Roger's side in stating that no one could guarantee an error-free pick-up because the coach might be involved in a crash on its way to the hotel, or some other situation that was beyond any human being's control. Clive would have none of it. This was an example of what those working close to Clive had to experience on many occasions.' Clive yearned to work with people who had the same eagerness to succeed and the same sense of perfectionism as he had.

Before the second Test, Clive received some bad news. His father had passed away and Clive flew home for the funeral after the match, leaving Uttley in charge. 'But the most bizarre thing happened,' said, Walters. 'Don Rutherford took over instead, and started changing much of what Clive had been working on.'

Uttley, meanwhile, found the time of Clive's absence far more peaceful and pleasant.

'The hotel was a different place without him,' said Uttley. 'There wasn't this feeling of panic. You weren't worried all the time that he would burst in with his next demand. The players all looked more relaxed. It reminded me how enjoyable international rugby can be.'

For Clive, success at international level was always the route to happiness. When he returned from England, it was with renewed determination to get everything right. He flew back in time for England's second game against New Zealand, dead set on making sure the team was doing everything he wanted. England lost 40–10 and Clive vowed to toughen up. When the team flew to South Africa, he was handed the opportunity to show just how far he would go to get things done on his terms.

The team travelled to their hotel, the Holiday Inn Garden Court Motel in a suburb of Newlands, where they would stay in advance of their game against the Springboks. To say the standard of accommodation did not meet the criteria of Clive's new professional expectations would be an understatement. The hotel was noisy and the food barely edible. The arrival of the South Africa Under-21s side at the same hotel infuriated Clive. While he became increasingly concerned about the accommodation, to ease tensions, Jayne had booked dinner on Thursday night at the Mount Nelson Hotel in Cape Town, nicknamed the Pink Palace. It is one of Cape Town's finest and most famous hotels, situated in nine acres of garden at the foot of Table Mountain. They went to the hotel that evening, just as the German football team, fresh from a pre-1998 World Cup training camp, were leaving, freeing up forty-five bedrooms. It was a beautiful hotel. The one they were currently in was dreadful. He decided to move the entire England team over there the next day and paid for the whole thing on his credit cards. Not only was it a much better hotel, but moving the team would also make a point about his expectations for this team and the lengths to which he would go in search of perfection. It was the storytelling that Paddi Lund had spoken about – the process of creating stories for people to tell about you, like the big coffee machine, the bone-china cups, the infinite range of teas. The story was that, with Clive, the players would have the best they could possibly be given and they were expected to give the best they possibly could.

'Clive put a note under everybody's door saying, "Be in the team room by 8.30 a.m.",' said Walters. 'I was there at eight and people were coming in asking, "Is Clive quitting?" I actually didn't know what he was going to say. He walked in and said, "We're moving out of here – it's a dump." Everybody had been drilled not to complain, because that's part of our rules, but they shouted, "YEAH!" There was lots of cheering. Everyone was delighted. It was absolutely the right thing to do. The players deserved better and Clive knew that it was his job to give them better.'

Not everyone was thrilled with the idea. Cattermole and Uttley both believed that Clive was in danger of gravely upsetting their South African hosts with his decision to move hotels. They were also desperately concerned about the financial implications of such a move.

England went on to lose their final tour match 18–0 and returned home, where yet more trouble awaited their coach.

Chapter Twenty-two

Judge me on the World Cup

'Nothing can resist the human that will stake even its existence on its stated purpose.' **Benjamin Disraeli**

Clive walked out of Heathrow Airport and straight into the arms of Don Rutherford, who had been dispatched by the officers of the RFU to meet him and take him to Twickenham to write a report about his extravagant hotel-hopping. Clive refused and Rutherford left empty-handed. The hotel bill was eventually paid by the RFU after they had slapped Clive on the wrist. For Clive, it was an important moment. Slap or no slap, he had won.

Clive's relationships with the RFU and the clubs were difficult. The disputes with his masters (the RFU) and the masters of his players (the clubs) combined neatly in the signing of the Mayfair Agreement. This document, designed to formalise arrangements between the clubs and the RFU, was signed during the 1998 tour. The agreement stated that the number of games each player undertook should be limited to thirty-seven a year, not including pre-season friendlies or international tours. In New Zealand, twenty-five was the absolute maximum. Clive was furious. He believed it was less an agreement and more a compromise, verging on wholesale surrender. Clive felt hit from both sides – the clubs let the international team down by first denying him the opportunity to take the best players on tour, then pushing for an agreement that would compromise the welfare of the country's best players; and the RFU had let him down by agreeing to the clubs' demands so readily. It was Clive and Team England against the world. He pulled his team more tightly around him and they withdrew into themselves, becoming a very separate organisation from the RFU, operating independently from Rutherford's department. They would mould themselves into an élite fighting force, distinct from the everyday foot soldiers in the Union. Clive rarely communicated what the team was up to, other than to ask for financial support. Rutherford, who had previously placed himself at the heart of successive England rugby teams, found himself severely sidelined.

Clive explained his vision to the team, enthusing players and coaches. There was one hitch, though. Everything within Team England was not as rosy as it appeared. Uttley and Woodward mistrusted each other and, increasingly, could not work effectively together. Clive found it difficult to work with someone part time. He wanted his manager to be in the RFU with him, working alongside him. He felt it was a throw back to the amateur days that Uttley held down a full-time job at the same time as acting as manager for the England rugby team.

Today, Uttley is back at Harrow School, where he has taught rugby for most of his adult life, his years with the national team long behind him. His role was to be a buffer between the coach and the rest of the world. When Clive was appointed, the idea was that Uttley would manage the press and the administration of the team, reporting to the RFU and being the team's 'manager' in the purest sense of the word. Clive would coach.

Of course, with hindsight, it's clear that this arrangement has much in common with a very fast train heading towards a very large brick wall. Business acumen was Clive's forte. His ability to marry business strategy with sports coaching had formed the backbone of all his coaching pre-England. Bringing someone in to do this for him was never going to work. Clive saw the link between managing England and being the head coach of England as seamless. His coaching had a management twist to it and his management of the team was directed by his views of them as the head coach. What he needed was a sharp administrator and organiser to pick up the pieces around him and make sure that his management strategy was implemented effectively.

Added to the confusion about job roles was the fact that the two men were vastly different personalities.

Uttley had been England coach before, and he had a sense of what the job entailed. Clive wanted to throw the rulebook out of the window and start all over again. They wanted different things, they had different views, and they were effectively doing the same job. Clive was full-time, so he took the principal role and Uttley was left with the rest. Clive wanted every detail attended to, so Uttley found himself submerged in dealing with what he felt were the petty obsessions of the new coach. The buses had to run on time, the food had to be of the highest quality, the rooms had to be the best in the house. Uttley was a former international player and former England head coach. He had been employed in a senior position – he didn't take kindly to being told that his new job role was to panic about late buses.

'I was supposed to chase around and make sure everything was perfect,' Uttley says. 'The bus would arrive a minute late and Clive would be screaming and shouting about sacking the coach company. He was extremely hard to work with, extremely hard to please. I hate to criticise Clive because it seems like sour grapes. It was a very difficult two- or three-year period for me – very up and down. He could be a charming man, but there were times when he wasn't charming at all. In fact, there were times when he could be extremely hard work and very unpleasant.

'He created such a pressure-filled environment that everyone, in the end, agreed with him. He just did what he wanted. For example, there was an open-door policy in the hotel. We were all supposed to leave our doors ajar and visit one another in our rooms, but Clive's door was often closed. It was "me and them" with Clive. He wanted to set himself apart. People will be reluctant to talk about that because Clive did, eventually, win the World Cup, but the cost of that was a miserable time for many.

'Clive loves power and hates to share it. He and I used to have stand-up rows about things – all to do with control. He'd want to have an impact on every area of the other coaches' lives. He'd arrange team meetings for seven a.m. so we couldn't go out with the players the night before – things like that. It got to the stage where I don't think he wanted me to do anything right – whatever the consequences for the team – because he wanted to show that he was in charge.'

Uttley's role would eventually be filled by Louise Ramsay, who arrived at the RFU in the summer of 2001 after working for the British Olympic Association (BOA) on the organisation and planning for the Summer and Winter Olympics, including Sydney 2000. Ramsay finished working for the BOA in April 2001.

'I sat and wondered what I should do next,' she said. 'I thought it would be hard to find another job to challenge me after the Olympics – I'd worked at the very top level with élite athletes. Where do you go from there?' She enjoyed rugby and decided to write off, on spec, to the Union, enquiring about possible jobs. Her letter was well timed. Clive was searching for a great organiser and administrator to work for the team. He needed someone with exquisite attention to detail. Someone willing to work long, hard hours and get everything right. Ramsay was perfect. She started working with Clive in 2001, and they developed a close professional relationship.

'Clive was always very positive. I liked him as soon as I met him because he was extremely professional, but there's more to Clive than that – he's also a genuinely nice guy. He was very welcoming and was always good fun to be around. He has a great sense of humour and is very charismatic. I'm not sure people realise this about him. You only tend to hear about how professional he is.'

Ramsay thrived in the 'no excuses' culture. 'It was an environment that I loved working in. Clive was responsible for everything on the pitch and I was responsible for everything off it. I felt we worked together well from the start. We were a good partnership.

'I never felt Clive was over-demanding because he had a very clear vision and explained exactly what he wanted. We all just worked towards it. He's a stickler for detail but so he should be. I thought that was a very positive attribute. I'm a stickler for detail, too. You have to be if you're working with élite athletes. There's no other way to be. I don't think that's a negative thing at all – I think it's very positive. I always enjoyed working with him. He thrived under pressure and lifted his performance. He was never negative. He just kept moving forwards and trying to improve everything. I thought the environment he created was second to none and working with him was always great fun, challenging and rewarding.'

In the summer of 1998, after the tour to hell and before England began the countdown to 1999, Clive went to visit the University of Colorado and Denver Broncos American football teams to examine their set-ups and pick up any tips for managing England. He had been told by Rutherford that the RFU could not pay for the trip, so he contacted Nike to find out whether they would fund it. The total cost was less than £1,000 and they agreed instantly, causing the RFU to backtrack and come up with the money themselves.

'My first experience was a two-hour brain-storming session, which included six defensive and six offensive coaches,' says Clive. What interested Clive was the level of focus on defence. For a great deal of the time in rugby, players are in defence (defined as the time when you do not have the ball in your hands). This is not dead time but the opportunity to defend territory and fight to get the ball back. Traditionally in rugby union, much of the focus of coaching had been on the man with the ball in his hands.

At Denver Broncos, Mike Shanahan had had a hugely successful run as coach when Clive visited, having just posted the most wins in pro football history in a three-year period (forty-six in 1996–98) and was the first coach in history to win two SuperBowl titles in his first four years of coaching.

How do I know all this? Because when you phone up and ask anyone at the club what they put their success down to, they say straightaway that it is the coach. The respect for coaches in the National Football League compared to rugby union is huge. There is a recognition that excellence in coaching is an important precursor to excellence in playing. Take this example from the Denver Broncos' website, referring to the coach:

'His stunning record as the Broncos' mentor places him in the legendary class of Vince Lombardi … [Shanahan is] arguably the finest head coach and most fertile football mind in the game today … one of the brightest offensive strategists in football – an intense and personable man.'

Way to go! Take a look at the website – it tells you all you need to know about the gaping disparity between the treatment of coaches in this country and the US. It may tell you all you need to know about why the US has such a winning culture – because they invest, nurture and respect the people who can bring about victory.

'Clive came over here and I remember him being surprised that our greatest coaches weren't great players,' says Jim Saccomano, vice president of public relations at Broncos. 'I remember him talking to the coaches about "the art of coaching" and how that was different from playing. We've got a wide receiver here who's the best in the league. Ask him, "How do you do what you do?" He says, "They chuck 'em, I catch 'em." He can do it but he can't explain it and he certainly couldn't teach it. There's no reason why he should. Players play and coaches coach.'

Clive returned to England fired up and ready to transform the national team. Two months later, in October 1998, Francis Baron became the new chief executive of the RFU. He drove into Twickenham in his green Aston Martin and set about turning a rather conservative and fusty sports governing body into a bright, commercially adept, profit-making organisation. Clive took to him initially because of Baron's business focus. Ironically, it was Baron's single-minded business focus and failure to recognise that success on the pitch was fundamental to business success, that caused unmanageable tensions in his relationship with Clive.

'I hadn't met Clive before I started,' says Baron, 'but from the first meeting, he came across as being a real live-wire, a-buzz with ideas. He explained how England had to make radical changes in the way they played. He's never changed – he's always been like that and he's always wanted to change things. He had just come back from the 'Tour from Hell' when I started and there was a lot of concern about whether Clive could actually do the job because he wasn't the RFU's number one candidate. That didn't deter him. He had massive self-confidence. He believed he could deliver. I always think of Woody as being a very creative person and he reminds me of when I was in the TV business – you get people who are very creative and bubbling with ideas. Woody has got good management skills but he's not an administrator. He's an ideas man, a motivator and a doer.'

Baron's job was to manage the RFU as a business. Since the main product of the Union, and its most powerful business tool, was the England team, it was vital that England started winning.

'The management of creative people is entirely different from the management of accountants or marketing people. I treated Woody very much as you should treat a creative person in a media business – you have to give them a lot of room, a lot of living space and leeway, because that's where they thrive. If you try to manage them on a sort of strict management by objectives basis, you don't get the best out of them. They don't like being constrained in a disciplined environment. I let Clive have that room and breathing space, but I kept tight control of what money he could spend.'

In these early years, while Clive was establishing himself, he managed to ease any positives that he could out of the largely negative results. When England played Australia at Twickenham in the autumn of 1998, England were ahead for most of the game, then lost 12–11 after John Eales kicked a dubious penalty in the closing minutes of the game. Clive did not understand why the penalty had been given. The players didn't either. Rather than sulk and complain, Clive learnt an important lesson – matches can be won or lost on refereeing decisions. He decided to bring a refereeing adviser into the England set-up to offer help in rule interpretation and in predicting how other referees might judge certain points of law on the field. Clive ensured that, from then onwards, a full-time referee was at England training sessions.

After Australia, it was South Africa – an important match for the visitors. They were enjoying a long-running winning streak, having just equalled New Zealand's record of seventeen consecutive Test wins. If they beat England, they would break new ground. England won 13–7. This victory was a defining moment. Francis Baron came to the dressing room afterwards and hugged the players. There was genuine warmth and Clive felt he had a real ally. After an impossibly difficult twelve months, England approached World Cup year with a little more optimism.

In January 1999, Clive's focus was on the forthcoming Five Nations Championship – the last to be played. With Italy joining in 2000, the Five Nations would become the Six Nations. He continued to build in 'critical non-essentials' at every opportunity. Anything that would make the players feel better and more inspired, or help develop 'teamship' in the side, was brought in. Clive had always recognised the importance of good communication with the players. He told them they were welcome to visit him at home any time.

'We often received invitations to dinner, or were invited, with wives and girlfriends, to drinks parties and barbecues at Clive's,' said Austin Healey. 'I don't know whether he ever thought that we would call. The invitations stopped once you were out of the team, but while you were in, you were really "in".'

Despite Clive's best efforts to make the players feel as if they were a close-knit group, communications were hampered by the disparate nature of the workforce. They were based all over the country and employed full-time by a range of different clubs. What should he do? How could he aid communication? Laptop computers! Clive went to see Michael Spiro, chief executive of Elonex computers, and an old friend. He suggested that the company might like to donate computers to every player. Spiro agreed to provide Clive with what he was after. The players would, henceforth, be able to communicate with one another and download programmes and training tips. Elonex would provide computers and an Internet dial-up account for each player as part of their team induction kit.

Clive's other major preoccupation was with trying to facilitate the movement of rugby league players to rugby union in time for the 1999 World Cup. He had been clear from day one that he saw this as a crucial step in creating the right team to win the tournament, but had faced opposition and difficulties all the way. Finally, he was told that, for financial and political reasons, the league players would not be signed. This was something Clive found barely tolerable. How could this vast pool of talent remain unused for nebulous and, in his view, unacceptable reasons? Clive had seen how well Scott Gibbs, in particular, integrated into the 1997 Lions team and became a valuable player on tour. He was so determined to have the best rugby league players in his team that at one stage he rushed home, declaring that he would remortgage the house and buy them himself. In the end, no such remortgaging took place and the league players remained in league. For Clive's World Cup preparations, this was a huge blow, although he did eventually sign rugby league players, and Jason Robinson, in particular, made an enormous impact.

On one dark January evening in 1999, Baron was in his Twickenham office. He had asked his secretary, Lavinia, to stay late. He called her in and asked her to ensure that Clive Woodward was in his office the next morning at 7.20 a.m.

'Certainly,' she said. 'Shall I tell him what it's about?'

'No,' said Baron. 'Just tell him to be here.'

No one but Baron knew why Clive was being summoned. He had kept his counsel during his first four months in the job, rarely talking to people, just looking. He had analysed the business and was clear about what had to be done. Cutbacks were needed. He had examined the personnel and it was clear what had to be done there, too. Heads needed to roll.

Clive took the call from Lavinia, and laughed. '7.20? Why such a precise time? What's going on?' he asked.

'These are the only instructions I've been given,' she said, with absolute honesty. She had a list in front of her containing the names of most of the people working at the RFU. She had been instructed to call them and arrange for them to come in and see Baron for ten-minute meetings. The precise timings enabled Baron to see everyone.

The next day, at precisely 7.20 a.m., Clive sat in his office and waited for Baron to enter. 'I felt like a schoolboy,' he recalls. 'I looked out of the window and could see everyone was in their offices waiting for him to visit.' Baron read out a list of people whom he had decided to make redundant, including Roger Uttley and Don Rutherford. Both Clive and Baron say that the cost-cutting measures were Baron's decision. Rutherford and Uttley are sure that they were used as a perfect opportunity to get rid of anyone with opposing views to, or anyone who stood in the way of, Clive. Around forty people would be asked to leave that day. Rutherford, who had been with the RFU since 1969, was told to clear his desk and leave the building.

Uttley wasn't based at Twickenham, so he wasn't subjected to the soul-destroying 'clear your desk' scenario that his colleagues suffered. He worked from Harrow School. Clive was asked to drive to Harrow to hand the letter to Uttley personally, while Baron was tied up seeing everyone at the Union. While Clive got into his car, Rutherford collected his things and left the building for the last time. The RFU's technical director, who had worked for the Union for the majority of his working life, was just a few years off retirement.

Baron had been so eager to prevent news of the impending redundancies from slipping out that he had typed every single redundancy notice himself. No one else was involved, he says. The redundancies were approved by the management board just the day before. That's why all the phone calls had been made between 7 p.m. and 9 p.m. – once the board had given its approval.

Clive walked into Rutherford's office and said that 'it looked like it had been ransacked' – such was the haste with which the technical director had left. Clive never called Rutherford after his departure, which he deeply regrets. When Clive wrote *Winning!*, a book about his rugby and business thinking, he asked his researcher to visit Don and talk to him for the book.

'When I heard the tape of the interview I was very sad,' says Clive. 'I realised how utterly tragic it had been for him, how life changing. I bitterly regret not calling him after it happened. I should have made contact with him.'

Don Rutherford lives in Penzance today, in a small farm cottage in beautiful countryside near the sea. The drive to it takes you past St Michael's Mount, up a steep hill. He has an office in the garden, tucked away in this tranquil spot.

Rutherford's redundancy ended a lifestyle. As part of his package, he lived in a house next to Twickenham stadium, owned by the RFU. He had to leave that house when he lost his job. He also had to give up his car and lost the full pension that he was three years from receiving. His family had been very involved with his job. His wife, Sue, had taken an important unpaid role with the England team, assisting in looking after the players' wives and girlfriends. His son, David, had organised the travel, ensuring they got the best possible rates. The end of Rutherford's time at Twickenham was the end of an era in England rugby. As Sue recalls, 'It was a desperate, desperate time.'

Sue went back to work full-time as a college lecturer to support the family, while Rutherford looked for work. He ended up moving to Portugal to coach for a few years, as he fought to put his experiences at Twickenham behind him.

'The worse thing about it was the timing,' says Rutherford. 'I was planning to go. Everyone knew that. I had reorganised the department so that I could retire without letting anyone down, then I was made redundant because I was no longer needed. It was disgraceful. Just appalling.'

At Harrow School, Clive talked to Uttley and handed him Baron's letter.

'It was almost a relief,' says Uttley. 'I loved working with England and would dearly like to work with the national team again some time, but not like that.'

While Baron dispensed with staff in order to cut costs, Clive continued to make England the most sophisticated and professional of organisations.

'Players used to have to fly at the back of the plane,' said Baron. 'Woody put them all in business class. He started to allow wives and partners to come on tour in the summer and that had cost implications. Lots of demands came through from him – he wanted more people involved and a better environment. He was sure that this was the way to win. You had either to believe in him and go with him, or sack him. There was never any question of the latter, so we went with him and tried to give him all the support we could.'

The final game of the 1999 Five Nations Championship was played at Wembley stadium. Clive was like a boy in a toyshop. The home of

English football lay before him – a shrine to the sport he loves. He wandered through the ground, walking into a reception room where the crossbar used in the 1966 World Cup final resided – the bar struck by Geoff Hurst when he scored that famous goal. 'I had a dream, as a youngster, of mounting the steps at Wembley and picking up the trophy,' Clive mused, romantically. He'd dreamt of doing it as a footballer. Now it looked as if he might do it as a rugby coach.

The Grand Slam was there for the taking by the time the players arrived at Wembley. All England had to do was beat Wales. The ribbons were practically on the trophy. Actually they were literally on the trophy. I have a clear recollection of that game, and of watching them tie the white ribbons on, carefully streaming them down the sides of the cup. Then, in the second half, England lost discipline and gave away six penalties. In a dramatic ending, Scott Gibbs scored in stoppage time to give Wales a one-point victory. The girls in the tunnel tore the ribbons off and dashed around looking for the blue ones. England's last gasp capitulation had gifted the tournament title to Scotland.

Clive learnt a lot from the defeat. In the heat of the battle, the players had reverted to type, despite being well prepared. They needed to be taught how to think correctly under pressure. Where could they go to absorb the discipline to keep composed when the minutes ticked away?

'The Marines,' said Walters, enticingly. 'Shall I see if we can spend a day or two with them?'

In early June 1999, Clive was at home with his family when the phone rang. Walters recalls how Clive's twelve-year-old daughter, Jessie, answered it.

'Dad, it's for you,' she called. 'It's someone from the *News of the World*.'

The call was from Piers Morgan, then the editor of the Sunday paper.

'Clive, sorry to ring you at home. I'm ringing out of courtesy to tell you we are running a story on the front page of tomorrow's edition. I would like your reactions to this story and a comment. We are exposing Lawrence Dallaglio as a drug taker and drug dealer. We have an exclusive interview with him and he has admitted this and given us some graphic and lurid examples that we are quoting in full in the paper. Perhaps you would like to comment?'

Morgan offered to fax the front page. Clive walked through the garden to his office and picked up six pages of Dallaglio's drug 'confessions'. This was serious. When Morgan phoned back, Clive declined to comment on the grounds that he refused to believe what they were printing. He told Morgan, 'Lawrence is the last person I would expect to be involved in something like this.' Morgan told Clive that he should comment. As coach of the national team he had a duty to offer his views on such a damning indictment of the England captain. Clive continued to refuse.

Late on Saturday night, Clive was still struggling to get hold of Dallaglio. All he knew was that the captain was at a hotel somewhere in the West Country. Clive was desperate to warn him about what was in the paper before he saw it, and before the papers got hold of him. He didn't want Dallaglio to wander innocently into breakfast and be confronted by dozens of guests all reading about him. Eventually, Clive left a message, urging him to call. By the time Lawrence awoke the next morning, he had hundreds of messages on his mobile phone. He ran out of the hotel, bought a copy of the *News of the World* and rang Clive.

'He asked me what he should do and I replied that he should pack his bags immediately and come to my house complete with his family. He arrived at about eleven,' said Clive.

Jayne and Alice Corbett, Dallaglio's partner and the mother of his children, stayed in the house while Clive and Lawrence went to Clive's office at the bottom of the garden. Clive told Dallaglio to tell him everything, no holds barred.

Dallaglio explained that he had been approached by PR personnel acting for Gillette, via his agent, Ashley Woolfe. He had met up with them at a London hotel, where they chatted to him about a big six-figure deal to promote male grooming products. First, though, they wanted to hear a little more about him. What sort of guy was he? Did he like to go out and have fun, or was he just a dull rugby captain? They plied him with champagne and urged him to talk about the fun side of life as a rugby player – the parties, the women, the booze and the drugs…

Dallaglio sat with his head in his hands and explained to Clive that he'd woven them a story about how wild he could be on tour. He'd drunk too much of the champagne and been beguiled by the prospect of a massive advertising contract (around £500,000). He'd exaggerated the parties and reinvented himself in the image they insisted would win the deal. He told them what he thought they wanted to hear in order that they might present him with a massive advertising deal. In fact, he was telling them what they wanted to hear in order that they might present him as a drug-pushing loser on the front page of one of the world's bestselling newspapers. Clive instantly and unequivocally supported his captain, and worked with him to limit the damage that the revelations might cause.

Clive understood the perilous position in which his captain found himself. He, too, had experienced an attempted tabloid entrapment – such is the world of modern, professional rugby. Clive and Tony Biscombe had been sitting in the bar of the Pennyhill Park Hotel having a drink one evening, when a girl and her boyfriend looked over at them. They asked Clive for an autograph and the girl smiled beguilingly at Clive. 'Ah, you never lose it, do you?' said Biscombe, teasing Clive. They laughed and joked and the moment was forgotten. A few minutes later, the waiter came over with a beer mat for Clive. The girl had written her room number on the back of it with a short note in which she asked Clive to come up in twenty minutes and she would be waiting. She added, rather alarmingly, 'My boyfriend will join us there later.' The waiter warned Clive and Biscombe that the couple had been hanging around the bar all evening and he had overheard their conversations – he suspected they were journalists. A little investigation proved that they were from the *News of the World*. They were ejected from the hotel.

Clive backed his captain, publicly and privately, through the whole drama. First, he made sure the players were on side and would close ranks around their captain. He phoned the key England figures. Meanwhile, in the newspaper world, things were reaching fever pitch. There was mild hysteria over the Dallaglio story as every editor screamed for a new angle and every writer called everyone in his or her contacts book, trying to get a new, fresh and hopefully controversial response.

'It was an incredibly difficult time,' said Jeremy Guscott, the England centre who found himself implicated in the whole thing because the

News of the World had used his picture in shadow next to the picture of Dallaglio. 'There were silhouettes of two other players from the Lions tour in 1997. Any rugby follower would have worked out one of the silhouettes was mine.'

Dallaglio lost the captaincy and his reputation was slightly tarnished by the incident.

'It was just naïvety,' says Guscott.

'He got stitched up,' says Jason Leonard. Martin Johnson was appointed England captain for the 1999 World Cup.

The team headed for a training camp on Couran Cove in Australia, trailed by journalists eager to chat to Dallaglio or extract any comments from his team-mates. The players closed ranks and interest in the story slowly dissipated. While at Couran Cove, Clive brought experts over from Brisbane to teach the players how to operate their laptops properly. Dave Reddin would design personal fitness and diet programmes for them that could be downloaded. It was an interactive coaching tool with great potential, but there was a downside – the laptop would prove an impersonal way to communicate bad news.

'He told us in Australia that team announcements would be done by email,' says Matt Perry. 'That was a step too far. I guess if you're in the team, hearing it by email isn't too bad, but if you're not in the team, it's galling.'

England played Australia in the Cook Cup, the one hundredth match between the two countries, and lost 22–15.

Humphrey Walters landed his helicopter at Lympstone in Devon, and went in to talk to the senior officers in the Marines. Clive wanted to find out whether they could organise a training programme for the players that was similar to the one for recruits.

'They said they could but would like press coverage,' said Walters, 'so I rang Clive and asked if that would be OK. He said it was, as long as it was on the team's terms, so I fixed the whole thing up.'

The next day, Walters received a call from Clive, saying, 'It's all off. Forget it. The whole bloody thing is off. I've just been rung up by the *Daily Telegraph* asking, "What's all this about you going down to the

Marines?" How the hell did they know?'

Walters had no idea. He went back to the Marines to talk to them. It turned out that a Royal Marine had rung someone in the Ministry of Defence to get sanction to use helicopters to transport non-military personnel. The Marine at the Ministry of Defence had mentioned to the defence correspondent of the *Telegraph* over coffee that the England team would be training with the Marines. He'd had no idea it was a covert operation.

'I couldn't believe it,' says Walters. 'I'd been through all that effort and agony and it almost didn't happen.'

Eventually, Clive relented and plans were made for England to visit the Marines twice before the World Cup. Brigadier Andy Pillar and Lieutenant Nathan Martin would be in charge of the training.

'The great thing about Clive is that he can be terribly het up, really cross, but he'll still do what's best for the team,' said Walters.

Lt Col George Matthews RM was responsible for Royal Marines public relations at the time.

'We had to be careful,' he said. 'Clive was eager for the Marines to get the publicity they wanted – to attract new recruits and be seen in a positive way – but he didn't want the players compromised, especially after what Lawrence Dallaglio had been through.' Matthews said that Clive was 'an absolute joy to work with' because he was so clear about what he wanted. 'He wanted us to work on the team dynamics, and to identify leaders. When he came to Lympstone with the players, it became clear straightaway that there was a squad within a squad. The old players who'd been around a while and would contribute a great deal, and the new players just coming on to the scene, who didn't feel they could contribute.'

Clive explained that on match day, players were putting their bodies on the line. It was important that the newer, younger players learnt that they could contribute as much as everyone else.

'Clive was trying to develop his ethos of "we're all in this together, so everyone has a say". A new guy might have an idea that resulted in a few extra yards, which allowed a try to be scored and won the game, so it was vital for everyone to speak up – not just the older, more established players.

'He also wanted to develop personal accountability, so that if players found themselves with the ball in hand, they would be able to make decisions. You need to take that decision for better or worse – you need to be unafraid of making decisions. That was the key thing.'

The Marines wrote a number of programmes that incorporated team-building skills. They explained 'dislocated expectations' – best-laid plans can go wrong. How do you cope then? The players would have to deal with plans changing every five minutes, the 'enemy' being spotted somewhere other than where they'd been told, organisational changes and not sleeping properly for four days.

The England rugby players were sitting and waiting in the commando training centre at Lympstone when in walked fifteen Royal Marines – smart uniforms, shoulders back, staring straight ahead at the players. The players stared back.

'There was a kind of stand-off,' says Matthews. 'The groups stared at one another. Once they started to talk, though, the barriers just tumbled down.'

Matthews describes looking after the players as being 'like herding cats'. 'They were civilians and when we said, "Be here at five to ten," they might think about heading over at ten-ish. That's completely alien to our culture.'

The next problem was getting them into Marines gear for some of the exercises. 'You've never seen anything so funny as trying to get Martin Johnson and Jason Leonard into Royal Marine-size trousers. Can you imagine trying to get a shirt to fit Leonard – he's just not got a Marine-sized neck, we had to send out for some bigger sizes.'

Not everyone was keen on doing this kind of training – Matt Dawson and Jerry Guscott didn't see the point of it. 'But Matt eventually threw himself wholeheartedly into it. He was one of the people to emerge as a potential England captain during that process. One of the things that Clive had specifically asked us to look at was who were the guys with leadership potential.'

The players were put through a range of mental and physical tasks, designed to test them under pressure. When they were exhausted after an assault course, could they organise a group to change a tyre on a

Land Rover while wearing respiratory masks and with no tools?

'We worked out fairly early on who the emerging leaders were. It was also obvious early on that if you've got a player who's in the twilight of his career and this is his last shot at international rugby, it's hard to change anything about him.'

The tasks were divided into those for which a leader was nominated, in order to see how that leader coped under pressure, and those for which there was no nominated leader, to see who emerged.

'Richard Hill was unbelievable. He stood back, looked at the situation and worked out what to do, while the others just ploughed in there and tried to fix it. He had to shout three times to make himself heard above the noise of people trying to fix something they didn't understand. Once he'd got their attention, they did it straightaway.'

They competed in a Tarzan course – swinging across gaps on ropes 20ft above the ground to reach a target. There was the endurance course, a pool in which they had to go underwater without knowing where they would end up, and a giant boat that had to be saved from sinking by plugging holes in the side, which demanded diving under the water. The boat sunk anyway, causing pressure to mount on the leader, who had to keep the team motivated and then decide when to abandon ship.

The players went down to Lympstone ten weeks before the 1999 World Cup, then again, four and a half weeks before the tournament. 'We couldn't push the guys to the limit physically in case they got injured, so we made it hard in terms of commitment and mental toughness,' said Matthews.

The Marines identify the characteristics of leadership with the acronym JUBWICK:

Judgement
Understanding
Bearing
Willpower
Integrity
Courage
Knowledge

'If you lack moral integrity in your own life, it's difficult to lead. Leadership is a strand that runs through lives. If you are a leader, it's 24/7. If you're on shore having five pints with your mates and you see something going wrong, it's your duty to step up, to do something. That's what leadership is,' said Matthews, who cites great leaders as being people such as Tony Benn, Lord Nelson and Ellen MacArthur. At sea, MacArthur has to make thousands of decisions every day to stay alive. His view of the England players he met?

'I'd take ninety per cent of those guys in the Marines tomorrow.'

Clive learnt three key lessons from the stay at Lympstone. First, the Marines looked much more 'élite' than the England squad – they were smart, punctual and efficient. The squad had to tighten up in that respect. Second, the ability to cope with the unexpected was vital – 'dislocated expectations'. Third, the 'jumping out of the helicopter' test – would you be willing to jump out of a helicopter behind enemy lines with this man to support you? Do you trust him implicitly? If not, should he be in the team, regardless of his rugby skills?

For Clive, the experience of being involved with the Marines, where teamwork is everything, led him to think of the negative influence that one person can have on a team. He needed to eliminate anyone who might 'sap energy' from the team. Henceforth, he would divide everyone into 'energisers' or 'energy sappers'. He told the players that he thought energy sappers were the biggest obstacle to success. He explained that he would not tolerate them in the group and would not select them for England. The ability to play rugby was crucial, but they had to play rugby with their hearts, souls and brains, as well. They had to be 'in' the team in every way. They had to be as passionate about winning as the Marines were and never, ever moan or groan in a way that sapped energy from the others.

Clive chose his squad and, as he had warned, told players by email whether they would be travelling to Australia for the tournament.

'I trained like a dog that summer,' says Will Green, 'then Clive emailed me to say I wasn't in and I remember being gutted. It [email] is not the way to communicate. Even Clive admits that now. I totally disagree with it. You're talking about people's dreams and livelihood. It's a job. If a coach looks you in the eye and says you're not good enough because of A, B and C, then fine, a player can accept that. But to send an email is a complete cop-out. You wouldn't do it in business. It's a disgraceful way to treat people. You put years of hard work into it. For a manager of an organisation to lose that personal touch ... and you don't leave a message on a phone either, you make sure you speak to the player concerned.'

For those who had made the squad, however, this was it – the big one, the World Cup 1999, the end of the millennium. Would it also be the end of the southern hemisphere's reign over rugby? Clive certainly hoped so. England were ready to take on the world. 'Judge me on the World Cup,' he said, although he denies it now. (He did say it – I still have the tape to prove it.)

In the build-up to the tournament, Clive continued to develop the team's thinking under pressure that would be so crucial. He'd arrange a series of games and tests. One was a treasure hunt between the backs and forwards. Each side was given a list of clues and the forwards charged off – in the rain – in an effort to follow them and find the treasure first. The backs, meanwhile, sat down and read through the clues. They noticed that the last letter of each clue, when rearranged, spelt 'boathouse', so they ran straight to the boathouse and found the treasure while the forwards were still foraging in the rain, hunting for clues. The lateral, six-f thinking techniques were beginning to make an impact on the players.

So, the rugby World Cup arrived, the first tournament of the professional age. England had a professional coach, professional players and great confidence in their ability to succeed. There was just one big hurdle on the horizon – from the moment the pool stage fixtures were announced, it became clear that success in the early rounds was desperately important. Five groups of four had to be whittled down to eight quarter-finalists. The top team in each pool qualified automatically and the second-placed teams had to play an additional match. Finishing top of the group meant a much easier ride through the remainder of the tournament. If you came second, not only did you play an additional match, but you also faced the big rugby superpowers, one after the other. England's group also included Italy, New Zealand and Tonga.

They beat Italy 67–7 in the opening game and Tonga 101–10 in the third game but, sandwiched between them, was the crucial match against New Zealand.

Clive thought they should adopt a strategy of attacking Jonah Lomu, the huge New Zealand wing, and playing the ball very quick and wide. A massive amount of video analysis had convinced Clive that Lomu was vulnerable when he was attacked, particularly if you got him to turn. Going forward he was awesome, so avoiding giving him possession was vital but, under the pressure of playing what they knew was their biggest game of the competition, England crumbled and kicked away valuable possession, gifting Lomu the advantages they had planned to deny him.

Wilkinson played at fly-half. He would go on to make the position his own but, at the time, he was new to it. Clive now regrets that decision. He wasn't ready for the number 10 jersey. He wasn't ready for the crucial role that would mean him having to run the whole game.

Losing 16–30 at home was a massive disappointment. A lot of thought had gone into the match and it was a 'must win' game. Now England faced a play-off game against Fiji, then a likely quarter-final against South Africa, a semi against Australia and the final against New Zealand.

England beat Fiji 45–24. Fiji battled physically, throwing everything into it because they had nothing to lose – this was their big match. Battered and bruised from the encounter, England had just three days' recovery time before the quarter-final against South Africa in Paris. The South Africans had been in their French hotel for a week. They were rested and ready for action. England had beaten the Springboks 13–7 at Twickenham the previous November, so knew they were capable of victory but, of course, this was not Twickenham. England lost 21–44. Jannie De Beer kicked five dropped goals and England were out of the World Cup. They hadn't even reached the semi-finals. It was a devastating blow.

Clive went into the dressing room and saw his players slumped across the benches, worn out and feeling utterly dejected. Some wiped away tears as he addressed them. He told them how well they'd done. He said that the defeat did not make them a bad team. They were still talented players and this England team would go on to do great things.

He said he was proud of them. Later, he would be more critical and point out to each player where he went wrong, but this was not the time for that. He said they should look to the future, forget about 1999 and begin thinking about 2003. He told them they would win the next World Cup. He said this defeat marked the beginning of something great for English rugby. Walters watched him as he spoke. 'To be honest, of all the things that Clive does well, public speaking, or certainly emotional public speaking like that, is not one of them. Yet, here he was giving the most tremendous speech.' It was one of Clive's finest moments.

'The way the defeat was handled by Clive got us all thinking about the future,' says Johnson. 'We realised that most of us were young enough to be playing in 2003. That defeat was a turning point – we felt close afterwards, and we felt we never, ever wanted to lose like that again. The defeat changed Clive, too. He realised that winning was important – not style. He bounced back after that and became more determined to change this into a winning side.'

Back in England, Clive was immediately asked to produce a report about what had gone wrong. Officers of the RFU were desperate to find out from Clive why the team had lost. During his two years in office, Clive had railed against post mortems after a defeat. His feeling had always been that you should sit down and work out exactly what had happened after a good performance – learn from the positives. 'After a defeat, you should go out, have a few beers and forget about it,' he said. 'Learn from the mistakes, but don't obsess about them.' In contrast, four years later, when Clive won the World Cup, he found he couldn't even get a meeting with anyone, let alone be asked to produce a report. In 2003, he was eager to take things further and to talk about how they could develop, but no one wanted to talk to him. In defeat in 1999, they were all over him like a rash.

Clive's report identified a lot of problems that he felt needed to be remedied before the 2003 World Cup. He wrote that he felt the team had been operating in a 'fingers crossed' environment. He highlighted problems that were out of his control – player access, the scheduling of the tournament so that England had to play back-to-back big games. Clive laid himself bare in the report, highlighting every difficulty and trying to make the management board understand, in twenty-six pages of type, how hard the job was when there was no structure within which a winning environment could be created. A few days later, he found his words splashed all over the front of the newspapers – it had been leaked.

'He was very down after the South Africa defeat,' said Cotton, who met Clive at the College Inn, just outside Windsor. 'Clive was desperate. He was so disappointed and hurt by all the criticism. He was clearly uneasy about the future. What's remarkable to me, though, is that's the only time I ever saw him down. After that, he seemed to bolster himself up and was full on for winning it next time.'

Clive vowed to continue as he had been doing but wanted to up the intensity considerably. He moved the team from the Petersham Hotel in Richmond to Pennyhill Park Hotel in Bagshot and, just before Christmas 1999, he got together his key players and the BBC – Brian Baister, Baron and Cotton. Clive made Johnson the permanent England captain and set about building a team for the 2003 World Cup. Clive would make sure everything was perfect – no more 'if onlys'. Everything had to be right from now on. He would employ the best people, pick the best players and never take 'no' for an answer.

Chapter Twenty-three

The 'bible' and the disciplines

'To the illuminated mind the whole world burns and sparkles with light.' **Ralph Waldo Emerson**

Rugby is a product to the extent that it can be marketed, promoted and developed, but it is not a product in the purest sense of the word. It doesn't really 'exist' in any meaningful way. It is the interaction of thirty players in a given space, with given laws and in a given time. Rugby is just people. That's what sport is – that's why it's endlessly fascinating and deeply frustrating. People are flawed, so achieving perfection, even identifying perfection, is close to impossible. All you can do is control everything that is controllable and leave as little to chance as possible. The fewer things left to that dreadful, victory-sapping, demotivating devil called chance, the better.

Many problems in sport stem from the fact that 'sport' itself is something of an abstract concept. When clubs battle to be successful, they do not do it in the same way that businesses do. Major commercial organisations seek to do one another out of business. If Tesco had 100 per cent of the market place, they would be delighted. If Saracens had 100 per cent of the market place, there would be no sport to watch. You cannot produce rugby without an opposition. In sport, the paradox is that your fiercest rivals elevate your business even while they challenge it. If you draw a great team in the Cup, your gate receipts will increase while the chances of succeeding decrease. It is good, commercially, to come face to face with a fierce rival. Sport and business are a fascinating fit because they don't really fit at all. Sport was never designed to be a business. If you think about it, sport is an obscure business proposition.

Regardless of this, when Clive took over the England team, it was with the very clear plan to take business principles into it. The way he made this work was by using the principles of top team performance accrued from his experiences in business. The guidelines for developing élite teams are generic. Clive quickly identified that to build a successful élite team demands getting two things absolutely right – the personnel and the environment. The issue of personnel was particularly vital in rugby because, as we have established, players are all there is. So when it came to creating the right environment, his concept of 'right' was entirely dictated by the needs and wants of the players. They were consulted at every step and the joint thoughts of the management and players were laid down in a document known as the 'bible'.

'The players were always consulted,' says Johnson. 'Clive would ask me what the players thought at every stage. If players thought they would benefit from a particular coach being brought in, that coach would soon appear. One of the funny things from the players' point of view was to play the game of working out which coach he was most influenced by in any one week. If we saw him having a drink in the bar with Dave Alred, you'd know he'd come to the session the next day and preach the importance of kicking. We'd see him chatting to Phil Larder, then next morning, he'd open the session by saying, "Defence, defence, defence." We'd have bets on which coach had influenced him most in any one session.'

People, people, people. They are what make a business great. Get the right people and then get them doing the right job, but get the right people on board before anything else – so far, so obvious. What Clive did differently was to venture outside the sport to find experts who did not necessarily have rugby backgrounds. He also employed experts in areas that had previously had no such input.

Of course, filling the team with experts does not guarantee success, and an ability to manage those people – their expectations as well as their time with the team – was essential. This was Clive's key to making things work. 'Clive recognises that the more experts you have, the more carefully you have to manage the time of the players and make sure that not too many demands are put on them,' said Phil Larder.

The coaches already employed by the Union formed the core of Clive's élite coaching team. When part-time assistant coach John

Mitchell returned to New Zealand in 2000, Andy Robinson took on the job full-time. Nathan Martin joined the RFU as Clive's assistant in 2000. Clive had met him at the Royal Marines. Martin then moved to become the performance services director and was replaced by Louise Ramsay, who joined in 2001 after working for the Summer and Winter Olympic teams. Alred continued as the kicking guru and Larder the king of defence. Larder had coached the Great Britain rugby league side before switching codes. 'Defence is not just a matter of settling on a system and sticking to it,' he said. 'You prepare for South Africa, who play a tighter game, differently from the way you prepare for New Zealand, who like to get the ball wide. You never stop fine-tuning.'

Several other people had been brought into the team. Tony Biscombe was an RFU divisional technical administrator from 1989 until 1998, when Clive grabbed him and put him in charge of video analysis. Brian Ashton joined as an assistant coach specialising in attack, and Simon Hardy became throw-in coach part-time in 1999, then full-time lineout coach in 2000. Phil Keith-Roach became scrummaging adviser.

Alred expanded his repertoire from being just kicking coach to also working on the team's mental preparation. 'The most fundamental change in the years leading up to the 2003 World Cup was the whole issue of mental preparation – trying to ensure that players always perform at or near their potential, whatever the interference. If there's anything I can do to get a player to go where he's never been before, in terms of the level of his performance, that's my job,' said Alred. He had joined Clive's team part-time in 1997 but moved to full-time in 2000. Reddin was the fitness expert.

Dave Reddin sits in his large Twickenham office, next to the one that Clive used to inhabit. The office is bursting with the tools of his trade – boxes of nutrients, supplements and protein drinks line the shelves. On his desk there is a DVD about yoga.

'We look at everything,' says Reddin. 'Anything that will make the team play better.'

Reddin started working with the England rugby team in October

1996 when Jack Rowell was in charge. Previously, he'd spent two years as the fitness adviser to Leicester. He says that under Clive, the fitness work he did became very focused. He was challenged to produce players who were not simply universally 'fitter' but better able to perform on the pitch. The fitness tests had to be relevant to the game.

'There was no point in testing how far they could run in twelve minutes just for the sheer hell of it. We wanted to make everything more specific so that you would see players' fitness scores improving, and their games improving correspondingly.'

Under Clive's instruction, he would have regular meetings with the specialist coaches to assess what they wanted from the players. His job was to ensure that the players were physically able to do what was required of them on the pitch. Therefore, if Clive identified that not enough ball was being won from set pieces, he would contact Phil Keith-Roach (the scrummaging coach) about it. Keith-Roach would then shore up the scrummaging side of the game. If he thought players weren't scrummaging well enough because they weren't strong, powerful or flexible enough, he'd bring Reddin in with specific demands. 'We need the back row to be quicker,' for example.

'Then I would work out how we could achieve it and whether it would be worth the time it would take,' he says. 'There's no point spending a lot of time trying to get Jason Leonard's speed time over ten metres down by 0.1 of a second – is that really going to make a difference to his game? Trying to keep his endurance levels at a very high level and improving them by 10 per cent is going to be a better use of his time.

'I get involved in all planning/selection/management meetings because it's important for me to have a very good feel for what the coaches want. There's no point in me going off in one direction with a player if it might be irrelevant.'

All the specialists worked on long-term programmes, trying to tie in with what the players were doing in the clubs. It was vital for Clive, with his huge entourage, to make sure the management team worked closely together and interacted with one another. They were encouraged to evaluate and praise one another. Clive called this 'cross-boundary team working'. They would meet as a group for an hour to dissect the game, before going away separately to work on their own areas of expertise.

Understanding what their own responsibilities were made it easier for coaches to help one another in a non-threatening way.

Clive arranged for a workshop to be held to establish ways in which every member of the management team could work to take England to the 'n'th degree – as high as they could go, beyond number one. The results were made into a booklet entitled *England Management Team – Beyond Number One Workshop*. It gives a fascinating insight into how the England management team worked, and the close relationships that developed between the individuals in it. It also sheds light on exactly what Clive did, where the boundaries lay and how the management team bonded so effectively.

The document outlines Clive's role, which is clearly strategic and forward looking. He had external focus and an eye on the future, while the coaches were immersed in the detail. The job of the assistant coach (Robinson) was much more focused on the actual coaching of the team. Clive's job was to create a winning environment for the whole squad. Robinson's was to create the right environment for every individual session. So Robinson's objectives were to develop the forwards to be physical and skilful, coach unit skills (lineout and scrum), coach contact areas, assist Clive in selection, analyse the opposition, and the very curious 'maintain humility among team'.

The penultimate member of Woodward's dream team was Dr Simon Kemp. Kemp was working for Fulham football club when he saw an advertisement in the *British Medical Journal* for a doctor for the England rugby team. The job was full-time medical officer based at Twickenham and working 100 per cent on England rugby medical issues.

'Clive received a hundred and twenty applications from all over the world,' says Kemp. 'The whole process impressed me greatly. It was a very professional way of finding the right person. In so much of professional sport, appointments are not even advertised – he advertised across the world and wanted to attract rugby experts and non-rugby experts. He just wanted the best person.'

The selection process was rigorous – applicants were interviewed by doctors, by Clive and by Baron. Kemp was chosen.

'I got to see what an incredibly professional organisation he ran. Clive's very good with new starters and his wife is very good, as well.

Jayne welcomed my wife and kids, which meant a lot. As a management team we were away a lot and it was nice that they felt part of it. He did nice things – the first December, after the autumn internationals, a large Christmas hamper arrived at our house. I was blown away by the size of it.'

The only time Kemp came into conflict with Clive was when he couldn't deliver what Clive wanted.

'If a player's injured, a player's injured. I can help speed up the recovery process but I can't just make him better,' says Kemp. 'Clive's expectations were high and, with the best will in the world, I sometimes just couldn't get the players he wanted fit.'

An added complication was that Kemp was at the mercy of the club doctors who treated the players on a regular basis and would also be making medical decisions.

'Sometimes there was a grey area, where the player was not definitely fit to play and not definitely unfit to play – there was a call to be made.' Clearly, Kemp would have called for the player not to play in a club game, whereas the club doctor would have urged him to play. 'The World Cup in 2003 was great because we had the players for two months beforehand, so I could get them fit, and we went into that World Cup with all players injury free.

'When we did well, Clive would always tell us. His feedback skills were good. Working for Clive was incredible. He took us on a journey and sold us his vision. You know he never doubted England could do it. I never saw him have doubts. He didn't deal in doubt. He's changed the way that I think and practise. He inspired you in any way he could to achieve the standards he set. If you did achieve them, he acknowledged it. Not a single medical opinion was challenged by him, he just challenged the speed and extent of the work we could do.'

The final signing to Woodward's team was possibly the most controversial. Vision specialist Sherylle Calder was drafted in to improve the peripheral vision of the players and 'train' their eye muscles. Calder became involved after Andy Robinson bumped into her on a scouting trip to South Africa, where she was doing research for a PhD in vision technology. Clive was impressed. Why could the eye muscles not be trained if every other muscle could be trained?

Calder recognised that 'seeing the gap' would be a lot easier if players' eyesight was better. She designed a computer programme to be used by the players on their laptops. They had to progress through one level before reaching the next. Guess who worked hardest on it in the run-up to the World Cup? Yep, Jonny Wilkinson.

Clive knew that the whole team had to believe in the concept and the style he was espousing, and that everyone, players and management, had to understand exactly what their role was and what his vision for the team was. The booklet containing all his thoughts, plans and views for the team was based on Paddi Lund's 'welcome book'.

This was Clive's handbook for success – his 'bible'. It contained all the information to define and shape the England team and turn a group of great rugby players into a World Cup-winning side. 'We are in the business of inspiration,' it says boldly across its top. 'Our goal is to inspire the whole country.' It reflects the extent of Clive's ambition from his first day in the job.

The purpose of the 'bible' was to put into words the discussions and thought processes of the England team and management. It changed as the years passed, reflecting the change in Clive's outlook and his new thinking for the team. On the last page of the booklet it says, 'Is there anything you would like to see included, amended or improved? Your input is vital – it is your document, your team, your success.'

One of Clive's great skills when working with England was to encourage ownership by everyone of everything within their sphere of influence. He was outstandingly good at making everyone well aware of exactly what the aims were, and where the team was heading, while being very specific about individual roles. His mantra was 'Coaches will coach, managers will manage, medical staff will look after the players, and technical staff will do the technical work. PLAYERS WILL PLAY.' The 'bible' shows clearly what Clive expected of his players and the staff who worked for him. If he created the best environment for them to work in, they in turn had to produce the best rugby they could on the pitch.

Off the pitch, they had to conduct themselves in 'a manner becoming an England rugby player'. Such conduct includes absolute confidentiality and allegiance to the team. All members of the playing and management team were told not to discuss, let alone write about, their time in Team England. Non-selected players were to discuss their disappointments with Clive personally, and not 'moan or complain' to teammates. They should always congratulate a player selected in their position immediately. 'We must be the best in everything we do,' says the 'bible'. That includes dress, punctuality and language. 'You are representing England at all times – not just when you arrive in the hotel. The highest standards are expected at all times.'

The 'bible' sets out separate roles for senior players, who are to become leaders and help the younger, less experienced players. 'Take the trouble to get to know them,' the booklet instructs. It suggests that senior players offer to act as mentors to newcomers. 'Display a positive attitude. Set an example of high personal discipline. Come up with suggestions for improvements rather than criticising existing methods. You are a senior player – act like one.'

The tone of the 'bible' is interesting – it doesn't preach and in most sections it doesn't present hard and fast rules (the code of conduct is an exception to this). Instead, it reminds players of all the implications of everything they do, urging them to make the right choice.

On the subject of sex, it says, 'Sex before training or matches is not a bad thing. However, staying up all night trying to get it is!' The advice for the drinkers in the group is rational and fair: 'Alcohol is a vasodilator – this means it causes the blood vessels of the body to widen, resulting in increased blood flow. If you have been injured, one of the major tasks initially is to restrict blood flow – hence RICE (rest, ice, compression and elevation). So if you have been injured in a game, don't drink too much that night.'

On match days, players are told to drink water out of Lucozade bottles, and consume bananas, wine gums and jelly babies before the match, bananas and sandwiches at half-time and bananas, sandwiches, fruit, tea and coffee after matches. Tony Biscombe goes to the team room five minutes before half-time and puts up notices with up to four key points for the players to consider. At the half-time whistle, the 'bible' says in bold type, 'I want us down the tunnel in front of our opponents if possible.'

The level of detail is staggering. You wouldn't imagine that the players would need help with 'proper use of the sauna' but apparently there is a correct way to do it. 'First, take a warm shower but leave your hair dry. Next, sit on the lower level of the sauna for 2–3 minutes. After this, move up to the top level (lie down if you can) and stay up there for 6–7 minutes. After this, take a cool shower for 30–40 seconds, then alternate with a warm shower for a few minutes. Repeat the shower sequence 4–5 times.'

The purpose of the 'bible' was to ensure that the players understood the level of detail needed to make it to the top. It was also to ensure that they bought into Clive's plans, hopes and dreams.

Chapter Twenty-four

Many a slip twixt Cup and Cup

'Success is the ability to go from one failure to another with no loss of enthusiasm.' **Sir Winston Churchill**

The period between the 1999 and 2003 World Cups was tortuous for England fans. They watched in dismay as a team that was clearly vastly improving every year threw away four Grand Slams with defeat in one match and by less than the score of a converted try every time.

'But Clive wasn't thrown off course at all by the defeats,' said Walters. 'We just continued blue skying and blue skying. We'd have meetings all the time to think of ways in which we could make the team better. You know – "the sky's the limit". We tried to think of everything.'

At Pennyhill Park, the Pecorelli family, owners of the hotel, began working on ways in which Team England's home could be improved to cater for the specific demands of the players. Over the next four years, the hotel would undergo a stunning transformation as a larger gym, specific diets and a rugby pitch were developed on site.

At the end of 1999, Clive called the players and his management team together at their new base and reinvigorated them about the future. He told them that no stone would be left unturned and no effort missed as they battled to make England the best team in the world.

'Clive could be quite belligerent,' recalls Terry Burwell, the RFU's operations director. 'I won't pretend for a moment that knowing Clive was straightforward and easy at that time. Sometimes he'd send emails through and I'd look at them in disbelief and think, "We can't do that." I knew that if I did what he was asking, it would affect dozens of other things and I'd have a whole load of people complaining.

'Clive wanted to change things with a moment's notice. He wanted everyone to act when he clicked his fingers. We'd have major rows about it. It used to drive me insane but, to be fair, everything he asked us to do was for England, and when we looked at the full picture of what he was working on, we realised why it was vital that he got everybody pointing their noses in the same direction and working for Team England.'

In the first game of the 2000 championship – the first Six Nations tournament – England kicked off against Ireland with some fantastic, free-flowing rugby, beating them 50–18. It was a great result and, more importantly for Clive, it showed England playing the sort of rugby he always hoped they would.

After the match, Tony Biscombe sat in his video analysis room, looking at the screen in front of him. He studied the statistics from England's recent games and noticed a worrying trend. While England started well and played exceptional rugby in the crucial opening ten minutes of a game, they did not do so in the first ten minutes of the second half. It was paramount that they started the second half as powerfully as they started the first half, to establish themselves early on.

'Clive explained the situation to me,' said Walters. 'I was mulling it over when three important things happened. First, I overheard some women talking about how they hated to wear white trousers because it made their bottoms look big. I thought straightaway of the England shirt – the bright white shirt, and how big it made the players look when they first ran out. I thought about how much of an advantage that was and wondered how we might make more of it. Then I was at Granada Studios and heard someone talking about how much bigger the television cameras made people look. Again, I thought of the players, but wasn't sure how we could maximise the impact of white shirts, television and making the players look big and intimidating.

'Then I watched Pete Sampras playing at Wimbledon and he changed his shirt on court. This great big hairy guy changed on centre court and, bloody hell, suddenly he looked fresh as a daisy. I watched and realised that Sampras almost always picked the moment when his opponent thought he was about to win.'

Could this work with England? Walters spoke to Clive and they decided to try sending England out in clean shirts at half-time. They would look bigger, fresher and, with a bit of luck, would replicate the dynamic start they achieved at the beginning of the first half. Could clean shirts give them a psychological advantage? What would be the impact on the opposition players if England suddenly came out looking fresh?

'We used it for the first time in the Stade de France,' said Walters. 'When England came out for the second half the French looked at them and thought, "Have they changed their whole squad?" Psychologically, it gave them an advantage and made them look fresh and bigger.' Added to this, Clive encouraged the players to think of the second half as a new start.

Against France, England looked hugely impressive. They faced the biggest pack in French rugby history and pulled them apart. Wilkinson kicked five out of six penalties, scoring all the team's points. England went down to thirteen men in the second half but still managed to win 15–9.

'This game was the turning point in my career,' said an elated Clive afterwards. The team went on to beat Wales and Italy and then they faced Scotland for the Grand Slam, but on a rainy afternoon in Edinburgh, Scotland raised their game, determined to deny England their moment. Punch-ups broke out all over the field and England lost self-control. At the break, England were one point ahead. They lost 13–19. Ten years after Scotland had memorably beaten England to deny them the Grand Slam in 1990, they'd done it again.

Through the disappointment, and accompanied by the sound of sharpening knives, Clive tried to learn from the experience. He looked at the statistical analysis of the match and watched the video reruns of the game carefully. England were playing too much rugby when under pressure. In the last six minutes of the Scotland game, they had adopted a high-risk strategy. He pulled out the video of the 1999 match against Wales – the same thing applied. In the last five minutes of the game, England had started risk-taking under pressure. He began to talk to the players about this. 'It takes twenty seconds to score a try,' he said. 'You need to keep calm, keep thinking properly and don't get panicked into throwing the ball around too much.' He called this 'coaching between the ears'. There was nothing wrong with his team, he deduced – they just needed to think properly under pressure.

One of Clive's key attributes during the troubled period between World Cups was his ability to stay focused, determined and utterly committed to making England a better team. No matter that the players seemed to stumble over their shoelaces in the final game of each championship in a manner resembling a comedy routine – Clive believed in them.

On the 2000 summer tour to South Africa, England drew the series after winning the second Test 22–27 – the first win by any northern hemisphere national side on Tri Nations soil since England's quarter-final win in 1995, and only the third England win there in twenty-eight years. It marked the beginning of a run of eleven successive England Test victories against southern hemisphere teams. The twelfth victory would be against Australia in the World Cup final. John Mitchell, Clive's part-time coach, returned to New Zealand just before the tour and Andy Robinson came on board full-time.

The first match of the 2000 autumn internationals was a landmark victory over Australia. England beat the visiting Wallabies 22–19. It was an important stepping stone on the path to World Cup glory, but those weeks in mid-November 2000, in which England took on and beat the best team in the world, will be forever remembered for one thing – the day the players went on strike.

To the outside world, the strike appeared to happen suddenly, without warning and without any particularly good reason, even with a touch of arrogance. The word 'strike' is such an emotive one, conjuring up images of soot-covered miners choking on coal dust and factory workers struggling to feed their families. It sat uncomfortably on the shoulders of men earning hundreds of thousands of pounds a year for playing rugby.

However, the players felt strongly that their course of action was the only one available to them. Consider it from their point of view – the Union had signed a massive multi-million pound deal with Sky Television, bringing in more revenue than ever to add to the international match ticket income. The RFU were using the players' image rights to make yet more money, but the players were getting a tiny proportion of it. As Matt Dawson said, 'There isn't a company in the world that pays its performers five per cent of the turnover. Everyone was making money out of the England rugby team except the players.' The players wanted £4,000 per player with a £2,000 win bonus. What the RFU offered was the opposite – £2,000 match fee plus £4,000 win bonus.

The players had been arguing with the RFU about this for six months. The strike came about after months and months of prevarication by the RFU.

'We kept bringing it up and the RFU kept batting it away,' said Martin Johnson. 'There was nothing we could do in the summer – you can't threaten to strike when there are no games. So, as soon as the autumn internationals started, we decided to act. We approached Baron and told him we were serious. He had to start paying us properly.'

Five days before the game against Australia, three players' representatives – Dawson, Dallaglio and Johnson – went to see Baron at Twickenham to discuss the situation once again.

'It was an appalling meeting,' recalls Johnson. 'I sat there and listened to this bunch of men arguing like schoolchildren. Baron was deeply unimpressive.'

They told Baron that the England team would honour the RFU's commitment to their sponsors that week only if Baron reversed the offer. Baron offered £3,500 match fee and £1,750 win bonus. The players were not happy. Why would he keep back £500 per man from the match fee and £250 from the win bonus? The RFU could afford to pay the players. Why wouldn't they? The players decided it was a matter of principle and rejected the offer, which was then withdrawn.

'It wasn't about the £500,' says Johnson. 'It was about the need to be listened to. It was about the fact that we had been having these negotiations for months and months and we knew that this was the moment to force the RFU to treat us properly. We couldn't accept it. Their offer was unacceptable.'

The players decided that if Baron wanted to make money off their backs for the RFU without paying them what they believed they were worth, they would make it extremely difficult for him to do so. They turned their training shirts inside out to hide the Cellnet and Nike logos. Johnson phoned Clive to tell him what the players were doing and he gave some hint of the madness that was to come by going absolutely nuts. He said that any player who wore his jersey inside out in training would not play against Australia. He told the players that as long as they did nothing to upset the sponsors, he would make sure that a meeting took place after the match, at which the RFU would listen to them properly. Normality was temporarily resumed. The players wore their sponsored shirts, they beat Australia and all was well with the world.

'We thought, after we'd beaten Australia, that it would be easier for us to have the discussions with the RFU. We thought they might agree to our demands because we were all playing so well,' said Johnson.

So Dawson, Dallaglio and Johnson – the most unlikely trio of trade unionists – contacted the RFU and tried to bring them back to the negotiating table. They were told that officials couldn't find the time. This was after Clive had promised that a meeting would take place. The players felt they were fast running out of options. Argentina were the next opponents, at Twickenham, at the end of the week.

'We debated whether to stay in the changing room for ten minutes at the start of the match but that would upset the television people,' said Johnson. 'We had no issues with them. We just wanted the RFU to sit up and take notice. What could we do?'

Suddenly, the 's' word was being mentioned more and more frequently. The camp appeared to be divided according to age over the issue of strike action – the younger guys didn't want to rock the boat, while the old hands were fed up with the RFU and their intransigence. Neil Back suggested taking a vote. The players were overwhelmingly in favour of action. Now they needed to tell Clive. They all looked at Johnson. The big man shrugged.

'I took the phone and dialled his number, thinking, "The guy's gonna go up the wall."'

'You're going to do whaaaatttt?' shrieked Clive.

Clive's position in this dispute was not an enviable one. His role sat precariously balanced between the RFU and the England team at the best of times. While the players are paid by their clubs, the national coach is paid by the RFU and is an RFU employee, reporting to Francis Baron. The team had his loyalty and his every waking hour was directed towards making their lot a happier one, but the RFU were his employers. Given the difficulty of his position, the great surprise is the way he charged in to the centre of the debate with all the finesse of a rampaging bull, exploding with indignation and rage at the players' plans and publicly berating them.

'He was really crazy,' says Austin Healey. 'I mean, we're talking REALLY crazy. We nicknamed the days of the week Mad Monday, Twisted Tuesday and Wacky Wednesday. He was going steadily more nuts as the week progressed. It was horrible at the time, but now I see it all for what it was – Clive's an emotional guy, he'd thrown everything into making sure we had the best possible chance of success and we appeared to be throwing it all away over a few hundred quid. He was just devastated – but nuts. My God, he went nuts.'

Matt Perry recalls, 'In truth, he lost his rag. There was talk of a division one side turning out for England instead of us.'

'It was a frightening time,' agrees Johnson. 'I didn't know whether that was it – England career over. We were threatened with never playing again. It was a real performance from Clive. He was desperately hurt and nothing would make him realise that we were actually going to do this. I looked Clive in the eye and said, "We're striking. You need to understand that, Clive. This is not about you – it's about the players and the RFU. You can threaten us all you want, but we're in this together."'

Clive rang each of the players individually and asked them to reconsider their decision. Some of the younger guys were desperately nervous. When the strike started, I was the rugby editor of *The Times*. I had calls from players who played their messages down the phone. They were being warned that they would never play rugby for England again. The messages quite categorically told the players to extricate themselves from the strike and have a career with England or continue with this 'offensive action' and never be forgiven. Never wear the white shirt again. They had no idea whether their loyalty should be to the team or to the coach, who was adamant that they would never play for their country again unless they were on his side.

'It was a horrible time,' says Johnson. 'We never really considered that Clive would stand against us like that. I kind of always thought he'd back us.'

The first day of the strike was Twisted Tuesday. This was when Clive

pleaded with the players to change their minds. He warned that the
game would never forgive them. The players had revealed the verdict of
their vote to Baron at 11.30 p.m. the previous day, Mad Monday. On
the stroke of midnight, Clive had appeared at the hotel, ashen-faced.
For the first time since he'd taken over, he could not support his
players. He felt they were using the England jersey to achieve their
ends. 'If you're on strike,' he told them, 'get out of the hotel first thing
tomorrow morning. Anything on your room bills, you will have to pay
for yourselves.'

In that late-night speech, he told the players that they had let themselves down, let the fans down and let the shirt down. He threatened
that he would put out a team on Saturday from non-squad players.
Matt Dawson called his club, Northampton, and told Keith Barwell of
Clive's threats. Barwell immediately called other premiership club
chairmen and they agreed not to release any players for the formation
of an alternative England team.

Wacky Wednesday brought more of the same as Clive continued to
leave messages, attempting to pick off members of the squad whom he
thought were weaker and could be bullied into attending training sessions. His tactic of trying to isolate individuals in an attempt to get
them to break away from the main body upset a lot of the players. His
message was clear – if players did not turn up for training at 11 a.m. the
next morning, they would never wear their England shirts again. The
players' message was clear – if their contracts were not properly sorted
out, they remained on strike.

'It was all getting very nasty. Some of the younger players were desperately worried. Playing for England was a dream come true,' says
Healey. 'None of them wanted it to end over five hundred pounds, but
they knew that breaking away from the squad was a dangerous thing to
do. No one knew quite how the whole thing would end.'

Johnson helped to break the deadlock by phoning Peter Wheeler,
chief executive of Leicester Tigers, Johnson's club, and asking for his
help. Wheeler headed for Wentworth golf club to meet Baron, and suggested that £50,000 be taken from the bonus the players would receive
if England won the 2001 Six Nations and be divided among the squad
as an immediate one-off payment. This would not affect the RFU's
accounts because they had already budgeted for it and they could argue

they had not improved their final offer. At the same time, it gave all the players an extra £380 per game.

The offer was put to the squad at a big dinner that was being held to raise money for former England player Alastair Hignell, at the Café Royal. It was accepted unanimously. The following morning, as the clock approached Clive's 11 a.m. deadline, the RFU gave it the green light. Players and head coach were reunited and England beat both Argentina and South Africa. The chariot was back on its wheels.

'That strike was an important moment in the players' relationship with Clive,' says Johnson. 'If you look at the results, we hardly lost a game after that. When we called off the strike, the relationship with Clive was slightly different. He realised we had strong views and weren't afraid to exercise our powers. It was actually much easier. The squad were much closer and Clive was more onside. It was less teacher-pupil.'

Clive continued his efforts to improve things for the players and increase their chances of success.

'I knew Clive was back to normal when he approached me with his latest request,' said Burwell. 'He asked whether we could keep the grass a little longer in the five-metre areas down in the touchlines. He wanted to do that so when England kicked into those areas, the grass would slow down the ball and it wouldn't go into touch, requiring the opposing team to kick it, and giving England the lineout. He clearly thought this was a fantastic idea until I pointed out that it would be of exactly the same benefit for the opposition as well.'

Chapter Twenty-five

Twenty-stone men in tight, white Lycra

---

*'The great successful people of the world ... think ahead and create
their mental picture, and then go to work materialising that picture in all
its details, filling in here, adding a little there, altering this a bit and that
a bit, but steadily building, steadily building.'* **Robert Collier**

The 2001 Six Nations Championship. Surely this time England would win. Surely. They beat Wales 44–15 in Cardiff to get off to a blinding start, then pushed Italy aside 80–23 at Twickenham. The Scotland game produced a 43–3 win to avenge their defeat the previous year, then they took France to the cleaners, beating them 48–19. They were heading for a resounding Grand Slam victory. No team could stop them. What did halt them in their tracks was something bigger and more profound than rugby – foot-and-mouth disease. This led to a delay to the final game of the championship because the team and supporters were prevented from travelling to Ireland. The match would be postponed until the end of October. In the meantime, those England players selected for the Lions tour to Australia prepared for their trip, while those players not selected were left to contemplate a summer tour to North America.

Clive was one of the 'unselected' group. Graham Henry, the New Zealand coach of Wales, had been selected as Lions coach instead of him. There is no question that Clive felt deeply hurt at the appointment of Henry and it is not too difficult to see why. England were playing great rugby. Clive was a former England player and Lion himself. He had made it clear that he wished to coach the side but, instead, the Lions management opted for Henry, who would be the first foreign coach to lead the team. By a strange twist of fate, by the time Clive became Lions coach in 2005, Henry was back coaching New Zealand and was thus his opposite number.

So why wasn't Clive selected? Donal Lenihan, the manager of that tour, refused to be interviewed for this book. Some of those who happily submitted themselves to questioning thought that it was Lenihan's influence that robbed Clive of the chance to coach the 2001 Lions. There is some history of antipathy between the two. Lenihan was in charge of Irish rugby when Clive became coach of London Irish Rugby Club. One of Clive's missions was to bring more Ireland internationals into the side. One of Lenihan's principal aims was to keep Irish players playing in Ireland. To say the two clashed would be to put it mildly. Lenihan was furious with Clive and had no more desire to work with him on the 2001 Lions tour than to stick needles in his eyes.

Clive took England to North America and witnessed his team's three Test victories there. Then, he flew to Australia to commentate for Sky Television, biting his tongue throughout as he fought to be as polite and uncritical of the Lions management as was humanly possible.

In October, after the summer tours, England travelled to Ireland for the unfinished Six Nations Championship. They arrived in Dublin horribly unprepared, the coaches having had no additional days with the players. Meanwhile, Ireland had played all their away fixtures during this time, so were well prepared for England's arrival. England lost 20–14 and returned, once again, without the Grand Slam.

The good news of the year, though, was that they beat Australia again, winning 21–15 to win the Cook Cup. This was followed by a 134–0 win over Romania, and another southern hemisphere scalp – a 29–9 win over South Africa.

The players soon started to respond to yet more innovations that Clive was introducing, including the concept of 'nine winning behaviours' under the headings defence, basics, contact, pressure, kicking, team attack, self-control, tactics and leadership.

On a crisp Monday morning in early February 2002, Chris Baff walked into his office at Nike's headquarters in Amsterdam, switched on his computer and glanced through the messages that had arrived over the weekend. There was one from Clive Woodward. The head coach of the England rugby team? It couldn't be, surely.

'The email had been sent to Clive's Nike contacts in the UK after the Six Nations game in Scotland, and forwarded to me. It said, "Watch how many times Jason Robinson gets caught by his shirt during the match. We need to do something about this. We need to take off the collars or tighten it up or something." I was so pleased. We'd been working on some revolutionary new designs and we just didn't know how the management or players would react to them. That email validated absolutely what we'd been working on and it meant that we could now go full steam ahead.'

Lycra shirts had been tried once before. The rival sportswear company Adidas had experimented with them prior to the 1999 World Cup, hoping to send the New Zealand team on to the pitch in skintight black numbers. They had even gone so far as to design the shirts, but when the All Blacks used them in training, they found that the shirts restricted breathing and were uncomfortable. Nike picked up the baton and worked on creating shirts that would be tight enough to be 'ungrabbable', yet comfortable enough to be worn by the players without hindering them or preventing them from drawing breath.

England had won that first game against Scotland 29–3, despite the grabbing of Robinson's shirt. Clive had made some subtle changes to the way in which the team approached travel to matches. They learnt from the defeats at Murrayfield and Lansdowne Road, and decided that, in future, they would stay at their England base until the last minute, travelling to away venues just a couple of days before each match. This kept Clive in control of the training facilities and environment, and kept the players in the comfort and familiarity of Pennyhill Park Hotel for as long as possible.

These new travel plans paid off in that first game, but Clive wanted more. His appeal to Nike to sort out the shirt situation resulted in Baff and three members of his team coming to London for a meeting with the England team.

'It was interesting because we had this whole presentation lined up and we didn't actually show the designs until about halfway through it,' said Baff. 'I remember very clearly that Clive was leaning back in his chair. I'm sure he was taking it all in, but he didn't seem to be quite engaging with us. When we pulled out the prototypes it was just like someone had turned on a switch. He leant forward and got very interested in what was happening. He asked a lot of questions. The shirts were radical – skintight. Clive loved what we were working on and he opened the doors to the team for us.

'He was so positive and encouraging, it was fantastic. We were always welcome in camp to watch and work with the players, learning what they needed and seeing what we could provide.'

The shirt couldn't have too much 'give' in it or when an opposition player grabbed a handful of material, it would stretch out and negate the value of the tightness. As a result, the shirts were almost impossible to put on and take off, and scenes on the pitch after matches were not dissimilar to those acted out in Top Shop on a Saturday afternoon – the players were like a dozen schoolgirls, helping each other in and out of tight Lycra numbers.

'We made quite a few changes to the original garment before it was acceptable,' says Baff. 'The neckline for the forwards, especially, was a bit too high and tight, so we lowered it and loosened it for them because they've obviously got slightly larger necks than the rest. Then there were a few other little tweaks that we made. We kept working on the shirt. Kept trying to improve it.

'It was great to be working with Clive during this time because he was so focused and extremely organised. He had this amazing set-up at Pennyhill Park, and he was very personable. He would share a joke with you but still be very business-like. He would just make things happen. Any problems we had – we'd see him and he would sort them out. The level of understanding of the game that he had just blew me away.'

While the shirt men designed and sewed, the England rugby team played a magical second Six Nations game against Ireland at Twickenham. 'Perfect rugby,' enthused Clive. Their 45–11 win marked the fourteenth successive Test victory at Twickenham – a new ground record – but as the team prepared to travel to France, Clive's efforts to keep improving backfired. He decided that instead of flying, they would travel by coach through the Channel Tunnel. A mixture of delayed trains and traffic conspired to turn the journey into an eight-hour adventure and they arrived at their Paris base tired and fed up. Their hosts were waiting for them. The French managed to keep Wilkinson completely out of the game, and beat the visitors 20–15. England had again lost any chance of taking the Grand Slam and it was a different team who had denied them. England bounced back to score the biggest winning margin against Wales, 50–10, then beat Italy in Rome, showing extraordinary strength in depth with Johnson, Dawson, Dallaglio and Leonard on the bench.

'All I can say about that time now is that the defeats did help,' says Johnson. 'I wouldn't have thought that at the time, but if we'd won consecutive Grand Slams, would we have been as hungry come the World Cup?'

A visit to Argentina followed and Clive continued to wheel out new players – he awarded five new caps and had Phil Vickery captaining the team to a 26–18 victory. The Argentinians had just beaten the same French side that won the Six Nations, and England's victory was achieved with a second-string side. It was the strength in depth, the knowledge that he now had a vast squad of talented players to call upon, that pleased Clive most of all.

The autumn internationals of 2002 provided the biggest test imaginable. With just twelve months to go before the World Cup, England took on New Zealand, Australia and South Africa at Twickenham. Having failed to win the Grand Slam for four consecutive years, they bounced from victory to victory against these big rugby nations. First came the All Blacks, who fell to a 31–28 defeat with an inexperienced side. Then it was Australia with a full-strength team on show. England won 32–31 and lifted the Cook Cup again, making it three wins in a row over the Wallabies. Finally, the 53–3 victory over South Africa was the Springboks' heaviest Test defeat.

Another critical non-essential was introduced to the team before the start of 2003 – Prozone. This is a computer and video system that reduces players to numbers, so the play can be viewed rather like a chessboard on screen. It shows where the gaps are and clearly indicates what the best play in any given moment would be. Prozone also calculates the work rates of the players, indicating who's working hard – on the ball and off – and who's 'cruising'. It's rugby's answer to *Big Brother* – there is no escape!

Clive first brought Prozone to the attention of the rugby world when he announced, at a press conference after the New Zealand game in the autumn of 2002, that the All Blacks had an illegal method of blocking. He deliberately highlighted these illegalities by showing the Prozone footage. Years later, when coaching the Lions, he would use video footage to display the detail of the injury to Brian O'Driscoll and be greatly maligned for it. Back in 2002, he was considered clever – he had simultaneously highlighted illegal play and displayed his new computer system to his key opponents while knowing that his opponents would not have the time to develop the system for themselves before the World Cup.

The computer system works off images gathered from twenty specialised cameras placed around the ground. It gives as much information on the opposition as on the England team. Through the system, data can be sent to the players' mobile phones.

Clive had learnt from American football that defence was a crucial part of the game because it is what players do for most of the match. Phil Larder used Prozone's statistics and analysis to explain to the players the myriad ways in which they could improve their defence. He highlighted how crucial defence was, and how many tries England had conceded in the last twenty matches. In 1995, when South Africa won the World Cup, they had the best defensive record of any team. In the football World Cup, France conceded the fewest goals. Defence was crucial. Each player was told that he had to achieve 95 per cent success in his tackle rate. After each match, every player was given statistics to indicate how he had performed.

Away from the field, Clive tried to make the players feel as positive as possible about the fast-approaching tournament. He gave all the players a framed photo of the 1966 World Cup soccer team parading round the pitch with the trophy. At Christmas, he took the players to see *Saturday Night Fever*. He was eager for them to do as much as possible as a squad.

Also in December, England became the world's number one side for the first time in rugby history. They had gone eighteen matches unbeaten at Twickenham and a World Cup was around the corner.

Chapter Twenty-six

2003 and the World Cup triumph

'When you are right, you cannot be too radical; when you are wrong, you cannot be too conservative.' **Martin Luther King Jr**

It was evening in Sydney, morning in England. The score stood at 17–17 in the 2003 Rugby World Cup final. Mrs Philippa Wilkinson walked around her local supermarket while, on the other side of the world, her son Jonny walked around a rugby pitch, seconds away from metamorphosing from man to superhero with a speed previously matched only by Peter Parker and Clark Kent. Mrs Wilkinson filled her basket. She was too anxious to watch her son play out the final moments of one of the greatest World Cup finals ever staged. You rather understood how she felt.

Journalists in the press box watched through gently parted fingers as the seconds ticked down. The crowd screamed and the coaches paced backwards and forwards in their little glass box, their eyes never leaving the pitch. It was sport at its absolute best. You dare not whisper lest the atmospheric shield cracked and a little of the tension ebbed away. Everyone was nervous except, it seemed, the players. All the composure belonged to them. It was injury time and the England players, who had been dismissed as old and unfit, were on the verge of making history by becoming the first northern-hemisphere winners of the World Cup, after one of the most successful years in English rugby history.

The year had started on a sour note for England. The night before their first Six Nations Championship game, against France at Twickenham, news came that a young England player called Nick Duncombe had died from blood poisoning. The twenty-one-year old had won two England caps in the 2002 Six Nations. The whole squad was torn apart by the news. His Quins club-mate Jason Leonard, winning his one hundredth cap, led out the team under a cloud of disbelief.

England did not play well – and, given the circumstances, who could blame them? – but they won 25–17. To beat France while playing badly was a phenomenal achievement – one down, four to go. It was vital that they won the Grand Slam this year. Clive had told the team, 'If you don't win the Grand Slam, you won't win the World Cup.' He wanted them to feel pressure and come through it. More than anything, he wanted them to go to Australia as the best team in Europe. Against Wales in Cardiff, England won 26–9 in an improved game, but still lacked discipline. By the time they met Italy, they had improved enormously, scoring thirty-three points in the first quarter to win 40–5. Scotland were beaten 40–9, which meant the game against Ireland at Lansdowne Road would be the Grand Slam decider. This time, they did it, winning 42–6. In a phenomenal display of rugby they proved they were, without doubt, Europe's best rugby side. They had lost just four of their last thirty-five games.

'I think it was the Grand Slam game in Dublin that made everyone really sit up and take notice,' said Fran Cotton. 'That's when people started thinking, "You know, they could do this. They could win the World Cup." It's certainly when I started having absolute faith in them.'

In Sydney, the tension was mounting. Clive came down from the coaches' box and sat on the end of the replacements' bench, next to the guys whose role in this England team had been so incredibly important – those players who hadn't made it on to the field for the final game but whose hard work had put England there.

Clive watched as the teams kicked off after the penalty that had taken them to 17–17. Mat Rogers sliced his kick into touch after an attempted charge down by Lewis Moody, sending the ball out of play within 35 metres of the Australia line. This was England's big moment. They had control of the ball as the seconds ticked down. What would they do at the lineout? Steve Thompson walked to the front and prepared to throw the best ball of his life. It had to go long. It had to go to

the back for Lewis Moody so the forwards could provide quick ball for
the backs. If they did not do that, they would not get the vital score
they needed in order to win. Could Thompson do it? Johnson nodded
and Thompson called the move.

Clive saw the lineout call and knew they were going for the zigzag
move – a routine that would give them the best chance of a drop goal.
The move was designed to get Wilkinson in front of the uprights. It
necessitated the other players controlling the ball in contact and
making quick breaks to take the team farther up the pitch. Before any
of that could be achieved, Thompson had to get his throw absolutely
right. All the pressure was on him. He had been training with a visual
awareness coach and had a full-time lineout coach to assist him. What
difference would those small factors make now, under pressure in the
World Cup final? Could Thompson deliver? Yes. Clean over the line it
went. Lewis Moody flipped it down to secure the quick possession
they so desperately needed. The ball was in the backs and the posts
were tantalisingly close. The zigzag move was on. Clive leapt up off the
bench and screamed with all his might at players who could not hear
him.

After the Six Nations Championship of 2003 came the summer tour to
New Zealand and Australia that would add layer after layer to the
players' confidence. While the players were away, the pitch at Pennyhill
Park was dug up and relaid. Clive was still looking for those crucial
percentage increases, even as the World Cup loomed before them. The
summer tour provided England with an opportunity to impress upon
the rugby world how ready they were.

'There had been a big bust-up in the RFU about that tour,' recalls
Cotton. 'Francis wanted to do two Tests in Australia, but I was very
keen for England to be given the chance to play New Zealand. I
remembered 1995 when Lomu appeared and no one had expected
him. I didn't want that to happen again. No one in the England set-up
wanted any surprises, so I made quite a fuss about England playing
there that summer.'

Thank goodness he did. England beat the Maoris first, then went on to beat the All Blacks on New Zealand soil for only the second time in history, winning 15–13 in Wellington, despite losing Neil Back and Lawrence Dallaglio to the sin bin.

In Melbourne, they beat Australia 25–14, winning on Aussie soil for the first time in history. It was an astounding achievement and Clive was at his bolshie, confident best. He'd endured a week of Pommie-bashing and chose the post-match press conference as the stage for his retaliation.

'Test rugby is an unforgiving place and it is about winning. I think that one or two people in this part of the world have forgotten that,' he said, provocatively.

He was swiftly described as rugby's answer to Douglas Jardine. Clive read all he could about the controversial Jardine, captain of the England cricket team on their Bodyline series to Australia in 1932–33. Clive declared himself thrilled with the comparison, and announced that England would win the World Cup. The rest of the world silently accepted that they would be difficult to beat. The World Cup had just got a hell of a lot harder for the southern hemisphere sides.

After the tour, Clive insisted that the players travel to Perth, venue for the first game of the World Cup. They stayed at the hotel they would stay in for the tournament, and trained at the local school.

England returned to face Wales at the Millennium Stadium, winning 43–9, before moving on to Marseilles for their penultimate game, the first of a two–match contest against France. They lost narrowly, 17–16, despite not having their best side on the pitch – the French have never been defeated in Marseilles – but England won at Twickenham 45–14 with a full side.

The pre-tournament build-up was not over yet. England had ten weeks of non-stop training with the specialist coaches, and with Dave Reddin hovering over the players menacingly, beating them into shape. To have such a huge amount of time with the players all together at the hotel was, as Clive said, 'a dream come true'. At the end of it, he declared, 'We are ready,' and it did seem as if he had a point.

From Moody the lineout ball went to Mike Catt. Would it go to Jonny Wilkinson for the kick of his life? No. Think of the zigzag routine. Wilkinson needs to be closer to be sure of victory. Somehow, in the deafening din of the stadium, worn out and mentally exhausted, seconds away from victory or defeat in the biggest match of their lives, the players thought so correctly under pressure that even now, a few years later, their calmness seems staggering. They needed to get Wilkinson closer to the posts. He might have scored anyway – we'll never know – but 'might' wasn't nearly good enough. Catt recycled and passed to Matt Dawson, the scrum-half. Would he pass to Wilkinson? No. Don't take the easy option, take the right option. Dawson showed such courage, setting off through the smallest of gaps and making those extra strides, around a dozen of them, each one crucial in getting Wilkinson to within striking distance.

Dawson sent the ball back again and in came Johnson. How appropriate that the greatest captain the game has ever known should step into the fray now, when needed most. Johnson took it on. The seconds ticked down. Time was running out. They had to get the ball to Wilkinson, but Johnson knew it had to be the right ball. They would get one chance. Johnson went up the side of the ruck and laid the ball down carefully. Then there was Dawson. This was it. The clocks stopped ticking and hearts stopped beating as Dawson passed to Wilkinson. Millions of people all over the world knew what would happen next. Mrs Wilkinson was in the fruit and veg section at the time. Would her boy do it?

England's first match of the World Cup was against Georgia in Perth, where Clive had taken the team after their summer tour. They were familiar with the place so they settled in quickly and won convincingly, 84–6. Then came South Africa – the 'must-win' game. In 1999, England had lost to New Zealand in the pool games and created a difficult path for themselves through the tournament, which resulted in them crashing out against South Africa in the quarter-final. They had to win this one to assert themselves early on, develop confidence and get the best possible route through the competition. However, South

Africa felt the same way. They were aware that this was a 'must-win' game and they wanted victory just as much as England did.

Before the match, pictures were released of the South Africans training with tackle bags marked with the England players' shirt numbers. Certain tackle bags, including the one with number 10 written on it, were being attacked with particular vigour. Despite this, they were nowhere near good enough to beat England, losing 25–6. The men in white moved steadily on, beating Samoa by 35–22 and Uruguay 111–13, to set up a quarter-final clash with Wales. This was the first match of the knock-out stages. The winner would proceed to the semi-final, and be based at the Manly Pacific Hotel in Sydney. For the losing side, it would be all over.

Wales arrived in Brisbane fresh from a stunning pool match against New Zealand, in which they'd given the All Blacks the shock of their lives – in the final quarter of play, they had been leading 37–33. They lost 53–37 in the end, and by eight tries to four, but they had shown that they were coming into form at exactly the right time. England had watched the match and knew that their opponents were dangerous.

The staff at the Manly Pacific – the hotel where Clive had stayed twenty years previously – watched the match in a state of mild panic as Wales led 10–3 at half-time.

'We'd guessed that England would go through, and therefore be staying with us for the final two weeks,' said Richard Holt, the hotel manager. 'But Wales were putting up such a good fight that suddenly, it wasn't so clear. The England party consisted of fifty-one people and that was what we'd catered for. If Wales had turned up, we'd have had loads of empty rooms. We were all set up to welcome England and suddenly realised we'd have to change everything.'

However, England pulled back to win 28–17 and headed for Sydney, to Clive's old haunt.

'The England management team were very demanding but in an utterly professional way. They just wanted everything to be absolutely right,' says Holt. 'Louise [Ramsay, the team manager] sent over a ten-page document on how things should be set up. They wanted a war room and a team room. The war room had a lock on the door and keys were given to Clive, Louise and Andy Robinson. Anyone wanting to go into the room – to replenish food and drink, for instance – had to be accompanied. There was even a shredder in the room so that when the guys came to empty the bins, they took away shredded documents with nothing that could be used.

'Then there were the food requirements. The team chef had been in touch by email and designed the menu for the players. They wanted loads of food in very small portions to aid digestion.'

In due course, the team arrived at their new base to prepare for a semi-final against France. There was a stunning difference between the preparations of the two teams, which exhibited itself at every level. England player interviews, for instance, were monitored and access to the hotel required a pass. At the French hotel, you could just wander in and chat to the players. I interviewed the French captain while walking along the prom eating an ice cream. The England captain gave few interviews and those he did give were short, sharp and desperately lacking in revelations of any kind. The French seemed relaxed, happy and confident. The English players seemed dour and unforthcoming. There was a mild fear that France would turn up, spin the ball wide and end all England's dreams. Happily, that didn't happen. England dominated the semi-final, winning 24–7, despite not scoring a try.

'Beating France was the best game of the competition,' said Cotton. 'I had lunch with Clive in Manly before it, and sat with a totally confident man. He was genuinely very confident. You couldn't help but predict an England win.'

Jason Leonard became the most capped player of all time in that match, and Johnson became the second Englishman in history to lead a team into a Rugby World Cup final. Will Carling was the first in 1991, when England lost to Australia at Twickenham. Would things be different this time?

The world's greatest kicker stood in front of the posts. This was the moment he had been training for and the moment that Clive had been preparing for. He lifted his right foot, kicked the ball and shattered a million Australian hearts. The ball flew clean over – 20–17. Clive prowled the touchline at the restart, screaming at England to boot the ball into touch as soon as possible. Catt did not hear his words but the

England centre knew what had to be done – he blasted the ball away. The referee lifted his whistle to his mouth and the rugby world tilted on its axis. England had won the World Cup.

Clive ran on to the field amid scenes of jubilation. 'Swing Low' echoed around the ground as they were all presented with their medals – beaming, muddy, blood-encrusted faces filled the large screens around the stadium. Then the trophy was handed to the magnificent captain. The players touched it and handed it to Clive. The crowd roared their approval, and Clive just looked down, deep into the gleaming golden Cup in his hands. He stared at its shiny surface as you might gaze upon the face of a lover, lost in thought and mesmerised by its beauty. Tickertape rained down around him and the crowd's chant changed to 'Clive, Clive, Clive'. Fireworks filled the night sky. He began to lift the trophy above his head, a smile creeping across his lips.

A different life lay ahead now. The rejection of being sent away to school and the horrors of life at HMS *Conway* were all behind him. The joy of Loughborough and the delights of Leicester with Jim and Chalkie – what giants! Rank Xerox and working in Australia, then Henley and the great triumphs, London Irish and shirt swapping, Bath, England Under-21s, then England. Especially England. This England. These men. This moment. This Cup that he promised he would win. One man, one mission, one giant, resounding victory – the biggest three points in the world. He lifted the Cup aloft, smiling out into the distance as the cameras flashed all around him.

SECTION FIVE

Chapter Twenty-seven

Stormy knight

---

*'Once we'd won the World Cup, we thought nothing would ever
be the same again. Everything was great. Perfect. Wonderful. And it
always would be. We thought every day would be like that. Then you
come back down to earth and realise that it won't.'*
Martin Johnson, England's World Cup-winning captain

To be fair to Johnson, he was almost right – maybe not perfect forever,
but the period of national celebration following the World Cup win
was all consuming and quite unprecedented. The Queen watched the
match on television and sent a telegram congratulating the team on a
'great victory'. Tony Blair watched the game at Chequers. He wrote,
too, declaring, 'This was a fantastic day for English rugby and for
England. The team can be proud of their performance, their spirit and
above all their character.'

Ministers rushed to add their sentiments. William Hill the book-
makers said it was the biggest ever rugby match for betting, with £5
million gambled. The telegrams kept coming. David Beckham and
Sven-Goran Eriksson, the England football captain and coach respectively, added their words of praise. 'You could see the belief they had in
themselves,' said Eriksson. 'We must give credit to Clive Woodward and
every single player. Congratulations to them all.'

The players' beaming faces filled the front pages of every newspaper,
while vivid descriptions of their heroic actions crammed the back.
Columnists rushed to compliment them – even the Australian newspapers spoke of the remarkable achievements of the England team – but
while the celebrations moved into overdrive, Clive's focus had already

moved to the future. England had won by three points in the final seconds of extra time after all the work that had been done. Hours, days, weeks, months, years in preparation and they had won by the narrowest of margins.

He was aware that the World Cup-winning team would not be together in four years' time. While far from being the 'old men' that Australian newspapers had labelled them, it was certainly true that many of the players were approaching retirement. If Clive was to have a chance of keeping England as the world's number-one team, and push for a second World Cup win, something that had never been done before, he had to start work straightaway. In 1999, England's defeat in the World Cup had been the beginning of the campaign to win in 2003. He needed to do the same this time to have a chance of victory in 2007. Urgent meetings were undoubtedly being called in New Zealand and Australia, as had happened in England in 1999. The coaches would be starting immediately on lifting the standard of their game. Clive's fear that this would happen proved justified. Just a year after the World Cup, the New Zealand team started using Verusco Analysis – computer systems designed to prepare complex statistics and videos by breakfast time the day after an international match. They were brought in as a direct response to Prozone, the England team's system.

On the lengthy flight back to Heathrow, many of the tour party continued celebrating while others chose to catch up on missed sleep. The plane had been renamed *Sweet Chariot* for the occasion. The World Cup was paraded down the aisles, players chatted to the fans aboard and all was well with the world. While they partied, their coach was busy jotting down notes. England had won because they had what Clive described as 'a freakishly good group of players' and because those players believed they could win it. That had taken a lot of time, thought and hard work. Now they had done it and were returning with the most precious trophy in the game, Clive hoped the RFU would realise what he could do. After all, he had proven that, with the right support, he could deliver at the highest level.

It had been England's ability to cope under extreme pressure that had led to the triumph. Had they not thought properly in the closing minutes of the game, they would not have won. T-Cup (Thinking clearly under pressure) had done it; all that preparation had done it.

Could he take the players down to spend time with the Marines again? Could he create an environment in which the match-day pressure was replicated? To do that, he would need more time with the players, and just how much time he would have depended on the outcome of crucial ongoing negotiations (which eventually resulted in the Elite Playing Squad programme) between the clubs and the RFU. Talks had begun back in March, some six months before the World Cup kicked off, and no agreement had been reached. Behind the scenes, debates were raging all through the tournament. Clive wanted the RFU to negotiate harder. He'd had the players for twenty-two days in season 2002–03 and felt he needed them for longer than that if he were to take them to a higher level.

The arrival at Heathrow Airport was tumultuous with thousands of people at silly o'clock in the morning, all desperate to catch a glimpse of the players. Most of the players looked tired and dishevelled as they filed out of the terminal. Jonny Wilkinson, though, beamed his youthful smile and looked for all the world as if he'd spent three weeks on a health farm. Clive wanted them to stay together, but they were bundled on to two separate coaches so that corporate sponsors could mingle with them *en route* to Pennyhill Park Hotel, where they were to go straight into a press conference. No one had told Clive about that, either, and the players recall him becoming increasingly frustrated. He'd had total control for months but now, in the hour of their greatest triumph, they were slipping away from him. No one was consulting him; no one was consulting the players. Nothing would ever be the same again for Team England.

As it was for the team, so it was for the individuals. Their lives were changed beyond recognition by the victory. Suddenly, they were superstars and the calls on their time were overwhelming. It wasn't just the dinners, lunches, awards and press interviews; there were also charity requests and individual requests. Autographs had to be signed at every turn and players felt themselves pushed and pulled all over the place as everyone fought for a slice of the heroes.

After the press conference, Wilkinson said goodbye to Clive.

'How are you getting back?' asked the England coach.

'I'll grab a taxi back to Heathrow and jump on a plane,' replied Wilkinson.

'You can't do that,' said Clive. 'You'll be mobbed.' Wilkinson had no idea of the level of fame to which he had been raised by that kick.

'I'll be fine,' he insisted.

In the end, Clive leant Wilkinson his car and driver and the new golden boy of British sport travelled home in style.

As the players dispersed, Clive headed home, eager to start planning England's next campaign. Clive's reaction to victory is unusual. For him, the thirst to win is not sated by victory. Each success spurs him on to strive for more, to keep searching for challenges. World Cup 2003 confirmed to Clive that he was doing something right. Now, new players had to be brought in and the management team would need to be shaken up. He could waste no time, but at the RFU, his renewed vigour and determination found no parallel. When he tried to arrange meetings, he was batted away. No one wanted to know.

'No one had the time to see me. I was banging on doors, trying to get people to talk to me, but it was no good,' he says. In truth, no one understood why he wanted to see them. He had done it. He had won the World Cup. Why not relax and enjoy the moment, then replicate the success in four years' time? What was the problem? Clive's frustration was boiling over.

In 1999, after defeat in the quarter-final, he'd been called straight in and asked to produce a report. This time, no one cared. The contrast bit deeply. It was fundamentally at odds with his own frequently expressed views on management – learn from the positives. Gather all the information you can about the things that go right, and don't obsess about the things that go wrong.

In an interview that I conducted with Clive before the World Cup, he said, 'In business, if you're winning, you tend to go down the pub and open the champagne. When you lose, it's the eight a.m. crisis meeting. To me, it should be the complete opposite – when you've done something really good, have an eight o'clock meeting to find out why. If you lose, go down to the pub and have a beer and stay cool about it. If you keep losing, you've got to change things dramatically, but if not, then carry on doing things right and carry on believing you can win next time.'

'I remember talking to Clive immediately after the World Cup,' says Tessa Jowell, Minister for Culture, Media and Sport. 'He said he was already thinking about how they could win in 2007. Everyone else was enjoying the victory but he'd moved on. I thought that was extraordinary.'

There were urgent issues that Clive wanted to discuss with his employers. First, he needed to establish whether there would be any more money available for him to spend on the team. He was eager to make even more changes at Pennyhill Park. He wanted to get the care of the players absolutely right. Clive had visited the laboratory at AC Milan football club in Italy, where the club analyse and devise programmes for all their players. AC Milan have the smallest squad in world soccer by keeping the players they have in the best possible health and fitness. This philosophy appealed to Clive and he wanted to create a similar set-up at Pennyhill Park. He spoke to the Pecorelli family and jointly they established that it would cost around £10 million for such a centre of excellence to be created. In order to keep working on 'thinking correctly under pressure' – the mantra that he had chanted before the World Cup – the new facilities would include a 'Performance Zone' where the players could practise their skills with jeering, cheering, wind, litter and rain to contend with. The aim of the centre was to replicate match-day conditions as closely as possible.

When Clive eventually got to see Baron, and to discuss the future with him, Baron refused to part with any more RFU money. Clive was incensed that £100 million was being spent on the redevelopment of the South Stand at Twickenham, but no money could be invested in a centre that he strongly believed would lead to greater success for England rugby. He had thought the World Cup victory would change everything and it hadn't changed anything, not in any real sense. Attitudes remained the same. He felt as isolated as ever.

Outwardly, everything seemed rosy. On an unforgettable Monday in December, a victory parade through the streets of Central London attracted more than 750,000 people. No one had an inkling of the anger Clive was feeling at the organisation of the parade, with the players again split between two buses. Clive was desperate for them all to be together – no superstars, just one team, in it together. The parade was followed by an appointment with the Queen at Buckingham Palace and a Downing Street reception hosted by the Prime Minister. By the end of the year, Clive had been knighted and won numerous awards. His entire team were weighed down by accolades and exhausted from celebratory parties. Clive continued to push for changes and improvements, determined to find a way of making his plans for England work – with or without the RFU's support.

'He had become a national hero overnight, and quite rightly so,' says Baron, 'but he suddenly found he was able to talk directly to a cabinet minister. He was bypassing the normal channels and when you do that it just upsets everybody. OK, it's nice to be invited in to see the Secretary of State and think you're doing a deal with her, but it just pisses off all the officials. He was a very restless soul after 2003. I sensed that, in a way, he felt he was operating on a bigger and higher platform. I just noticed changes in him and we did have some very difficult discussions because, as I say, he was suddenly talking directly to ministers.'

Why would he be 'talking directly to ministers'? To whom was he talking that so upset the RFU?

Tessa Jowell smiles politely as she tears around her Central London office, trying to deal with a dozen questions, phone calls and reminders while eating her lunch. Her office has the look of a hotel suite – plush, thick carpets and panoramic views over London. She whisks me in and settles me on to the sort of plump sofa that rarely exists away from film sets and furniture-shop advertisements.

'Just a second. I have to have a quick word with my private secretary,' she says, disappearing into a side room where a collection of civil servants are bashing away on keyboards and answering phones. Jowell discusses the afternoon's activities.

'Yes, we need to check that with Tony first,' she says, over her shoulder as she walks back into the room.

'And Prince Charles's briefing at five,' shouts her assistant.

'Of course,' replies Jowell, retrieving a banana from deep inside one of her desk drawers and coming to join me. 'Do you want half?' she asks, indicating the banana.

How entirely disarming. I don't think anyone has offered me half a banana since I left junior school. There is something warm and hospitable about Tessa Jowell. She has a wide-eyed, enthusiastic quality and the same understated authority that Clive displays. It's not hard to see how they might have got along so well.

Jowell first got to know Clive when she invited him and Jayne to dinner at the House of Commons to congratulate him on the World Cup victory. The two had previously been introduced at what Jowell describes as 'semi-formal' functions, but it was on this occasion that they talked properly.

'And I was impressed,' says Jowell. 'He is an utterly inspiring man. There is something about his certainty and the confidence he has in his judgements that is very inspiring.'

Over dinner, Clive mentioned the idea he had for a centre of excellence, incorporating a zone where moments of intense pressure in any sport would be replicated. Jowell thought it was a fantastic idea.

'I just thought it was absolutely right, just what was needed. One of the things about Clive is that he views élite performance as just that, regardless of sport. I wanted it to work, so I put him in touch with Sport England.

'Sometimes you back people. The funding for the stress centre [Performance Zone] wasn't my decision and I wouldn't have sought to influence it, but from time to time you think, "This is someone special, he's outstanding. I'll back him." Sometimes organisations are not good at bending to adapt to the needs of an extraordinary individual, and I think Clive has some extraordinary talents.

'I think Clive is a giant in British sport. If he says he's going to do something, he will just do it. He inspires people to follow him and you always feel a bit taller when you've spent time with him – which is a rare gift.'

Clive was put in touch with Roger Draper at Sport England, but it was corporate money that he really needed to get the whole thing off the ground. He approached Dianne Thompson, chief executive of Camelot, who advised him to talk to the National Lottery's corporate sponsorship department, which he duly did. Two representatives came to Pennyhill Park, together with sponsorship adviser Tim Stemp.

'We walked in and there were three chairs in the middle of the room,' says Stemp. 'Around us sat the coaches and the owner of Penny-hill Park. We were surrounded. It was a very odd set-up.'

Clive went through his speech about the centre, assisted by Dave Reddin, Dave Alred and Tony Biscombe, with Mr Pecorelli confirming the hotel's commitment to the project.

'It was all very surreal because the project had nothing to do with the RFU at all – it was an independent project that they wanted to do for Team England. It was impressive but, in the end, we had to say no because it was hard to back something that did not come from a governing body. It's difficult to pour a lot of corporate money into a project when there's just an individual in charge. If he left, would it all stop? It's a shame the RFU weren't on board – then the whole thing might have worked. Having said that, perhaps he wouldn't have got to that stage if he'd been waiting for the RFU to take a lead – who knows?'

Clive became increasingly agitated by the whole situation. If the project had been backed by Baron, it could possibly have attracted the funding. Now he was facing an uphill struggle to get the centre under way when he was confident it would reap massive benefits for the team.

At the end of 2003, England played their first match since the World Cup, against New Zealand Barbarians at Twickenham. Clive was eager to use this game to bring the players back together, dust off the cobwebs and begin the new era. In the event, he was told that he could choose no more than three players from each club. Even when he complied with those strictures, he found the players he wanted were unavailable and he was offered alternatives.

He left for his Christmas skiing holiday with stirrings of concern. Martin Johnson, the England captain, announced his retirement – the first of many leading England players to do so – and Clive was feeling ostracised by the RFU and not in control. In order to regain some sense of authority, he organised a major coaching conference at the end of January 2004. It was a three-line whip for all coaches. Brian Ashton was also asked to attend, to give his verdict on new players.

Clive wanted to start building for the future, so he had told the England players that if they were not available to tour in the summer of 2004, they would not be able to play in the Six Nations Championship. It was a decision he would live to regret as players retired earlier than they would have done.

The coaching conference was titled 'With passion – nothing is impossible'. All coaches were instructed to be ready to 'examine every area of what we are doing, and what we have to do to go Beyond Number One (BNO).' The conference ended on a positive note and, shortly afterwards, England played their first match in the Six Nations Championship, against Italy in Rome. Lawrence Dallaglio was made captain and the team won 50–9. After that, they won in Scotland by 35–13, but Clive remained unhappy. The amount of training time he had with the players was insufficient. New players were coming in and not being guided properly. Players were being drafted into dinners in international weeks that Clive knew nothing about. Companies were organising functions at Pennyhill Park so that players could be brought in to say a few words. Against Ireland, it all caught up with them. Ireland won by 19–13, bringing to an end the record run of twenty-two consecutive wins at Twickenham. They had gone into the match on the back of two training sessions. The last time they'd done that had been in 2001 when they'd lost the Grand Slam in Ireland. It was as if they had gone back in time.

Before the game, Clive had set the team a challenge to try to score seven tries in the match. Many of the other coaches thought this was a mistake but, rather than speak up, they kept quiet. In the build-up to the World Cup, they'd often challenged one another but then the environment had been conducive to authoritative and confident behaviour. Everything had changed now. There wasn't enough time to work on the team. Random targets were set. Nothing was coordinated. All the control had gone.

England went on to beat Wales by 31–21 at Twickenham but standards had slipped. They travelled to Paris and lost 24–21, despite a great second-half comeback. The defeat allowed the French to win the Grand Slam. England dropped from their position as the world's number-one team.

There is no question that the exodus of top players accelerated

England's decline. Other very talented players were waiting in the wings to take their places, but to lose so many experienced players in such a short space of time, without having the training days with the younger players, was catastrophic. Clive has apologised publicly for his role in precipitating the break-up of the team. With hindsight, it was an error to force so many of his key men into early retirement in his determination to recruit players for the future – and it appeared to contradict his long-held belief that a coach should always pick on form and have only the next game in mind.

Neil Back and Jason Leonard were on the wrong end of Clive's ruthless selection policies. Back was left out of the squad for the match against Italy and England missed him. He spent his time away from the squad contemplating his future – would he ever get back into the first team again? Clive called him after the game in Italy, and told him he was being selected for the next one. Back was thrilled but explained that he had done a lot of thinking and had decided not to tour in the summer. Back was not picked for the next game after all – an England career ended.

Leonard also received a call from Clive before the Italian game, telling him that he would not be in the team or on the bench for the next game – that place would be taken by Matt Stewart. 'Clive thought it was time to blood new players and look to the future,' says Leonard, who reacted angrily to the news, suggesting to Clive that he put Stewart straight in the team to test the young prop in an international match. 'He'll get murdered,' said Leonard. 'Just put him in the team and you'll see. I'll be back in the team next week then.' Clive did not change his plans and Stewart was on the bench.

The following Monday, the England players and Clive were all at an O2 sponsorship lunch in the Spirit of Rugby restaurant at Twickenham. When Leonard went to the toilets, Clive followed him. As they stood side by side, Clive said, 'Julian White is fit, so he'll be in on Saturday.' Leonard looked at Clive in amazement. In that short sentence, Clive had ended the longest international career in rugby history.

'I felt like turning round and pissing all over his shoes,' says Leonard. 'There is so much about Clive that is great. He had moments of brilliance as England coach, but I could hardly believe he'd done that. I would never play for England again. Never get to run out at Twickenham again. I just couldn't believe he would tell me like that. In there.'

The summer tour to the southern hemisphere consisted of two Tests against the All Blacks and one against the Wallabies. As Clive selected his players, he realised that he would not be able to take twelve of his World Cup squad with him because they were injured or exhausted after returning from Australia and going straight into club fixtures.

The tour was a disaster. Clive described it as being so much worse than the tour to hell that he had endured nine months into his appointment. He felt he was right back at the beginning again. They lost 36–3 and 36–12 to New Zealand. Then they lost 51–15 to Australia in Brisbane. Just five of England's World Cup final starting team ran out to face the Wallabies. The next day, 26 June, the final outcome of the protracted negotiations between the clubs and the RFU was announced to the world, encapsulated in a document called the Elite Playing Squad (EPS) agreement. Under the agreement, Clive would have just sixteen days a year with England. He returned from Australia harbouring serious doubts about the future. The disappointment of discovering that Twickenham would not back his plans to build a state-of-the-art training and conditioning centre that would help England to move on to the next stage had deeply wounded him. The signing of an EPS programme that prevented him having the time he needed with England made him realise that even if he built his centre using independent finance, it would be pointless. Without enough access to the players, the greatest training systems in the world were futile. These two events made him contemplate his future with England and, once he had started having doubts, he wondered whether he could carry on. After he returned from the tour, something else happened to convince him that he couldn't.

Chapter Twenty-eight

Why did Clive really walk out?

---

*'The true mystery of the world is the visible,
not the invisible.'* **Oscar Wilde**

At 10 p.m. on Saturday, 28 August, the *Match of the Day* theme tune burst into sitting rooms around the country and sports fans settled on their sofas to catch the highlights of the day's play. One of the featured games was Southampton versus Chelsea. Chelsea had battled to a 2–1 win and the cameras panned around the crowd as the final whistle blew, settling on the directors' box where Rupert Lowe, the Southampton chairman, sat chewing his fingernails in anxiety. Also present was Sir Clive Woodward, watching intently. The focus returned to the studio for expert opinions on the match. 'What do you reckon?' asked Gary Lineker. 'Sir Clive Woodward to coach Southampton?' Oh, how they laughed in the studio. Alan Hansen thought it ridiculous beyond words and they agreed wholeheartedly that Clive was not there with any aspirations to coach the team. He couldn't be. He was a rugby coach. He was friendly with Lowe. Wasn't that it? Surely that's all it was. The men in the studio laughed again and returned to their match analysis.

On Monday, 30 August, the *Daily Mail* broke the sports news story of the year. Jeff Powell, chief features writer and one of the most experienced and respected sports journalists in the country, announced that Clive was quitting rugby to go into football. 'Eh?' said the nation. You can only imagine what Hansen said. Clive's goals had changed, claimed the piece. From now on, he would work to become the new England football coach.

Could it be true? Had Powell gone nuts? If not, had Clive gone nuts?

It was certainly one or the other. Most of the sensible money was on Powell as the day began but by lunchtime it was clear that Clive was indeed leaving the RFU. Conflicting stories circulated about whether he was really going in to football, but Powell's story gained credibility as the day progressed. Clive would be attending courses in an attempt to earn the badges that would be essential for him to progress as a football coach. He was planning to leave rugby for football. People would have been less surprised if Clive had announced that he was planning a sex change.

However, it wasn't quite the case that Clive was leaving rugby for football. Powell's report was right. Clive had offered his resignation as coach of the England team, and he intended to work his way through football coaching courses with the aim of taking a position at a football club to learn the ropes, but what has become abundantly clear during the research for this book is that Clive did not leave rugby *for* football. He decided to leave his job as coach of the England rugby team for four clear reasons that were unrelated to his ambitions in football.

Clive was first approached by the Football Association before the World Cup had kicked off. If he'd had any immediate, burning ambitions to go into football, it would have made absolute sense for him to have gone straight afterwards. Why wait? Why charge around the country trying to set up a new training centre at Pennyhill Park? Clive returned from Australia believing that he could take the England team on to greater things, and determined to push the boundaries farther on critical non-essentials, bring in new coaches, new players and new ideas. He knew there was much more to do and believed the RFU would back him in his efforts to do it, despite his volatile relationship with his employers, but they weren't. Clive became so disillusioned that he left and the first reason for this was the dreaded EPS agreement, which caused such bitterness and resentment between the parties involved. In my view, it lies at the heart of Clive's decision to go but is by no means the only reason.

When rugby went professional, the clubs signed up the players and so the national side has to barter with them for players' time. This bartering used to take place annually and resulted in an agreement – most recently called the Elite Playing Squad agreement – that was signed by the RFU and Professional Rugby Ltd (PRL), the organisation that represented the clubs. The agreement was due to be renewed by 5 September 2003, just before the World Cup, but this time the RFU was eager for it to cover the four years up to the next World Cup in September 2007. This would enable the national coaches to plan their training programmes in advance and spare everyone the painful process of annual negotiations. So far, so good.

The trouble was that the two sides were polarised, wanting entirely different things. Naturally, the clubs wanted their players with them as much as possible, while Clive wanted more access to them for England. He wanted to be able to work with his squad as the southern-hemisphere countries work with their players. He wanted to take England into tournaments on the basis of professionals against professionals. He wanted a level playing field.

This club-versus-country debate is pertinent to rugby more than to cricket or football. In cricket, the players are signed to the national team via central contracts. In football, they are signed to clubs, but this is the case around the world. If Brazil were to meet England in the World Cup final, both sides would know that they had had roughly equal amounts of preparation time as a team, because of players' club commitments. This is not the case in rugby. Clive wanted central contracts for rugby, like the other nations had, but whenever he suggested it, he was told by the RFU that it was too difficult. If they tried to do that, there would be revolution. Clive thought that, after seeing the reaction of the fans to the World Cup, the RFU would realise how important it was and change everything to make sure England won it again, revolution or not. They didn't – they just opened the floodgates to more bargaining. The clubs wanted primacy of control, whereas Clive felt that England should be in charge. In areas such as fitness, nutrition and medicine, this was vitally important. How could two doctors with entirely different aims negotiate on the medical welfare of players?

'Sometimes a player is fit to play, other times he is clearly unfit to play. That's simple,' says Dr Simon Kemp, 'but there are times when it's not clear, and the doctor has to make the call. Any number of doctors may make a different decision about what's best. It's very difficult to be in the position where you think a player is unfit to play, then see him run out for his club the following week because the club doctor thinks differently.'

A draft document had been compiled by the RFU and sent to PRL for discussion at their board meeting on 19 April. The proposal was circulated by Baron, with a note attached: 'I expect we are not at the very end of the process but unless we start to put some pressure on PRL they will still be talking about this next year.' In other words, the RFU were keen to get the proposal pushed through as quickly as possible. Clive was not. He was appalled by the proposed document and contacted everyone he could to express his dismay. He objected to several specific points:

1. The number of proposed training days.
2. Primacy of control still rested with the directors of rugby at the clubs and Clive felt strongly that the national team should have that.
3. England were allowed to use players in ten matches, whereas the clubs could use players in thirty-two. What disturbed Clive most about this rule was that only 'full matches' counted, so players brought on as substitutes, coming off injured or playing up to 40% of a game may find themselves playing vastly more rugby than this. It all meant that England players would be exhausted by their club commitments and suffer more injuries and fatigue than any other players in world rugby.
4. In the same vein, Clive was eager that players should have a proper rest period in the summer. Guided by injury audits and medical reports, he was adamant that players should have an eleven-week rest period in one continual block. This was interpreted in the document as players having a total of eleven weeks off, including 'rest weekends' and *ad hoc* weeks through the season. Clive and the England medical team felt this negated the whole point of the long break.
5. Clive had been told that he would be in control of 'when and where' his England training days would be, but in the document it stipulated that most of his training days would be on a Monday or Tuesday, when players were still battered and bruised from Sunday matches.
6. The number of players he was permitted to have in his squad had been reduced from fifty-five to forty.

Clive's heated contributions to the negotiations, and his unwillingness to compromise on any issues that he believed adversely affected the players' ability to play well for England, led to him being ostracised from management meetings. This left Chris Spice, the performance director, to negotiate for the RFU against Howard Thomas, then the chief executive of Premier Rugby, and Peter Wheeler, chief executive of Leicester, who were heading up the negotiations on behalf of the clubs. Baron stepped in to assist with negotiations when they appeared to be breaking down.

The clubs played hard ball. Their opening stance was for no training days. Under pressure, they offered ten and the figure crept up from there. This was traditional bargaining. Everyone has done it. When you put an offer in on a house, you offer way below what you are willing to pay. The vendors come back with a figure higher than they are willing to accept. Somewhere in the middle, a compromise is reached. Clive wanted the players full-time, and the clubs offered no days at all. Neither side wanted to compromise. Clive eventually suggested twenty-four days – an increase of just two days on the previous agreement. The clubs suggested sixteen days.

As the team were making final preparations to leave for Australia, a deal was struck whereby Clive agreed to the clubs' demand for sixteen release days a year and twenty in the next World Cup year in return for a guarantee that he could pick the release days. He also insisted that the players have an eleven-week rest period. Nothing was quite as simple as that, though. While he was at the World Cup, he received information that the EPS agreement had been changed without his consent. There would now be fourteen training days and twenty in World Cup years. He wrote back angrily to Baron, saying that the document did not reflect the needs of the team. He added, 'Please make sure everyone knows that this has nothing to do with me.'

Clive consulted Fran Cotton about the situation, much to the annoyance of Baron, who told Clive he wanted to meet him in Perth to discuss the matter face to face. Clive was trying to manage the World Cup campaign and negotiate an important document for the future of England rugby at the same time. The arguments dragged on until the following summer. The rest of the negotiating committee, consisting of Graeme Cattermole, Robert Horner, Malcolm Phillips, Fran Cotton, Jonathan Dance, Paul Murphy, John Owen, Bob Rogers, John Spencer,

Peter Wheeler, Nick Eastwood and Chris Spice, were eager to get the proposal signed. Then, while Clive was pulling the team back together after the 51–15 defeat in Australia, it was.

This was a huge blow to Clive, but it was not the only thing troubling him. More generally, he was also concerned about the way he and his coaches were treated by the RFU. His failure to receive support for his new, all-singing, all-dancing centre at Pennyhill Park was one thing, but he also wanted to make sure his coaches were properly remunerated, and he felt that he was worth more, now that he had proven his credentials. Clive was being offered jobs with other governing bodies, with Sport England and with various businesses. He was turning down a great deal of money to stay with the RFU and felt that they should compensate him. The answer from the RFU was always that the coaches were being paid the market rate, but how can that be defined in this context? What is the market rate for a coach who helps to bring the World Cup to the northern hemisphere for the first time? There is no market.

The third reason for Clive's resignation was the backbiting and in-fighting at the RFU. Clive had felt this keenly when he first arrived and had had many battles with officials on his road to World Cup glory. After the EPS agreement, he felt as if he had many opponents inside the Union and too few allies. Articles appeared in national newspapers doubting his abilities, and he believed the source had to be from within the Union, so he complained. Nothing was done. It would be fair to say, although Clive may disagree, that the only firm ally he had inside the RFU was Fran Cotton.

These issues were brewing in Clive's mind once he returned from the summer tour. Then, on 1 July, he went for his annual appraisal meeting with Baron. That meeting tipped him over the edge and forced him to realise that resignation was the only option if he was to have any chance of keeping his sanity. Not unnaturally, he was expecting a fairly good appraisal, having won the World Cup, but instead, he was presented with a handwritten report more suited to the first year of secondary school. It congratulated him on his victory but marked him down for having lost since the tournament, and for his inability to communicate properly with the commercial department.

This was the final straw. Those who saw Clive leave the meeting at

Twickenham report that he was furious with the fact that he had been so harshly judged. 'He stormed out of the office, clearly very unhappy,' said one observer. 'He hadn't been given five out of a possible five, as everyone would have expected, and he felt patronised.' He was angry for three reasons. First, he was the only person in the entire organisation being judged on England's results, yet his ability to deliver depended on others negotiating time with players. He felt they should all be judged on England's victories. Perhaps then the RFU would be more supportive and accommodating. The second reason was that he could see England slipping farther and farther down the world order because he was being denied the time to do what he needed to do with the players, so his reports would get worse and worse. There was no way of improving the team unless he could spend more time with them. Third, Clive felt that he was being judged by people who knew little about coaching. During his summer holiday, Clive decided not to continue and on his return he went to see Baron.

'The resignation came out of the blue,' says Baron. 'Clive came back from holiday and took me to lunch at the Glass House in Kew and just said that he wanted to take on other challenges. In a way, that's typical of Clive because he can move fairly quickly from one position to another. I mean, if he has a new idea or a new passion, everything has to happen immediately. He's not a reflective person. He's not the sort of bloke you can ask to think about things over a weekend or something like that. When he wants to do something, it has to be done now and I can almost see him in his villa in Portugal, sitting around the pool and just saying to Jayne one day, "You know, I think I'll resign when I get back," which is in effect what he did.'

This seems a slightly harsh summary, considering that Baron must have been aware of the resentment that his appraisal of Clive had caused, and surely he had some indication of the frustrations Clive had been feeling for almost a year.

A formal meeting had already been arranged for three weeks' time, 1 September. Baron insisted that Clive think about his position and they would talk again on that day, but Clive had made up his mind. At the meeting, Clive told Baron that he would see out his contract and the twelve-month notice period, which would mean remaining in the job for the three autumn Test matches. Then he would stand down and work on British and Irish Lions tour planning. Baron insisted that if he wanted to leave, he had to do so straightaway.

'I had this funny feeling that everything wasn't right,' says Fran Cotton. 'You know – when you get this feeling in your water. Clive said he wanted to see me and that he would travel up so we could talk. I met him at the station and said, "You're going to stand down, aren't you?" He just nodded. I thought it was a tremendous shame and a great loss to the game, but he'd had enough.'

Graeme Cattermole was chairman of the management board during this time. It would be fair to say that Cattermole did not enjoy friendly working relationships with either Clive or Baron. So there were tensions between senior RFU officers as well as between Clive and the RFU, between the RFU and the clubs, and between Clive and the clubs. The complications this caused and the extent that this contributed to Clive's frustrations are unquantifiable. In May 2005, Cattermole resigned, and Martyn Thomas was elected as chairman of the management board.

'It's a great source of regret to me that Clive left before I started,' says Thomas, 'both from a personal point of view because I would have enjoyed working with him, but also as a rugby fan. I like to think that it would have been a different scenario if I had been there. I'm sorry that it was frustrations with his employers that led him to leave.'

Thomas is entirely in agreement with Clive that Twickenham can be a frustrating place to work. He accepts wholeheartedly that Clive's desire to spend more time with the players was because he believed this to be the only way in which he could lead them to continuing success. He adds that he is now working hard to make sure the clubs do not run away with the sport's most precious assets.

'The Longform agreement that was originally signed between the clubs and the RFU, back in 2001, was a giant compromise and that's where many recent problems stem from. We need to stop building on that as a way forward and start doing things properly. We need to grasp the nettle and take control of the players.'

This will be of little comfort to Clive, but Thomas is determined to change the way in which the England management relate to the players. He has called the clubs to a series of meetings in which he has demanded more cooperation from them for England, or he will suggest central contracts for the England players.

'We need to sort this out,' he says. 'Clive was right when he complained about the EPS agreement. It is incredibly difficult for coaches to work in those conditions – seeing the players for a couple of weeks a year. I spent a lot of time with the New Zealand committee on the Lions tour – they have total control of the management of players, and they have the sport's best interests at heart at all times. All the successful countries manage their players centrally except England and France. I think it's time to act.'

Thomas says that Baron is firmly with him on this issue and that the two of them are seeking to redress the balance for England. 'We cannot allow the professional game to take over,' he says. 'We are prepared to do whatever it takes to get this right, and to get England winning again.'

Time will tell whether Clive's departure eventually precipitates central contracts for England players. There will be a certain irony in it, if it does. Clive is convinced that with such contracts, he could have taken England to the top of the world order and kept them there.

🏈

At his final press conference, Clive fired shots at the clubs he felt had not supported him and at the RFU officials who had let him down. He says he regrets that press conference now, but it was a masterful performance all the same. He buried his co-interviewees – Baron and Cattermole. He grinned throughout it like a man who simply didn't care any more, a man who was tired of skiing uphill. Then he walked out of Twickenham to a new and very different life.

Chapter Twenty-nine

Clive on Clive

'Things are only impossible until they're not.' Jean-Luc Picard

On a miserable morning in the Midlands, wind-driven rain lashes through the car park of the Telford Conference Centre. It's barely 7 a.m. and still dark – cold, early and wet is not an alluring combination. This time yesterday, Sir Clive Woodward was in Geneva. The day before, he was in South Africa. Today, he is here, inside this cavernous building, pacing up and down and talking to imaginary people, smiling and engaging with empty seats. He clutches a paper cup of tea in one hand as he enthrals the empty room with his witty repartee. He laughs, shrugs and smiles at emptiness. Then he goes back to his notes to make some refinements.

Outside in the car park, the traffic is building. By 8 a.m., the queue has grown to such an extent that the attendant has had to abandon the warmth of his little wooden hut to man the barrier permanently. He has been resisting this up to now, choosing to make the short walk to the barrier every time a car pulled up rather than stand there, battered by the winds and soaked by the rain. He hasn't let go of his tea, though. He holds tightly on to it as he stamps tickets and admits cars. He has found a way of flicking the barrier up with one hand and checking credentials with the other while still holding his mug. It's quite a skill. Finally, by 9 a.m., the traffic is subsiding. He's let around two thousand teachers in for the annual sports colleges' conference – the biggest PE and sports symposium in Europe. One final car arrives. The driver is angry and fed up. He can't find his tickets anywhere, but the passenger

– also a teacher – has so much paperwork associated with the event, all of it bursting out of a scruffy looking sports bag, that the friendly car-park attendant decides to let them in anyway. Then he ambles back to the warmth of his hut and puts on the kettle. The car park is packed. He's got a good couple of hours before anyone arrives or leaves. The rain is still pouring down. He sits on his small wooden stool and takes a tea bag from the plastic container by his side. I don't think a man has ever looked happier.

It's 9.10 a.m. and the two flustered teachers arrive at the main doors. Their frustration with the weather, early morning, traffic and life generally is palpable. They hurl their sports bags over their shoulders and charge through the doors. The man with the scruffy bag drops half of his paperwork, and a woman wearing a bright red buttonhole helps him to retrieve it and directs the two of them to the lecture theatre. Her kindness does nothing to placate them. They moan, audibly, about having to attend. 'I hate these bloody things. They're a waste of time. We never learn anything.'

Clive is standing at the side of the stage in the main lecture theatre, one hand pushed deep into his pocket. He's stopped talking to himself but still looks lost in thought as he stares out across the rabble in front of him. He is dressed smartly in a dark suit, white shirt and red tie. He wears shiny black shoes and clutches his notes in his unpocketed hand. He looks fresh and relaxed, like a man just emerged from a couple of weeks off and a good night's sleep. He's had nothing of the kind, of course. He left his Cookham home at around 5.30 a.m. after three hours' sleep. Lack of sleep is part of the lifestyle. He spent most of the previous week working with Jake White, the South Africa coach who invited the World Cup winner to his coaching conference, desperate for input from the man whose name has become synonymous with sporting victory at the highest level. Before that, he spent a week with each of the home nations. There have also been trips to Brazil to watch football coaching sessions. It's an exciting time.

Clive is in the spotlight now. The angry teachers still look angry. They keep their coats on in an act of minor, silent rebellion. Clive introduces himself and explains that when he took over the England team, in 1997, they were ranked sixth in the world. This is lowly enough, but when you consider that it's the same position they occupied fifteen years before that, when Clive played for them in the early eighties, it's indicative of something of a rut. Whatever England were doing needed to be changed. They needed to think differently about the process of building a successful rugby team. He's in the middle of the stage, slightly nervous, and blinking a little under the bright lights that flood the platform. Half of the lights are blue, half of them are that unflattering halogen explosion of white that makes the healthiest of men look like cadavers. The blue lights trace through the turquoise carpet and bounce off the back wall where Clive's first slide awaits us. 'The Winning Mindset' it says.

'What I'm going to do today is tell you why England won the World Cup,' he says, alluringly. 'I'll explain how England were transformed from a team ranked sixth in the world to a team ranked number one. I'll explain that we did that by changing the players' mindsets,' he says.

There's a shuffling forward in seats. A rustling for notebooks and pens, then a heavy silence settles. He's got them now.

'There are five points – five things you have to do to create a winning mindset. I'm going to explain them. I'm going to explain how my mind works. These five points are crucial. They mean everything. I have them on my mobile phone, on my screensaver and on my laptop.'

The first point is enjoyment. You have to enjoy what you're doing. Harvard Business School reliably informs us that 75 per cent of a person's life is spent at work, so it's vital that time there is enjoyed.

'I believe that if you're an élite athlete, it's a commitment one hundred per cent of the time, so you really have to enjoy what you're doing,' Clive explains. He gave the England players lots of feedback questionnaires to assess what constitutes enjoyment for them. Two factors were mentioned time and time again. First, the England experience must be of a higher quality than their club rugby – they must feel like they are taking a step up in order to fully enjoy it. Second, their definition of enjoyment was coming to an environment that was at the cutting edge of world sport. 'They wanted to be challenged, they were not scared of being ridiculed, they wanted to try new things.'

The second point is lateral thinking. Clive explains to his audience about Dr Paddi Lund. They laugh as he explains that a crazy Brisbane dentist influences much of his thinking on successful environments.

'Paddi redeveloped his business to suit his needs by starting with a blank piece of paper, ignoring everything that had been previously said about how to run a dental practice and totally reworking the model,' he says. Clive describes this as starting with a big empty room, all white. Then you throw out every preconceived idea and everything you do and bring in only what you have to. Question everything. Don't copy. Question everything and see if you can rethink how you run your business.

Along with the notion of questioning everything, central to the Woodward method is the notion of detail, detail, detail. So you throw everything out and think very carefully, examining every possibility for improvement before allowing anything back in. Clive describes his six-f way of thinking, and invites the audience to study the sentence and count the fs. Most count three.

'When I showed that slide to the England team seven years ago, not a single person saw six,' he explains. 'I realised that if England were to be the best team in the world, we had to become a six-f-thinking organisation. We had to notice the detail because the chances are that our main competitors – New Zealand, Australia and South Africa – would be seeing only three.'

So you start with your empty white room, having thrown everything out of the window, then you bring everything back in after analysing it with six-f thinking. 'Paddi thinking is known as thinking laterally, and six-f thinking is known as thinking vertically,' he says.

Clive shows a clip of Jason Robinson, flying through the defence. Opposition players reach to tackle him, but he slithers away, thanks to Lycra. Robinson wouldn't have scored had he been wearing the old baggy shirt. Did the changed shirt lead to England winning the World Cup? No, but it was one of the details that added up to victory. Lateral and vertical thinking won the World Cup. Clive is sure of that. Thinking differently won the World Cup – as it wins most things.

The third point in Clive's five-point strategy is the concept of critical non-essentials. Clive asked himself how many sides, in all honesty, could win the World Cup. Probably eight, on their day, could win, so why does one of these teams win and not another? Better players? No, not always. Better coaches? No, not always. In knock-out tournaments, it's the team with belief, the team that believes itself to be the best. The things that set a team apart from others are the critical non-essentials, like all the players having laptop computers to aid communication and transform the learning process. Prozone was another critical non-essential. The machine traces players in matches and reduces them to counters on the screen so their movements can be easily traced through the course of a match and analysed. 'It gives you the best feedback ever. Coaching is all about feedback,' says Clive.

Another critical non-essential was Dr Sherylle Calder, the eye specialist. She believes that the eyes can be trained, like any other muscle in the body. She developed a basic computer programme for the players to work on designed to develop 'strength' in the eyes. The programme trains different aspects of vision, such as peripheral awareness. Players watch images on screen and respond to what they have seen by hitting keys. It measures response times, and a player cannot move on to the next level until he has achieved a certain response time at any one level. 'As far as I know, no other sports team in the world weight train their eyes. Certainly no other rugby team does.'

Did England win the World Cup because they had stronger eyes than anyone else? The team started eye training eighteen months before the World Cup final. The match was won with a drop goal, which came from a lineout. Steve Thompson, the England hooker, had worked with Calder before the game. He found himself in the position of having to throw a ball into the lineout under the greatest pressure he'd ever known, and he made the best throw of his life. Australia left the back of the line free because they didn't think Thompson had the bottle to throw the ball there under all that pressure. He did.

Did we win the World Cup by using Sherylle Calder and weight training the eyes? No, but when you add it all up, you create a winning mindset. You develop a group of players who believe they are better than anyone else. That is a critical non-essential. It's what sets someone apart from their major competitors.

Point four consists of the critical essentials – management and players. Clive broke down the team management into seven areas – coaching, medicine, fitness, nutrition, the management itself, the needs of the team and the psychology of the team. He had experts in every area, the best people he could find working in the best environment he could create.

As far as players are concerned, he looked at the ideal components that every player should have. He tried to identify what a winning player profile would be and established three key areas – skill, leadership and the X factor. The X factor, for Clive, is someone who is a natural winner. 'Is that X factor something we can coach, or is it something that comes from your background, something that's in your genes? We're looking at that very, very closely. In the World Cup final, we had nine players with all three components, which is very high. Obviously, players who have all three components are crucial for the team's success, but every great team also needs guys made up of pure skill to work alongside the leaders. It's vital that the balance in a team is right.'

Point five is no compromise – if you are serious about becoming the best in the world, winning World Cups and winning gold medals, you cannot compromise in anything you do. To be successful at sport, you cannot cut corners, because someone else out there isn't compromising. 'You start to compromise in any sport and you will come second. I have absolutely no doubt about that.'

As he finishes, the audience applauds, standing and cheering, as at the end of some virtuoso performance. Slightly embarrassed, Clive looks out into the sea of faces. Then they troop out, rather dazed by what they've seen. Deeply impressed, the two late-arriving teachers are beaming. 'Bloody hell,' they say, full of awe. 'If the rest of the conference is like that, it'll be well worth coming. Well worth it. Bloody hell. I'm glad we came. That was great.'

Clive was not paid a penny for giving the talk. He did it to help out Sue Campbell, organiser of the conference and his old college lecturer from Loughborough.

Chapter Thirty

Lions 2005

'Life can only be understood backwards; but it must be lived forwards.' **Soren Kierkegaard**

With the benefit of hindsight, it was mad for Clive to have involved himself with the British and Irish Lions. Bonkers. Crackers. He walked away from the England team for many reasons but largely because he felt he could not compete with the southern-hemisphere countries on equal terms. The antipodean coaches had so much more time with, and influence over, their players than he did with his. He felt his ability to progress with the team was severely limited. So what does he go and do? He agrees to take a group of Scots, Irish, Welsh and English who have never before played together to the other side of the world to compete against the number-one-ranked team, with just ten days' training. To say that these circumstances were not ideal for the man who likes to spend a lot of time with players, working his way into the fabric of a team and changing everything about it, from the shoes they wear to their attitudes and expectations, would be a complete understatement.

Why did Clive take on the job? I suspect that, like most of us, he was seduced by the romantic nature of the tour, the history of it, and the fact that he had toured as a Lion and longed to make improvements. He wanted to make his mark – and he loves a challenge. Even as Clive plunges his flag into one snowy peak, he is scanning the horizon for the next mountain to climb.

It was a mistake, though, and Clive knows that. It completely tarnished his reputation, albeit temporarily, and for what? Is there any coach alive who could have taken a mixture of players from the four home nations and moulded them into a team that would have beaten New Zealand? 'I don't think so,' says Lawrence Dallaglio. 'I don't think there's a coach who could have done that. I think rugby's changed too much. We might sneak a win every so often, but most of the time, the southern-hemisphere teams will win against a side that's been thrown together a week before leaving.'

Consider the position in reverse. Imagine if Graham Henry had been asked to put together a composite team of New Zealand, Australia and South Africa players to create a touring side to play at Twickenham when England were the number-one team. Carnage.

Aside from the particular problems of Lions tours, New Zealand is a difficult country to visit. Ten sides have toured there, but only one has won – the 1971 Lions, and that was in the amateur era. To win in 2005, with the weight of professionalism bearing down, is exponentially harder, especially given the way that the game is organised in Britain – in England, particularly – compared to New Zealand. An average Kiwi's season with his club involves a maximum of thirteen matches from 25 February to the end of May, and only eleven if the club fail to make the play-offs. No All Blacks were required for the provincial matches against the Lions, just the three Tests. If a player avoided injury, the third Test was his eighteenth match of the season. In New Zealand, the down period is sacrosanct – Graham Henry's team has a minimum eight-week break every year. After the Lions, the players didn't return to their Super 12 sides until July. In England, things are different. A player only has a break if he is injured. The third Test was the fortieth match of the season for some players. To mould exhausted players into what is, essentially, a scratch team, and take them to the other side of the world to play the number-one side was a huge task, but Clive took on the responsibility, so we should judge him on how he fared.

Clive was appointed head coach of the 2005 tour to New Zealand at a Lions committee meeting, held on 3 February 2004. He accepted the role straightaway, and began quietly by studying the mistakes made on the 2001 tour, and establishing the ways in which he might put things right.

By the time he walked out of his job as head coach of the England team, in September 2004, he had a pretty good idea where they'd gone wrong in 2001, and what he needed to put right. Many would later argue that he became too hung up on correcting the mistakes of the 2001 tour. His departure from England meant he could become more overt about his development plans for the Lions. Newly unencumbered by the role of national coach, he could spend time talking to the coaches of other national sides without appearing a threat, getting to know them and to understand their players. The first teams he visited were Wales, Italy and France, as they prepared for the arrival of the All Blacks in November 2004. Clive stayed with all three teams in their week-long build-up to the tour. He sat in on every meeting, spoke to the medical team and all the coaches. He said of these visits, 'They removed the barriers. It made a world of difference.'

Clive was invited to South Africa by Jake White, the Springboks' head coach, and he also met up with Eddie Jones, the coach of Australia, to discuss the New Zealanders. Australia and South Africa play against the All Blacks regularly, often beating them, and Clive was eager to try to gain an understanding of the Kiwi players' psyche from White and Jones.

Clive was based with France when the All Blacks beat them 45–6, taking them apart in the process. 'The New Zealanders have got better and better, and I have absolutely no doubt this is one of the best New Zealand teams ever,' he said. 'I can't see a single weakness at this stage, especially in their front five, which some people have felt was their Achilles heel.' It was the first glimpse into just how difficult the task ahead of him was.

Clive had a grand plan, aside from leading the Lions to victory in New Zealand. Although Lions tours would become increasingly more difficult to win, they should not be wasted time. If Clive gathered the very best coaches and players together, they would all learn from each other on tour and come back more experienced. It would be a giant training camp, a chance for the best to learn from the best under the stress of a major international tour. Clive's aim was for Lions tours to become massive learning experiences every four years, lifting the whole game in the northern hemisphere.

So he announced a twenty-six-strong management team to back him in his efforts in New Zealand. Gareth Jenkins of Wales was in the team. 'My first impressions of Clive were very good,' he said. 'His attention to detail is fantastic. He's done a lot of work reflecting and planning before doing anything. He's spent a lot of time learning the lessons of the last tour [to Australia in 2001]. He's really dismantled it, and he recognises how different this tour needs to be from that one. His track record speaks for itself, but it's his appetite and enthusiasm for the tour that has impressed me. What else can you do after winning a World Cup? It's taking a Lions tour to New Zealand and winning. I am going to be involved with the best coaching group that has ever been brought together. There isn't a better place for the Lions to go than New Zealand. It's the one.'

Clive is not one to be knowingly understaffed, so few were surprised at the size of the management team. Experts in every field and from most of the towns and villages across England, Scotland, Ireland and Wales were selected. If you owned boots and had any sort of coaching expertise, you could consider yourself unlucky not to be included. Every area appeared to be covered.

Then one winter's morning, a gaping hole was spotted. Dismay, shock and despair descended on the British rugby writing community. There was only one person in the media department. It appeared that Clive, alarmingly and uncharacteristically, was short on personnel. Surely, someone was needed to carry the pens and notebooks, and do the seating plans for press conferences. Representatives from the Rugby Writers' Club were dispatched to explain to Clive the importance of looking after the media, and he listened patiently to their views. They came away from the meeting thinking that the Lions coach may act on their thoughts. They considered that he may turn to a retired rugby player or someone in sports PR to help him pull together a coherent media strategy.

A few days later, Clive appointed Alastair Campbell. The government's spin doctor strode into the Lions management team in what must rank as one of the most 'eh?' decisions in the history of British sport. Campbell received the call from Clive when he was running on Hampstead Heath. He told Clive that he was reluctant to take up the post because he comes with 'so much baggage'. Clive didn't care. Campbell was recognised as being the best person to deal with the press, and Clive needed someone to do just that.

Campbell, the twenty-seventh member of the management team, made an immediate impression on Clive when he came along to observe the Lions coach at a press conference. Clive performed well, and he knew it.

'How do you think you did there?' asked Campbell afterwards.

'OK,' replied Clive, modestly.

'No, I mean what mark out of ten would you give yourself?' pushed Campbell.

'I suppose eight out of ten,' said Clive. Campbell nodded enigmatically.

'Why?' asked Clive. 'How many marks would you have given me?'

'About three,' said Campbell.

'Three?' said Clive, alarmed. 'Why only three?'

Campbell explained that Clive was judging himself on his ability to respond well to journalists. Campbell was keen for Clive to have a clear idea of what he wanted to say and to judge himself on his ability to get his messages across. He wanted him to be less reactive and more proactive. Spin or common sense?

'You're calling the press conference,' said Campbell. 'You need to make sure you say what *you* want to say, and don't just answer their questions.'

'What if I've got nothing that I want to say?' said Clive.

'Then don't call a press conference. Someone else can give a press briefing.'

Campbell advised Clive to have key things in his mind that he wished to convey to the public about the tour, and to try to lever these messages into every reply – for example, this is the best-prepared tour ever, and this is a tour that will reflect all that is best about the history and tradition of the Lions.

As 2004 drew to a close, Clive had enough of an idea of whom he wanted in his Lions squad to contact 140 players with a Christmas parcel containing the sort of motivational literature that they would soon get used to receiving from him – 'Who says we can't do it?' 'How do you want to be remembered?' The Christmas package was the first of six that together produced an inspirational dossier for the team. The package also included a wristband in scarlet, navy blue, emerald and white, bearing the legend 'Power of Four'.

Some people argue that Clive's overriding concern with avoiding the mistakes of 2001 distracted him from the task of winning in New

Zealand. Certainly, he believed the 2001 tour party was one of the strongest assembled, with Martin Johnson, Lawrence Dallaglio, Keith Wood and Jonny Wilkinson in the mix. So why hadn't they succeeded, and why had some of them come back saying it was utterly disappointing and they hadn't learnt a thing?

One of the reasons was the split between the coach and the players and even in-fighting between players of different nationalities. In order to avoid this, Clive instituted a campaign specifically aimed at generating team spirit. He called it the 'Power of Four' and pushed the theme at every opportunity, appointing coaches from all four nations, sending the squad those wristbands and having an anthem composed for the Lions.

Another reason was the extraordinary amount of travelling the 2001 Lions had to do. On this basis, Clive rethought the whole trip, and instead of sending the squad around New Zealand from hotel to hotel, he fixed on three bases where the team would stay. From there, they would travel out to matches. In January, Clive went to New Zealand to visit these three main venues – Auckland, Christchurch and Wellington.

After the Six Nations Championships, during which he spent time with Ireland and Scotland, getting to know the coaches and players from those countries, Clive picked his squad and made Brian O'Driscoll captain. He selected forty-four players (to become forty-five when Jonny Wilkinson was proclaimed fit), making it clear that this was not a case of twenty-two for the midweek side and twenty-two for the Test side, but based on the fact that the 2001 Lions had used forty-five players. That's how many players you need on a modern Lions tour. Although there would be one group of players, there would be two groups of coaches. The midweek side was headed up by Ian McGeechan and the Test side by Clive.

At a two-day conference in April, the members of the squad were given some insight into what they would experience under Clive – there were motivational talks, team-building exercises and videos of the greatest moments in Lions history and British sport. Clive then had just eight days with his Lions squad before they left for New Zealand. It was a temporary workforce with no time to establish real harmony.

'The British and Irish Lions had twenty-two club cultures and four country cultures,' says Humphrey Walters, whose services were retained for the Lions. 'The spread of expertise ranged from World Cup winners to people who had only just begun playing for their country. It was incredibly hard to instill the team values we sought in the few days we had with the squad.'

Clive drove home the critical non-essentials like never before – Prince William would come out and meet the players and be an ambassador for the tour and the anthem was launched. Clive was in his element, being as quick and creative as he could.

When the RFU got wind of his extraordinary efforts, they feared the England coaches involved were being distracted from working for the national team, so they contacted them all to advise them that they must not work on Lions business while being paid by the RFU. Clive's retort was sharp and immediate. 'Dear All,' he wrote in an email, copied to the RFU, 'please note that from 17th May to 10th July, you are contracted to the British and Irish Lions. The Lions are paying the RFU for your release and also paying you as well.' His email continued that those England coaches contracted to the Lions must spend no time thinking about England between those dates. 'I think it only fair that if you spend more than fifteen minutes thinking about England, you need to log it down and we will then invoice the RFU for this time.'

The tone of the email was humorous. Clive suggested that if coaches moved their arms and legs around at the same time as talking about the Lions, they should be charged extra because this is clearly causing tiredness and will affect their ability to do their jobs properly. Coaches were advised not to contemplate England rugby issues in their sleep, on the toilet or while eating. His point was clear, though. Clive would not tolerate any attempts by the RFU to constrain the coaches that he had selected for the tour. He delighted in making it very clear that he thought the RFU's stance petty.

Before leaving for New Zealand, the Lions played Argentina at the Millennium Stadium. The match was a fundraiser and played against a depleted Argentina side. Still, the Argentinians played well and the first stirrings of concern about how the Lions would fare in New Zealand grew into a small growl. The score was 25–25. Critics sharpened their knives, and Lions supporters shifted uneasily in their seats.

Clive was unperturbed. He boarded the plane to New Zealand full of confidence that the Lions would win 3–0. He said that the Lions may lose some midweek games around the fringes but they would win the Test matches. He absolutely believed that – either because he *had* to believe they would win to have a chance of them actually doing so, or because he genuinely thought that, when it came to the crunch, the Lions would pull a victory out of the bag.

One thing that is consistent in the Clive Woodward story is his almighty self-belief. It was justified when he coached England, but the interesting thing is that the self-belief was there long before the victories and it remained when the victorious phase had passed. It is as if self-belief is a personality trait rather than something that develops with experience and success. It lies deep within the man's character and is not thrown or disturbed by the flux of real events. After the Lions had lost the first Test, he believed they would win 2–1. Few could understand how he remained so confident, so convinced that the Lions would come back in some way. His views seemed out of keeping with the stark reality of the situation, yet he believed all the same. His belief was something quite separate from the events and results in front of him.

The early games on the Lions tour meant little to Clive – harsh but true. His interest in the Lions tour was in making sure the players grew in confidence, learnt more about their sport and each other and, more than anything, won the Test matches. He'd spent a year in planning and had appointed every expert under the sun. The document he prepared outlining how and why the Lions would beat the All Blacks is a stunning piece of work, an example of how to create an élite sports team. He considered every eventuality and looked at every possible scenario. He canvassed the views of those who know the All Blacks well and those who understand winning – people from outside the sport as well as in it. He arrived in New Zealand believing that he had done all he could to get the Lions ready for the battle. That allowed him to tap into his enormous self-confidence – but the Lions lost 3–0 and never looked like winning. Why?

The team that was chosen for the first Test was roundly criticised, mainly for the omission of Gavin Henson, who many thought one of the most talented players in the party. Jonny Wilkinson was selected out of position in the centre, despite having played very little rugby since his glory moment two years previously.

The team looked very much like one that had been put together with memories of 2003 in mind, rather than hopes for 2005. Clive disagrees with this entirely. He says he was right to pick Wilkinson and he stands by that because Wilkinson's defence and field kicking were fantastic. He cannot see how anyone would think of going into a tough match against the All Blacks without a player who could kick the team out of trouble. Clive admits that he picked his team for the first Test based on a lineout game, which is how he thought the Lions could win. He decided that Shane Byrne was the best lineout thrower and Ben Kay the best lineout organiser. He thought that if they secured ball, the backs he had chosen would be able to run the show. He still says that the thought of Stephen Jones and Jonny Wilkinson at fly-half and centre excites him and they were a joy to see working together in training. 'That left foot, right foot thing,' he says. 'I thought they'd be magic,' but they barely touched the ball. Much debate ensued about the relative merits of the backs, but the truth is they might as well have had my mum's ladies' tennis club out there for all the ball they won. J.P.R. Williams was furious that Gavin Henson was left out. It all seems rather a mute point because it had gone wrong in the forwards. Clive had changed the lineout codes in the week leading up to the first Test because he believed they had been leaked to the New Zealanders, and there was confusion. The New Zealand team played magnificently to win 21–3. Clive says that the inability to secure lineout ball was something from which the team, and indeed the tour, never recovered. But why go into the match with no plan B? It seems extraordinary at that level. 'The only way in which we could beat them was plan A,' he says.

Of the questions thrown at Clive through the tour, one is crucial – why did he not give the proposed Test team a run-out before the first game? Why wait until that first Test before trying them? Clive's answer is that there was not enough time. He could not play every conceivable combination and chose the one he believed would work best. He adds that more games should be played and more players should be taken on tours to allow the various combinations to be tested.

Clive changed the line-up for the second Test considerably, adding to the feeling that he had messed up first time round, but even with a new team they lost, this time 48–18. New Zealand were good, of that there is no question. The final Test was an effort to win back some pride but they lost again, 38–19.

However, the story of this Lions tour does not lie only in the specifics of the tactics on the field, or even in the pre-tour planning that Clive had done. It is to be found in the tremendous, crushing response to the defeats. Clive was lambasted. He was torn apart.

The tour cost an estimated £6.4 million and is expected to make a profit of £120,000. Around 400,000 paying spectators saw the Lions being outscored 107 to 40 by the All Blacks, and by 12 tries to three. It was the third whitewash in the history of Lions tours to New Zealand, and those who had always felt a little uncomfortable with Clive's aggressive confidence and winning mindset leapt in to attack.

It is interesting to consider why. What had he done to upset people so much that, given the opportunity, they would happily see him buried in defeat? The answer possibly touches on the peculiarly British response to success, that slightly cautious view of it, especially when it is sought and planned for as Clive did. Former England cricket captain Mike Gatting describes success as being like 'something you really have to disguise. If you win, you have to say, "Ah, it's only because the other guy had an off day. He'd have beaten me otherwise." You can't win and enjoy winning. I played in Australia for a while – everyone wanted to win and everyone liked winners. It's really not like that here.' Is that why Clive was vilified by the press? Because he had pursued and enjoyed victory so much that when he failed, the world produced a united smirk? 'Yes, definitely. There's also the fact that he was full of confidence. You're setting yourself up for a fall if you're like that because everyone wants to see you cut down to size,' says Gatting.

Jeff Probyn, the former England prop and Clive's nemesis, said, 'This Lions series has brought public perception of Clive's ability closer to the reality understood by those who know him.'

Suddenly, history was being rewritten. Clive's role in the World Cup win was now being challenged. Adversaries, forced into silence by his World Cup victory, were now able to voice long-suppressed views. What was reality? Had Clive been lucky with England and exposed with the Lions, or a success with England and unlucky with the Lions?

'The Campbell situation was a disaster and was always going to be a disaster,' added Probyn in the *Evening Standard*. 'The reality is that a rugby tour is not a political party. You can't spin results. The game is about winning. Campbell was there partly because of Clive's political ambitions. Why does a rugby team need a spin doctor? It's ridiculous.

The fact that Campbell gave a team-talk to the players is ludicrous and insulting beyond belief.'

Political ambitions? When I spoke to Tessa Jowell, she said, 'It's a shame Clive has no political ambitions whatsoever. I think politics would benefit immensely from someone with Clive's skills, but he's just not interested and can't be convinced.'

So Probyn had that wrong, but what about everything else? What about the fact that everyone was now delighting in Clive's fall? The environment had changed. Clive had laid himself open to attack and they were coming thick and fast. The Lions tour did Clive's reputation an enormous amount of damage. Some of the complaints against him had validity. Some did not. Clive went to New Zealand believing he could bring professional standards to a makeshift team from the British Isles. He thought that if he included critical non-essentials and bolstered the self-belief of the players before departure, they would be able to swing a three-match tour victory over a great rugby team.

Perhaps the world learnt something about Clive Woodward through the Lions tour, but not that much. What we really learnt was something about modern sport – great teams that have been together for three years tend to triumph over teams that have been together for three weeks. Every four years, we learn from the Lions that a team is more than the sum of its parts. Teams take time to develop and knit together. Lions tours are very difficult, and far more so since the advent of professionalism in rugby. Winning against South Africa once in a while may be possible – given the time difference – but Lions victories over Australia and New Zealand will become harder and harder as time goes by.

Finally, Clive learnt that taking a political spin doctor on a Lions tour, however amiable or talented he may be, sets you up for all manner of abuse on your return. No one will think of the Lions 2005 without thinking of Campbell, but he let in no tries, missed no tackles or kicks. If he threw any spin passes, they were off the pitch. To blame Campbell for the Lions tour disaster is to blame off-the-field incidents for the defeat. That is wrong. Everyone involved with the tour recognises, surely, that what went wrong with the Lions 2005 went wrong because the All Blacks played bloody well, and the Lions didn't. Some of this was down to Clive and some of it wasn't. He, though, must take the blame.

Chapter Thirty-one

Realising a childhood dream

'Some people are on the pitch. They think it's all over.
It is now.' **Kenneth Wolstenholme**

Geoff Hurst's goal in 1966 is one of Clive's fondest memories. It is the one that excites and entrances him more than any other. A love of football runs through him like an arrow through time, linking the little boy, clutching his ball and waving at planes as they landed near his home in Yorkshire, with the grown-up man, the knight of the realm.

A love of football remained a largely silent obsession throughout Clive's rugby career. Pictures of him watching football matches would appear in the papers occasionally, but rarely did he speak of his passion for the round-ball game, or his innermost desire one day to make a dramatic return to the sport he loved as a child. So his decision to turn his attentions to coaching football full-time left most observers bemused. Footballers, entrenched in their belief that only someone who has played at a certain level can ever coach at a certain level, stared deep into the eyes of rugby men, who expressed wholesale bemusement that a fine fellow of Woodward's sophistication would wish to ditch rugger to join the footie ranks. The consensus of opinion in football was 'How could he?' and in rugby 'Why would he?' Word from Clive was 'Because I want to.'

He believes that his ability to manage an élite performance team demands a set of skills that are eminently transferable to a new sport. For many commentators, shocked by the news that he planned to move into football, the cultural and social distinctions between the two games were more concerning than the physical, tactical and technical differences. Football is seen as the game of the people, with its roots in the working classes – muddy balls thundering against brick walls in back yards on tough council estates across the country. Rugby was conceived in middle-class schools with the aim of promoting muscular Christianity and, despite the many changes in the sport, it is still deeply associated with privilege. These are two different worlds, two different classes – at least that's the theory. Whether Sven-Goran Eriksson, Arsene Wenger and José Mourinho would agree is an entirely different matter.

What is important to remember in all this debate about the differences between the two sports is that much of what Clive came to dislike about working in rugby and the genesis of the obstacles strewn in his path, were the result of the clubby, cigar-puffing, blazer-wearing nature of the sport. The unwieldy decision making, people briefing against him and the complicated routes to success that he was forced to endure – the hurdling of egos, side-stepping round conformists and pole-vaulting over amateurish principles – were largely the result of the sport's dependence on, and respect for, tradition. It drove him nuts.

Football is considered a more aggressive sport than rugby – 'nastier' even. The wealth of football chairmen is inexorably linked with victory, as is the success and job security of club managers. Winning is everything. The raw pursuit of it is tangible and laudable. Contemplation and hesitation escape through the cracks in the windows of smoke-filled bars because of it. Professionalism has moved rugby further towards football in this respect, but it is still very different. Football is a foreign country, full of people who don't speak or behave like they do in rugby. Clive accepts that there are differences. 'In football, they stab you in the front. In rugby, they stab you in the back.'

Seven million adults and five million children play football in England. Tens of millions more watch it, support it, cry because of it, celebrate, laugh and scream as a result of it. The collective passion evoked by football is as great as the collective passion evoked by anything outside national disasters. Rugby evokes strong feelings, of course, but rarely on such a grand scale as the spontaneous emotion demonstrated by a football result, certainly not at club level. With the benefit of hindsight, football was bound to have an appeal for an ambitious man with an interest in building élite sports teams.

However, Clive's yearning to move into football is not based on an intellectual decision to take over sport at the highest level. It's an emotional decision. He feels a real pull back to his first love because he has such an extraordinary attachment to it, given the way the sport was denied to him at a young age. His decision to move is heart and soul, mind and body. Football left an indelible mark on his life and on his character when he was prevented from playing it as a boy. It left a hole that he has fought to fill with rugby union. His successes in rugby have been a chance to prove, perhaps, that the denial to him of football was not entirely in vain. As Clive enters his fifties, perhaps he feels it's time for him to do what he always dreamt of doing.

The question, though, is how? How would he even start to talk to football clubs, let alone the Football Association, about a move into the round-ball game? Just how would that conversation go? 'Erm, hello. This may sound daft, but I'd love to come and coach your side.'

It took an approach by one man to kick the whole thing off.

Mark Palios sat in his Soho Square office, flicking through the morning papers. It was July 2003 and he had just started work as chief executive of the Football Association. He was settling into his new world and adjusting to the demands of his new job, when an article caught his eye.

'It was a piece in the sports section – an interview with Clive in which he was saying that he thought he had skills that were transferable across into different sports,' says Palios. 'It struck an immediate chord with me because I believed that one of the things holding football back was its insularity, the idea that people from outside football can't contribute. That only perpetuates the current system and stops improvements being made.

'I started to wonder whether someone from a different sport would bring a new slant. I thought about what Clive might be able to offer. I made contact with him, but didn't get the chance to meet him straight-away.'

They did speak on the phone, though, and Clive's reciprocal eagerness to talk about opportunities in football appealed to Palios immensely.

'I could detect interest straightaway,' he says. 'I realised then that this might actually work. Having someone accomplished from outside the sport, with a real passion for football, sounded perfect. We'd found that it was foreign coaches and players who were making the biggest difference to British football and were beginning to realise that it was because people were coming in from the outside with new ideas.'

Palios runs his own company now, advising and helping to restructure businesses. He is working from his office at home in Buckinghamshire when I meet him. The large modern house is situated in a leafy street, not too far from where Clive lives.

'When I was at the FA, I was very keen on the concept that you don't have to be a good player to be a good manager,' continues Palios. 'In fact, you have to be a good educationalist. Essentially, you've got to get your ideas across and you've got to motivate. It's a totally different set of skills from playing.

'I wanted to bring in educationalists and businessmen with passion for the sport. I wanted professionals with real skills to work alongside the amateurs. I brought in Trevor Brooking to develop football – not because I wanted him as a coach but for his ambassadorial qualities. Members of the League Managers' Association were saying, "Look, Trevor Brooking hasn't even got a coaching badge." I never wanted him to coach – I wanted him for his knowledge of sport generally, his passion and enthusiasm for the right way of playing and his government connections. He was a big boost to the FA. He didn't have to put on a coaching session to prove that he understood the bigger picture better than most of the guys there.'

Clive was on the target list of people whom Palios was eager to recruit, but the two struggled to find time to meet. The summer tour led to the World Cup. Palios continued to 'make overtures' to Clive and, once Clive was back from the World Cup, they finally got together.

'You know how you meet some people and you can relate to them,' says Palios, 'they actually have the drive and energy to make things happen? Clive was like that. I thought, "Yeah, he would be good in the team." I'd always thought of Clive in terms of his skills, but when I met him, I found the qualities of the man as well made me think, "Here's a guy who could actually add something to football." He was worried about his contract with the RFU, though. He didn't want to break that, so we were always talking about an involvement longer term.'

Palios thought Clive might add value in two areas in particular, 'without limiting or pigeon-holing him. One was his ability to work with top sportsmen to generate that team spirit that he clearly had with the England rugby players. The other was all the off-field stuff – an open mind and his critical non-essentials, those little details he took to a new level. Bill Shankly, in the sixties and seventies, always used to say, "Look after the little things and the big things will look after themselves." I felt that Clive was taking that principle to a new level.'

How much credibility would Clive have had at the FA? Surely, you can't send in a rugby coach, however talented he may be, and expect footballers to trust him and believe in him from day one?

'That's the single problem Clive faces in football. He said straightaway that he was worried about credibility and would need to achieve immediate success. He'd have to be successful from day one, and if, after a brief period, he became unsuccessful, players being what they are, would say, "He's only a rugby coach. What does he know about football?" It was always going to be a big hurdle, but I believed there were ways of getting round it because what really impressed me about Clive was that he totally understood this. He was entirely realistic.

'We talked of the ways in which we could bring him in gently. He didn't have to pick the team or coach them full-on to have an enormous impact. He was interested in things such as teaching footballers to kick the ball. You might say, "Hang on – they know intuitively how to do that." Actually, they don't. He had lots of ideas about working with his kicking coach to get the players to hit the inside of the post on the penalty. I told him, "If I was the manager of a club and you came to me and said you could get my guys to hit the inside of the post nine times out of ten, you'd be brought in straightaway." As soon as you start to add value, you gain credibility.

'Then there was the sense that maybe he could work with the development teams, influencing our coaching across the FA with his ideas and getting to know the players who would eventually come through to the England team.'

Palios explained to Clive that he aimed to bring a number of talented individuals into the FA. Another was Gerard Houllier.

'I've heard people say, "Gerard Houllier – he's a failed manager, isn't he?" I'm not sure whether five trophies in one season counts as a failure, but I didn't want him for his management skills, in any case. I wanted him because French players are generally regarded as having very good basic skills. A coaching system is embedded throughout the country to promote and develop those skills and Houllier set it up. The system uses guys who are specialists at teaching kids at that age. Who better to get involved in our coaching system?

'After Gerard and Trevor, the third piece in the jigsaw was Clive. It was sad that I never got to finish all that off before I left.'

Palios is convinced that Clive could, and will, make it as a coach at the highest level.

'He's already operated at the top level, which is good. That's why I felt he could operate at the top level in football. The only problem was credibility, but you win that if you're successful. Look at the coaches out there – Houllier was not really a player, he was a teacher; Sven's not really a player, he's a teacher; Wenger's not really a player, he's an educationalist, and Mourhino. There are more. There's a theme coming through that some of the best guys are actually educationalists rather than players.'

How high could Clive go in football?

'I have no doubt that Clive could become the coach of the England football team. Apart from his personal characteristics, his willingness to learn and his experience of running élite teams generally, his experience of running an international team specifically persuades me that he'd be good. An international side has a different dynamic from a club side and few people have experienced that. It would be fantastic to see him be successful – it would change the landscape completely if he is, and I think that's healthy. I can't understand why people don't see it.'

In the summer of 2004, Palios resigned from the FA after a media storm over the discovery that he had been having a relationship with Faria Allam, an FA employee. It was revealed that Eriksson, the England coach, had also been having an affair with the same woman, and the newspapers flocked to pick over the bones of the hottest story of the summer. Palios walked away, and the FA's eagerness to appoint Clive took a temporary back seat. Then Brooking called Clive to discuss the situation further. The two met, but Clive decided to pursue his entry into football via a different route.

His international experience was a real bonus, his management style was deeply appealing and his personal skills were considered perfect for the new, all-embracing approach of the Football Association, but how to overcome the credibility gap? In September 2004, after handing in his notice to the RFU, Clive decided he would take the Football Association's coaching badges in order to be qualified, if not experienced, as a soccer coach. He decided to start off at a club and to build up, rather than stepping in at national level. If he earned the badges and gained experience quietly, working alongside an established manager, he would be better placed to establish just how far he could go in this new game.

At nine o'clock on a cold October morning in 2004, a year on from the World Cup – from Sydney in summertime to Buckinghamshire in wintertime – I am standing on the edge of an Astroturf pitch at Wye Valley School in Bourne End, as rain pours down. Ten teenaged boys, dressed in kit that does nothing to protect them from the elements, belt a football around with reckless velocity.

'Sir Clive came down here,' says Mitch Woodward (no relation), the school's head boy. Mitch has spiky blond hair, an affable, informal manner and wants to coach football in the United States when he leaves school. He charges in and strikes the ball so hard that it ricochets off the fencing and bounds back at him, nearly knocking him over. Clive is not with them today because he has travelled to South Africa on a fact-finding mission to help him plan the Lions tour. He cannot miss the session, though, so he will catch up by attending the class at a school nearby. The students are here to train for their level-two coaching award as part of their NVQ in football. They have done level one, described as 'a very basic badge'. Level two is where the proper coaching starts. Clive was granted dispensation from doing the first level. That's what winning a World Cup does for you!

In charge of this session is Jim Kellman, an experienced Football Association coach who watches intently as the teenagers take it in turns to run ten-minute sessions. They are given a particular skill to focus on every week, and are told at the end of each session what their task will be next time. They have to run sessions on all manner of things from ball control to heading (defence), heading (attack), goalkeeping and turning and shooting. Kellman's approach is not the didactic, watch 'n' learn strategy of old, but a refreshing way of encouraging the boys to find their own voice, run things their own way and display their natural flair for teaching. Afterwards, he steps in to correct mistakes and offer tips on how to improve their own coaching styles, rather than forcing his own style on them.

The boys respond well to him and are clearly enthusiastic about the course and where it may lead. Mitch recalls how he spent the summer as a ball boy at Chelsea, 'basically, catching and fetching, carrying and doing whatever they wanted me to do.' He got £35 for two hours' work, though, so it was a decent enough rate. 'And I was back by midday, so I could coach in the afternoon as well. It was great.'

This coaching course is run at the boys' school, and everyone on the course except for Clive is a pupil.

'We were told at the beginning that someone famous was coming along, but they didn't tell us who it was until the week before he turned up,' says Mitch. 'Then Clive walks in. We thought he'd play the big "I'm a celebrity" thing, but he took one look at the ball and just wanted to join in and play. He said, "Hi, my name's Clive," and that was it. After that, he was one of the lads. He loves it. At the end of the sessions, he's always up for a kick around before we go in. I was surprised by how good he is.'

What do they think of him as a potential football coach?

'The thing that stands out about him is how much preparation he does for the lessons. Some of us do a quick five minutes' planning in the changing rooms before hitting the pitch. Clive always turns up fully prepared and ready to go, with his key points written out. He's always spot on timewise, and he gets everything done properly. We should do that, too.

'He's a nice guy, easy to talk to. He has a nice manner. He doesn't shout or swear or anything. You'd think he would from coaching rugby players but he doesn't. He's good at coaching. I can't believe how he never shouts at anyone.'

'OK,' says Kellman. 'Gather round.' The head coach has appointed an examiner for the session, one of the boys who will mark his fellow pupils on their coaching efforts. Once the marks have been given, and notes taken, Kellman, the former manager of Newbury Town Football Club, adds his thoughts and advice. Then it's the next pupil's turn.

Once the session is over, the boys decide to stay outside and help coach some of the younger children, who have a PE lesson. Kellman goes inside and drops down on the sofa in the staffroom.

'Clive started doing his level two in September,' says Kellman. 'He will get through this quickly. He's clearly a talented and experienced coach and he knows his football, so he'll be fine.'

After the course, Clive has to attend review days, then have an external assessment. The award takes around ninety hours to complete in total. He attends these sessions at Wye Valley School most Fridays and when he can't make it, he catches up by completing the parts of the course that he's missed at nearby Parkhouse School.

Clive finished his level-two coaching award at the beginning of 2005 and did his external exam on 21 March. He had to organise small-sided games (six against six) in front of a visiting examiner. On 2 April, he began working towards his level-three award on an intensive nine-day Easter course. Following that, he had to practise with 125 teaching hours, attend two review days and then face an external assessment.

'Level two is about how to do things. It's a very technical course. Level three is more tactical – it focuses on where and when to do things. You have to understand the game in much more depth to pass that one,' explains Kellman.

For level three, candidates analyse the principles of attacking and defending, looking at movement to create and exploit space, support play, switching play, tackling, cover and balance. Passing levels one, two and three gives a coach the UEFA B licence. It is this qualification that Clive needed before joining a club.

'Once you have the B licence, you can manage a club, as long as you are working towards the A licence [level four],' says Kellman. Level four is a two-year project. Candidates must attend a one-year course, then come back for assessment after a year spent practising.

'Clive has a very different way of looking at things,' says Kellman. 'He looked at the course very differently from the way anyone else has looked at it. He wanted to change it all the time and think of new and better ways of doing things.'

Around 80 per cent of people inside football are unqualified, but Clive felt it was essential that he achieved the qualifications because of this elusive 'credibility' that he needed in football. Ironically, although his position in rugby gave him access to key people at the top of the sport, it almost lost him credibility with the grassroots because it linked him so closely with one sport.

Clive had a clear idea of the sort of football that he wanted to build towards. The fast-running, no-kicking, multi-dimensional rugby that he'd envisaged for England would have its footballing equivalent in a clever Brazilian style of football.

'We had lots of conversations about football and the way it's taught in this country,' says Kellman. 'We agreed that players weren't focusing on skills. Think back to 1966. The players didn't have Sunday league football then. They didn't have the number of matches they have today – they taught themselves by playing at school, in the yard, etc. They focused on practising. Nowadays, there's an obsession in the British game with big strong players piling in – it's an unintelligent approach to football. British fans have got used to players who give the ball away all the time, then battle to get it back – it's all ooohs and aaahs but it's not good football. I've seen matches when they don't have a sequence of more than two passes without giving it away. In France, they reviewed the way they were coaching children and changed it to focus on skills. French players are much better at the game because of this. British players can't retain possession because they're not skilful players. Too many coaches of youngsters want their side to win, rather than trying to develop the children and make them better players. We should be judging youth coaches on whether their players make it to the top and how skilful they are, rather than whether they can win all games.'

It was for this reason that Palios had been so eager to get the coaching structure of the FA right during his tenure there. His efforts to recruit Gerard Houllier were precisely because of these problems. He'd always felt that it was coaches who would make the difference.

In addition to having an idea about the football he wanted to encourage, Clive believed that much more was controllable on the pitch, during games, than most clubs realised. One day, in February 2005, as he drove home, the radio was on in the car. He listened to a match in which three penalty kicks were missed. He was appalled. 'You need to practise penalties – you can't have penalties being missed. I just know that Jonny wouldn't be missing them with such regularity.'

Other areas are ripe for change, too. Humphrey Walters, who worked so closely with Clive on the development of the England rugby team, says there are dozens of ways in which Clive can make an immediate difference in football by instilling discipline on the field and making the players more aspirational and harder working off it. On the field, he says that the propensity of players to run around the field celebrating after a goal, instead of running straight back to the centre circle, robs them of a key advantage. The opposing side are crestfallen after conceding a goal but have had time to think by the time the team come back. If the scoring team return quickly and utilise the momentum before the opposing side have had time to regroup, imagine how much more they could achieve.

Similarly, a throw-in should be a competitive advantage, but one player takes the ball and prepares to throw, then another comes up and says, 'It's my throw.' By the time they've finished messing around, the players are marked and the advantage is lost.

Clive had plenty of good, strong advisers from rugby and business, but he needed to absorb himself in football – to get out and meet people coaching and running the game, and to find models of good practice.

In October 2004, at the time when Clive was working away at his level-two badge, Ann Heaver was flicking through the magazine tucked inside her copy of the *Daily Telegraph* when she spotted an article about Simon Clifford, a thirty-four-year-old football coach from Leeds. She hadn't heard of him before but read on regardless. The interview was written by Alex Belios, a highly respected journalist and recognised authority on the world of Brazilian football. Something about Clifford reminded Ann of Clive. He had broken all the rules, was anti-establishment, liked loud Brazilian music to be blasted out at training sessions and was an extremely hard worker who rarely slept. Belios, who had stayed at Clifford's house while researching the article, described how Clifford had refused to let him go to bed, so eager was he to talk about the Brazilian football schools he has set up around the world.

'Four hours after allowing me to sleep, I am awoken by him showering me with a pint of cold water,' wrote Belios. 'The act – playful, eccentric and utterly domineering – gives an inkling of how he has managed to rattle British football culture. A policeman's son from Middlesbrough, Clifford has risen from humble football fan to international sporting guru thanks to remarkable energy, opportunism and a devil-may-care attitude with the powers-that-be.'

Ann cut out the article and passed it to Clive. He read it, picked up the phone and packed his bag for a trip to Leeds.

'This call came through,' says Clifford. 'It was Clive Woodward. I'm not a big rugby fan so it didn't mean all that much at the time. He said he wanted to come up and see me as soon as possible.'

Clifford is a former primary teacher who runs an empire of soccer schools – 150,000 in total – mainly in England, but also in the US, Australia and the Far East. His business is based on one guiding principle – if the best footballers in the world come from Brazil, then why not teach British children to play like Brazilians? He began running his first Brazilian Soccer School, with the aim of 'making football more beautiful, more entertaining'. He encouraged young kids to copy the flamboyancy and creativity of the great Brazilian players. Style isn't everything, however. Clifford is interested in producing winners and, less than ten years on, he has delivered four England and five Scotland internationals at junior level.

Clive arrived in Leeds and booked into a nearby hotel.

'I went to meet him for dinner and didn't really know what to expect,' says Clifford. 'I was just dressed in sports gear, as I always am, and he was smartly dressed. I thought, "I'm not really sure about all this." I wasn't sure we'd have anything in common but we started chatting about what I'd been doing and he told me about his plans in football. To be honest, I was blown away. He really knows football. He knows exactly what he wants to do, and his ideas were so similar to mine. It was as if he was reading my mind. We both felt exactly the same way about the sport and the way it should be taught. Even when it came to tactics on the pitch, he said things that I'd been thinking for a long time. I don't think I've had a conversation with anyone before or since who understands – really *understands* – football like he does.'

Clifford's great interest in Brazilian football was nurtured by his close friendship with Juninho whom he met quite by accident at a football match. As his friendship with the Brazilian player grew, he became fascinated by why Brazilians appeared to have many more skilful players than other nations. One of the key reasons was simple – they trained much harder and were more disciplined than those from most other nations. They spent a vast amount of time on their own, honing individual skills – something that British players rarely did.

One of the key things that Juninho did was to introduce Clifford to *futebol de salão* – an indoor version of the game played with small, heavy balls. In the summer of 1997, Clifford flew to Brazil to have a look for himself.

'People have this idea of Brazilian football being played on beaches and of the players being relaxed and just naturally good at it. What I found was that they worked extremely hard at their skills. The image of Brazilians kicking around on the beach all day comes because what you see when you first get to the country is all the beach football. If you really look at the areas where great Brazilian footballers come from, though, there are no beaches around. They work hard and play hard. They play *futebol de salao* to learn their skills.' In 1998, he founded the International Confederation of *Futebol de Salão* in the upstairs room of his house.

The day after the meeting of minds, Clive went to watch Clifford run a training session. Clifford's sessions are two hours long and focus on the development of core skills above all else. Loud music pumps out in the background. Every child is given one of the small, weighted balls used in *futebol de salão* and performs hundreds of repetitions of moves demonstrated by Clifford. Everyone in the class is expected to go away and practise alone for two hours every day, as they do in Brazil. Training becomes more difficult with the special balls because they are so much harder to manipulate than a conventional football. 'You have to be more precise with them,' says Clifford. 'You have to make clever passes – you can't just kick the ball in the air to get yourself out of trouble.' The fact that an area much smaller than a football field is used also helps the youngsters to develop their skills because the gaps are fewer and smaller.

Clifford is a likeable man – friendly, engaging and deeply ambitious. He has drawn up a twenty-five-year plan for himself. He knows exactly where he wants to be at every stage of his life. To date, he is well ahead of schedule. In addition to his football schools, he has recently bought Garforth Town Football Club, which he plans to take to the top of the Premiership. He predicts a day when the entire England football team will consist of his Brazilian football-schooled players. His self-confidence is immense. 'I'd like to make the perfect footballer, the foot-baller the world has never seen,' he says. There's only one other man I've met with the same level of surety – Clive Woodward.

If Clifford was impressed with Clive on their first meeting over dinner, it was Clive's turn to be impressed when he watched Clifford in action at the coaching sessions. 'They were phenomenal,' he said. 'Brilliant. He is extremely talented and very inspiring.'

Through Nike, one of Clive's sponsors, Clive travelled to Brazil to see first hand the game being played and taught. He returned more convinced than ever that his vision for football was right. He also knew that he wanted to work with Clifford. Somehow, though, Clive had to persuade the man who has turned down requests from many leading clubs and players in the past to join forces with him. With Clive's experience of managing élite-level teams, his development of critical non-essentials and leadership skills and Clifford's footballing experience, they could forge a combined vision for the future of the game. All they would have to do then is find someone in a football club somewhere willing to take the risk of employing them.

Chapter Thirty-two

Saint Clive

'Courage is being scared to death –
but saddling up anyway.' John Wayne

On a midsummer morning in July 2005, Clive Woodward pulls into the Southampton Football Club car park to begin the first day of the rest of his life. It is unfeasibly early and the man from rugby has an unfeasibly large job on his hands – to convince a sceptical public, uncertain players and a bemused manager that he is a credible addition to the backroom staff of this recently relegated club. None of these things matter to Clive, though. He's confident that he can make his mark and determined to learn all he can in the process. More than anything, he's thrilled to be working at a football club – finally, after all these years.

Clive is in his office by 7 a.m. Members of the press gather outside the gates at 8 a.m., wondering when the new boy will arrive. He has been in his office for nearly an hour and a half by the time they are told that he's already in position. Groans are heard among the assembled media. There will be no photos of him arriving for his first day in the job. That doesn't suit the media, but it suits Clive enormously. He is desperate to keep out of the limelight as much as possible over the next couple of years while he learns about the business and achieves his UEFA A licence.

Clive is operating under the title of technical director. It gives him the scope to prove his worth and the time to learn about his new environment. His aim is to learn all about football – the culture, organisation, processes and planning – as well as the hopes, dreams and aims of the club, its players and staff. He will busy himself by introducing the sort of professional standards to Southampton that defined his time with the England rugby team. He says that he will not replicate the England rugby experience at Southampton. Those who expect to see the winning formula shifted unchanged from Twickenham to the south coast will be in for a shock. What he will replicate, though, is the creation of a great coaching team. He has already confirmed that Simon Clifford will come on board to help run training sessions at the club, and over the coming weeks, he plans to bring in a number of new faces. 'It's a case of getting in there and seeing what needs to be done,' he says – except that's not strictly true, not from the master of forward planning. Even as Clive is parking and walking towards his new office he's already commissioned months' worth of research on trends in the sport, likely scenarios and possible improvements. He's asked more questions and sought more information 'than most football managers do in a lifetime'. That is the view of Ged Holmes, chief executive of Prozone, brought in to work with him at Southampton. Clive has advised on changes to the training ground, including having separate wooden cubicles in the dressing rooms. He has brought in new equipment, new ideas, and all this before he's even made it to his desk.

'Clive asked us to look at trends in football over a couple of years,' said Holmes. 'For example, he wanted us to look at every throw-in taken, to see what the outcome was.' What throw-ins were successful? Were quick throw-ins more successful than slow ones? Was there a real advantage in throwing in before the defending side had the chance to mark? 'He had certain views, certain feelings,' said Holmes. 'He wanted us to take a look at the evidence and see whether he was right. The thing with Clive is that he is always questioning – why can't we do this? Why not this? He wanted to explore trends in the sport and come up with data to consider before advising on possible changes.

'Clive asked so many questions and wanted so much done that we had four people working flat out for months before he started his job, just doing analysis. He was asking questions that have never been asked before. Most managers just want analysis on what happened at the weekend, and what lessons to learn for the next game. He wants to know all about football and to challenge all thinking and assumptions. He wants to know about long balls, short balls, the whole lot. There was about a year and a half's work to be done by the time he'd asked all his questions. We had to get a load of work-experience people in to go through it all and come up with all the statistics.'

The research is designed to show when and how goals are scored and how advantage is gained. Is it the in-swinging kick that is most likely to result in a scoring goal, or the out-swinger? Where in the goalmouth are goals scored from different kicks? Where and how are goals most frequently scored? The research has shown that the in-swinging kick struck in front of the goal is where most goals are scored. What skills do players need to replicate this? Should this be incorporated into training?

'The thing is, it's actually easy to do all this research. It takes time but it's not hard. The difficult thing is to take all the information and use it to improve a side. Clive wants to do everything he can – even if it's just a five per cent advantage, he'll take it. Every improvement is worth having.'

By establishing, among other things, how goals are scored, in what circumstances, and from where, Clive goes into Southampton with a pretty good idea of where players need to be and what they need to do to get themselves into scoring positions. That provokes thought on what broader changes can be made to the way they train, look after themselves and prepare for matches. All this, in turn, takes him back to his initial premise – you need excellent basic skills to play winning football and footballers don't work hard enough on these skills. As a result, Clive is convinced that players need to spend more time at the club, practising basic skills and ball play as never before, and the Southampton players will find that their presence is required from early morning until late afternoon. Think of Jonny Wilkinson. Think of David Beckham, even. For all the criticism levelled at him, he has a reputation for being first at training and last to leave.

There is more. Clive is eager to cover every area of sports science in his efforts to get the players on form. He will be equipping each player with the facilities to conduct blood tests on themselves at home before leaving for training. They must then email the results of the tests straight to the club so that a doctor can assess them and predict problems/dietary deficiencies or weaknesses before they have an effect on performance. When the players arrive, a doctor will be there to talk to them about any medical issues or advise them of any ways in which they might improve their health. In a game that is becoming more closely fought every season, the opportunities to steal advantages are rare, and such efforts will, Clive hopes, provide a number of small benefits that together should give the team the edge.

The aim of all this work is two-fold. The first, and most important aim, is to improve performance on the pitch. The second, the covert agenda, is the psychological advantages that his changes bring. They should make players feel like winners. If players feel they are in an infinitely superior environment, they respond to being treated as professionals by behaving like professionals.

Clive is confident that he can make a difference. He is also confident that he can forge a great working relationship with Harry Redknapp, the manager of Southampton and a man steeped in the game but less enamoured with modern scientific thinking. In theory, the pair should make the perfect combination, Clive working behind the scenes and reporting to Redknapp.

'He's going to get involved with the academy, the medical side and sports science. That can have a big impact on the game. I can't say I understand any of it. I understand football,' says Redknapp. 'Clive will come in and help us with those areas and you have to have an open mind about these things. He has got a lot to offer in terms of organisation and on the medical and fitness side. I don't think you should ever close your eyes to what people have to offer. Look at José Mourinho at Chelsea. He wasn't a player but he's done a fantastic job.'

The origins of Clive's move to Southampton can be traced back three years to a chance meeting with Rupert Lowe, the chairman. Clive first met Lowe when he went to watch Southampton play Chelsea (years before the match which led to his appearance on *Match of the Day*). They discussed, among other things, Clive's love of football and Clive explained the processes that he went through to transform the England rugby team. Lowe was impressed. He called Clive and suggested they might meet to talk further.

'We met at Pennyhill Park,' says Lowe. 'It was just before the World Cup, and I loved everything he said about organisation and planning. I thought those were things that were sorely missing in football and it struck me that he could contribute a great deal.'

Lowe confesses that while he had a vision of Clive coming to work at Southampton as soon as they met, he had no real idea of the capacity in which he'd come. He just believed that Clive could add real value so wanted him in the managerial team.

Once Clive won the World Cup, the offers from various institutions, governing bodies and clubs came in, but Clive was eager to continue with England. 'I kept thinking about what he might bring to Southampton, so I kept talking to him, letting him know that there was a role here for him should he ever decide to leave rugby,' adds Lowe.

'Footballers are naturally sceptical, so it's not going to be easy for him. When I became chairman, there was suspicion of me. It's even more pronounced for those involved on the playing side. Most managers played at a high level before becoming managers. That's what always happened in football, so that's what's considered right.

'As far as I'm concerned, though, the fact that there aren't any people like Clive in football is irrelevant. Football is a team game and a squad game. There's the playing side, but there's also logistics and analysis. What I wanted at Southampton was someone to come in to plan the campaign. We were relegated after nine years. We need to plan our club's future straightaway.'

What is clear is that Lowe is interested in Clive for reasons other than just to sharpen up the first team. He's eager to change the ethos of the game.

'Football is a closed shop,' says Lowe. 'Agents have enormous power. It's a "ring" and it's holding football back. Agents control the business in football. They are buying shares in players as they move from club to club. This industry is driven by greed. It's not ethical.'

Lowe says that he has brought in Clive for the long term. 'I don't have any short-term thoughts at all,' he says. 'Obviously, we want to start winning and we want to go back up, but I'll be looking at what Clive achieves after three or four years – not next week. It's not a short-term business. I want Southampton to play entertaining football. I want us to start "growing" our own players and developing a team of great footballers with great skills. I want the academy to flourish. I know it won't happen tomorrow but I believe it will happen, so I'm willing to wait. I happen to believe it will be an exciting wait.'

SECTION SIX

Chapter Thirty-three

Clive in the dock – was he any good or just a bloke who got lucky?

'If the trumpet shall give an uncertain sound, who shall prepare himself to the battle?' **St Paul, in his first epistle to the Corinthians**

In the dock he stands, arms folded, head bowed, as the clerk's voice booms out across the packed courtroom. Players and coaches past and present look up, a thousand or more cauliflower ears bulging offensively as Mr Justice William Webb-Ellis strides in, confident and powerful.

'All sit,' says the clerk, approaching the accused. The squeak of chairs echoes through the courtroom as those in the public gallery struggle to sit down. Twenty-stone men fight for every square inch as they squash into seats designed for twelve-stone bottoms.

'Please state your name and address.'

'Sir Clive Ronald Woodward,' said the man. He gave his address.

The clerk nodded solemnly and told him that he would be handing him a copy of the Bible.

'Of course,' says Clive, his eyes sparkling. He always knew that bible had been a good idea. Look how far it had come from those early days when he was squabbling for the money to make them. 'It's good, isn't it?' he said in a loud voice, hoping Don Rutherford could hear.

'Sorry, Sir?'

'The bible.'

The clerk regarded the accused as one might regard a mad, drunken man staggering down the street with a sawn-off shotgun. He handed over the Holy Bible and backed off. Clive's face fell.

'Oh, this,' he said, fingering the gold lettering on its leather cover. How much more powerful his vow to the truth would be if sworn on the smiling faces of Andy Robinson, Martin Johnson, Dave Reddin *et al.*

'You are charged that on 22 November 2003, you did, with malice aforethought, win the Rugby World Cup by virtue of luck and circumstance. You did inherit wonderful players, the greatest captain in world rugby and benefit from the finances available as the first coach of the professional era. You did not win the World Cup through your skills as a leader or manager. This was proven most conclusively during the Lions tour, when you lost the series 3–0. How do you plead?'

'Not guilty,' muttered the accused. 'Your Honour, I am not guilty. We threw the kitchen sink at it. We did six-f thinking and Paddi thinking and we had loads of coaches. Your Honour, there are some villages in Australia with fewer inhabitants than there were specialist coaching personnel in the England and Lions teams. If the Lions had employed an eyebrow technician and a manicurist, they would have had a bigger entourage than Jennifer Lopez.'

The counsel for the prosecution approached. 'If any previous England rugby coach had had the finances and personnel given so freely to the accused, they, too, would have won the World Cup,' he said. 'This is not about skilled leadership – this is about good timing. It is our contention that Clive Woodward is not the best coach in the world and that, furthermore, any coach could have achieved what he achieved, given the advantages presented to him.'

What should we make of Sir Clive Woodward? Is he the best rugby coach that England has ever produced because he won the World Cup final in Australia, or the worst rugby coach in history because he lost the Lions series 3–0? Indeed, what do these conflicting results tell us about him? Can a leader be good one minute and bad the next? Do certain leadership skills work in certain situations, or are they generic? How do we begin to assess Clive Woodward in light of the World Cup victory and the Lions defeats?

The World Cup

The final of the 2003 World Cup against Australia in Sydney turned Clive from good to great, but isn't a one-match victory insufficient evidence on which to base an assessment of greatness? It seemed to be enough evidence for the Queen, who was moved to knight the England rugby coach for his achievements, but perhaps her knowledge and understanding of modern, professional rugby isn't as good as it might be.

If Clive Woodward had looked up into the storm of flashbulbs on that stunning November evening as the coach of the losing side in the World Cup final, would that have made him a worse coach? He certainly wouldn't have been knighted, and his team would not have been feted and celebrated, but would he, in all honesty, be a worse coach? What if the team had lost for reasons out of his control?

Let us look at a silly example. Imagine if Wilkinson had eaten a dodgy prawn sandwich the day before the match, been sick all night and missed that kick. Clive would be perceived as a less effective coach than he is. The whole story would be different. As Wilkinson bit into the sandwich, he would have made Clive a worse coach. There would have been no calls from the government, no parade through London, no fame, no glory, no knighthood. Failed. Surely, that makes no sense at all.

Actually, it does. Let's take the example of the dodgy prawn sandwich again. The truth is that Wilkinson would never have eaten a dodgy sandwich the day before a game because Clive had taken a chef to the World Cup with him. Clive eliminates all doubts. He took experts in every field so that he had control over everything. The RFU thought it wasn't worth sending Dave Campbell, so they wouldn't provide the money and Clive found a sponsor – but what value do you put on Campbell if not taking him means Johnson or Wilkinson gets food poisoning and you lose the match? How much would Dave Campbell be worth to the RFU if he saved England from losing the World Cup? He would be worth everything. 'A chef, a chef. My kingdom for a chef.' After all, in 1995, some New Zealand players suffered food poisoning ahead of their final against South Africa.

Every detail that could be attended to was attended to in the England rugby team. That's why they won. The very thought that England might lose 'for reasons out of his control' would make Clive shiver. His entire England tenure had as its foundations the will to control all aspects of the game and attend to every detail that might make the tiniest of differences. Clive produced a team of men who never had to say 'if only'. A great coach controls all the controllables and Clive asserted that far more was controllable than had ever been imagined before. His drive to cover every base and leave no stone unturned was designed to eliminate these 'if onlys'.

The reason that Clive is held up as a national treasure is because all the things he did – taking England to number one in the world, inspiring a nation, dragging a thoroughly amateur sport into the professional age – had their most eloquent expression on that rainy night in Sydney. The detail, clever thinking, confidence, thought processes were all summed up in one match – indeed in one kick.

Every player on the pitch knew that Jonny Wilkinson would kick for goal. The skill was not only in Wilkinson's kick but in what it represented. Was it by chance that the greatest kicker in world rugby found himself in front of the posts with moments to go? Was it by chance that he had all the time in the world to make that kick? Or was it the meticulous defence of the forwards, the brilliant thinking of the captain, the sheer courage of the scrum-half? Wilkinson's kick was fantastic and should be celebrated because of what it represents – a team in harmony, a unit of men working as one. The hours, days, weeks and months of attending to detail – that's what brought the world's best kicker to the position in front of the posts with seconds to go in the World Cup final. So much of that was down to Clive Woodward – it's impossible to get away from that fact. He didn't kick the ball and he didn't hold back the Australian forwards, but the fact that the players could do it was down to him and his input.

However, if Clive is to be credited for the World Cup victory, so he must be criticised for the defeats on the Lions tour.

The Lions tour

Many reasons can be cited for why the Lions didn't win. The predominant two are that a Lions tour does not lend itself to modern, professional coaching techniques, and that the New Zealand team was a darn sight better. We must judge Clive in a context that he fiercely espouses, though – the 'no excuses' environment.

In the lead-up to the tour, Clive appeared masterful and totally in control as he swooped from country to country to analyse players, devise a strategy for beating the All Blacks and learn from the best coaches in the British Isles. He sought inspiration from outside the sport, visiting Ron Dennis, chairman and CEO of McLaren motor racing, and learning that to be successful, one must engage with a project 'body and mind'. He put a detailed document together outlining what the coaches needed to do in the limited time available, and he set about trying to make this huge group of coaches into the best-prepared and most sophisticated group of coaches ever. Yet, he was more unsuccessful than any previous Lions coach has ever been. What does this tell us about his leadership style?

Clive has a way of working that has been evident throughout his career, appointing cultural architects, building a team and making sure every part of it is challenged and improved. Clearly this was not right for the Lions. The Clive Woodward way was not appropriate. Perhaps Clive shouldn't have taken the job. Perhaps he should have approached the management of the Lions differently from the way in which he approached management of England. It may be that he tried to do too much in too little time with the Lions, with all the critical non-essentials and the barrage of information. But he was appointed Lions coach because of all he'd done in the past, so to take on the Lions and do it all differently would appear to be a recipe for even greater disaster. Perhaps he raised expectations too high with no real way of matching, let alone exceeding, them. On the other hand, what choice did he have? Could he really have sat before the world and said, 'We'll be lucky if we get a point this afternoon. New Zealand are simply too good.'

In an arena where victory is clearly defined and meticulously aimed for the value of a coach ultimately has to be viewed in terms of the successes he achieves – in other words, the extent to which he fulfils expectations. He wouldn't want the world to have anything other than the highest expectations of him, so the nation was shocked by the three defeats. You can look at the quality of the play, the off-field antics and the enjoyment that players derived on tour, but the point was to win more matches. Competition is what defines sport, what differentiates it from art, so the Lions were seen as failures and Clive as an unsuccessful Lions coach. It stands as a blot on his reputation but it does not undermine it. It establishes him as a certain type of coach – one who needs time with players.

What about the specific leadership mistakes he made? One of the things he was most heavily criticised for was the appointment of Alastair Campbell. That decision appeared to display the width, depth and extent of Clive's thinking – lateral, vertical and strategic. It seemed in keeping with some of the 'blue sky' decisions he had made with England, but did it, ultimately, display a certain naïvety and a lack of appreciation for the practical implications of taking a controversial political figure on a rugby tour? Or, more damningly, does it indicate an arrogance, an aloofness? Did he become more concerned with bolstering his own ego and career at the expense of the team he was managing?

The appointment of Campbell proved quite unpalatable to many rugby fans because of Campbell's image as a supreme spin doctor – someone employed to twist the truth to fit his employer's agenda. The effect of Campbell's presence was to provoke the entire media, and a fair chunk of the general public, to doubt everything said by the Lions, assuming it to be spin. Campbell had the effect of distorting people's perceptions of the whole tour by dint of his very presence. It meant that everything uttered by Clive on tour was questioned and the assumption was that Campbell was behind every word. Clearly, the New Zealand team used this to their advantage and cranked up the spinning accusations as much as possible. Given that situation, was Clive right to have taken him? It is clear that both Clive and Humphrey Walters found Campbell a real help on tour.

'He was really very good,' says Walters. 'He was popular with the players and stuck to giving advice and trying to help us organise the relationships with the media better. The idea that he was constantly spinning and interfering is utterly untrue. We were all amazed at the press response to him. He was a decent, hard-working guy who just got on with his job.'

Clive selected Campbell because the leading rugby writers felt a media expert was needed and Campbell was the most celebrated exponent of the art. Clearly, his presence on the tour would have been resented far less if the Lions had won. This is a crucial point to make about Clive's more creative urges. When they work, they really do make him look like a genius, but when they don't, he looks like a complete nutter for having tried. Is it fair to say that all that separates the madman from the genius is success? It would seem so.

Great leadership, as great sport, sits on the shifting line between art and science. There is no formula for creating a great rugby team. If there were, we'd all do it. There's also the fact that you can be a terrible leader and your team can still win. Conversely, you can be a wonderful leader and your team can still lose. Analysing the success or effectiveness of a leader cannot be wholly scientific. So is there any way of stripping back the emotion to look at the bare bones of what someone does as a leader and thus analyse whether they were any good? Whether what they did was any good rather than what they achieved? Or, does 'good', in this context, come inherently bound up with the results produced? What, even, is the role of a leader? What is the point of them? Are they any use at all?

Leadership

'One of the most universal cravings of our time,' wrote the American political thinker James MacGregor Burns, 'is a hunger for compelling and creative leadership.'

The majority of people yearn to be led, and those with the confidence and desire to stand up and offer this leadership are followed, as the history books so colourfully remind us, sometimes blindly and ill-advisedly, but often to make more of themselves and improve. In a sport such as rugby, in which each individual has a role to play in the context of a team, having someone to guide, inform and instruct that team is vital for coherent functioning. Two of the key attributes needed for a great leader are self-belief and an ability to persuade other people that what you believe is right and should be followed unquestioningly and unfailingly.

In his book *Hitler and Churchill: Secrets of leadership*, the historian Andrew Roberts says, 'During the worst days of the Battle of Britain, Churchill never stepped out of Downing Street and said, "I don't know what to do," or, "I'm lost." He walked out with a direction and purpose, even if he had to fake it.'

Clive is a good leader in this respect. Whether you agreed with him or not, it was hard to argue that he didn't always believe in what he was doing. After England had struggled to overcome Wales in the quarter-final of the 2003 World Cup and the entire world doubted England's ability to overcome France in the semi-final, Clive stood firm. He looked out at a packed press conference and said, 'We will win this World Cup. I have no doubt.'

'But what about France?' came the question.

'We'll beat France.'

'Based on the match today, how can you say that?'

'We'll beat France and we'll win the World Cup. Any more questions?' came the response.

Clive had never seemed surer of anything yet he cannot be immune to the insecurities, fears and anxieties that grip us all. He must have had his moments of despair. His skill was in not showing them, always being strong. The trumpeters' sound was always certain when he was in charge of the England rugby team.

Such certainty is bound to create an environment in which people also feel confident in their own ability, especially when backed up by the extraordinary level of detailed thinking that went on. Clive made the England players believe that they could be the greatest team in the world, which is the first step in them actually becoming the greatest team in the world. He managed not only to have unshakeable belief but to share it and convince others that if they followed him, he would lead them to World Cup glory. Then came the Lions. It was significantly easier for Clive to convince the Lions that they would win in New Zealand because he had a track record of delivering on his promises. Everyone believed in him – the players, the coaches and the public. That is why the defeats hit so hard. Two statements that Clive has often been heard to mutter are, one, you should always raise everyone's expectations of you, and two, always deliver above expectations. This is an incredible amount of pressure at the best of times but with a group of men who haven't played together before and with whom you have just a week of preparation? Certainly, Clive succeeded in raising expectations but didn't exceed them. Clive says he had no choice – he had to talk up the team's prospects, he had to instil confidence in the players. He had to go out and tell the world that this team was going to win, even if he, himself, was harbouring certain reservations. Only then could he have the power to influence the behaviour and confidence of the players.

This quote, taken from Roberts's excellent book, gives a fascinating insight into the powers of great leaders to persuade others of their abilities. Field Marshal Hermann Goering said, 'If Hitler told you you were a woman, you would leave the building believing that you were.'

The downside to such confidence in your own ability, and such utter conviction, is that when people don't fall in line, or don't believe you, what do you do? In Clive's case, he cut them out of the picture – not because of personal malice but because he believed he had to in order to get the job done.

One of the most popular modern management texts is *Good To Great* by the American author and business analyst Jim Collins. He concludes that 'great' companies are led by people who 'are fanatically driven, infected with an incurable need to produce results. They will sell the mills or fire their brother if that's what it takes to make the company great.'

Graeme Cattermole saw these characteristics in Clive. 'Over the years it became very clear that he would drop an individual if that person did not support him and his views one hundred per cent. Clive had many good points, despite being a difficult person to work with. I have to admire his single-mindedness and his relentless desire to win and be successful. His attention to detail was meticulous. He was able to instil in a small band of people total loyalty and support to the exclusion of everyone else outside that group. His leadership and motivation skills were immense and were admired by everyone who came into contact with him. If you agreed with him on every level, you were his friend. If you had a disagreement or he did not like your views, he would lock you out.'

Types of leaders

Adrian Atkinson describes Clive as being 'a stealth leader' – a man who does not charge in like a bustling sergeant major and demand attention, but one who encourages the group to buy into his way of thinking by showing/persuading them that it will work. Stealth leaders are good at working themselves slowly into the fabric of a team and being seen as the one who has expert knowledge and the ability to change a situation for the better.

'They achieve quietly and are more sensitive to their own strengths and weaknesses than the traditional image of an all-out leader,' says Atkinson. 'They have a strong understanding of the power of a situation, and a need for information and data. They are extremely well organised, not necessarily very competitive, more intellectual leaders.'

Cattermole sees these qualities in Clive, too. 'I did not recognise it at the time, [but] I subsequently realised that he would work in such a way as to soften you up in the anticipation that you would become one of his men by agreeing to all that he wanted.'

Richard Prescott was the PR manager of the RFU during Clive's tenure. 'Clive was able to walk into a group of players and say, "You over there," and, "You over here." There's no question that he could control groups. He could be very dictatorial, but it wouldn't be true to say that was his preferred style. He was always more carrot than stick.'

Atkinson adds, 'Stealth leaders like to be clear with people about how they will operate once they take charge – you are either in the boat or out. You can rock the boat but if you're in it, you stay in it and you don't rock the boat so much that people fall out. Stealth leaders always have to show they're in control because they are not highly and visually dominant and don't always manage conflict well.'

One interesting observation is that many modern sports coaches are stealth leaders – for example, Arsene Wenger, Sven-Goran Eriksson and Duncan Fletcher. Perhaps the level of leadership required to coach a sports team demands this style. The leader is not on the pitch with the players when they make the crucial decisions that will determine whether they win or lose. Perhaps that blustering, confident, all-consuming, Nero-style management that one associates with sports coaching is a thing of the past. Now it's all chalkboards and discussions about the winning mindset rather than running round the field until you're sick. The aim of high-level sports coaching is to produce a group of players who, above all, can think for themselves. A coach needs to make sure that his management is part of the process, not the whole process, or the players won't cope when he steps away. An interesting point to make is that stealth leaders 'need time' according to Atkinson – another reason, perhaps, why it all went pear-shaped on the Lions tour.

Leadership versus management

Clive showed clear, identifiable leadership traits throughout his time with England but he also involved himself in the intricacies of management. Mike Poulson has known Clive for nearly thirty years. He now works as a management consultant and management trainer. He says, 'If you're looking for the ideal person for a senior management role, you look for someone who can combine management and leadership skills. People who can do that are few and far between. Clive is an entrepreneur and an operator in one – it's very rare.

'When you watch how Clive works, you see how he will view a situation differently from the way in which other people view it. He has worked out that to win, you can't stay the same as everyone else. He's willing to try out all sorts of new things that other people wouldn't think of. When he brought the Australian players over to Henley, no one could believe it – but it made perfect sense. I remember him meeting up with Willie Phillips, a New Zealand player who was at Newbury. He wanted him to come to Henley, so he went to meet him in the Swan in Pinkney's Green. As soon as we knew Clive had got a meeting with him, we knew Phillips would come. Clive can be extremely persuasive. You believe what he says and he always delivers.

'Working for Clive, guys really understand their roles and how important they are to the whole effort. They feel valued and are constantly being told by Clive how much their contribution means – this is the best way to motivate people. It's not about flag waving, screaming and shouting. It's about making people know that their input is valuable.'

If Clive can be manager and leader in one, other paradoxes also define his management style. For example, he is focused towards goals but is easygoing socially. He doesn't have to dominate in a social situation or force his personality on everything he does. It would be unimaginable to find Clive at a party or standing at the bar, telling people about his achievements and how important he is. The Australians always found this hard to understand. He appeared to be without ego, and would fade into the background after work. He is inclined to be a student rather than a teacher. When he's not working, he learns from situations rather than dominating them.

Don Rutherford always thought this was an unwillingness to share information and help others. Rutherford contrasted this business way of thinking with the educational way. In education, he said, people share all the information they have with one another, but the businessman is secretive. Knowledge is power and is guarded and protected.

'I think that's just Clive's way,' says Walters. 'He's really quite shy and hates things like having to go to tea after the matches. You see him in the corner. He hates these occasions, including the dinner at the Hilton that we used to go to after games.'

Influences on management style

Atkinson says he senses signs of 'fear of rejection' in Clive's management style. Clive's unwillingness to have the conflict-resolving discussions with people that pepper the lives of most managers is symptomatic of this fear, as is the personalising of business decisions that go against him. He takes any feelings of perceived rejection in a highly personal manner. Cattermole says, 'What Clive wanted, Clive had to have, and when he was told no, he took it as a personal slight.'

'People who fear rejection – which would classically be someone who was sent away to boarding school – tend to push their ideas through and be resistant to public debate on them,' says Atkinson. 'It can make them appear as if they're behaving slyly because they're tenacious and quiet, and though they seek a great deal of expert opinion initially, they don't consult too much once they've made up their minds. Fear of rejection is very different from fear of failure, which Clive doesn't appear to have.'

Clive has confessed to being driven by an intense frustration that his father never believed he was good enough to play football at a high level – never believed in the talents that Clive knew he had.

'I have talked to many international sporting men and women and there is one common denominator that has driven them to excellence,' Atkinson continues. 'That is the frustration and hurt they have experienced from someone who has told them they would never achieve or be good at anything. They have taken this negative thinking and made a commitment to themselves to prove this person wrong and to cancel out this negative debt.'

As already mentioned, Humphrey Walters made a psychological profile of Clive that indicated he gains satisfaction not only from personal achievements but also from controlling other people in the process of getting results. Forming friendships is not high among his needs. This means that he will respond well to people who regard him as an important and significant person, seek his point of view and are good listeners. He likes clear action plans with specific and realistic targets, he likes meetings to be to the point without waffle and small talk, and he likes proof of the benefits of an action and that results can be achieved.

'You should never deal with Clive in a woolly, chatty way,' says Walters. 'He is very goal orientated, a bit of a loner and likes targets and goals. He needs feedback all the time. You can never deal with Clive on the basis that you're his mate. He has respect for people but he's not a close guy. I've sat in cars with him for hours and he just says nothing until you talk about the job.

'Clive is not the easiest guy to work with. He's quite brilliant but he's very passionate and therefore he's not easy. He's unpredictable. You sometimes do things that you think he will like and he really takes umbrage. He's very hard to read and he's quite moody as well – especially under pressure. People tend to avoid him when he's under pressure.'

The big question is why is Clive like this? According to all expert opinion, it's because of the environment he found himself in when a young boy.

'If you're a kid with an IQ of 130, and you're brought up in the East End of London at the same time as a boy with an IQ of 130 is brought up on a farm in Devon, you'll grow up differently because the environment's totally different, so your needs are totally different. If you think back to what drove you when you started your career, it's probably different from what drives you now. People will say you've matured. You haven't. Your environment's changed, therefore your drivers have changed,' said Walters.

Transformational versus transactional leaders

Traditionally, one tends to think of leaders and managers as being different types of people. Leaders are more visionary, less concerned with the minutiae, externally focused, looking forward and for ways to improve, whereas managers tend to exist in the detail of the moment. They look inward and manage a situation as it exists. Some management experts describe the difference as being between 'hunters and farmers'. Leaders are hunters, out there looking for new things to shoot. Managers are farmers, tending to what is already there. Once leaders have been separated from managers, they are further subdivided by management experts into transformational and transactional leaders.

Transformational leadership allows individuals and organisations to thrive at the edge of chaos as they are being improved. These leaders inspire innovation and creativity. They help to develop new products that lead to sustainable competitive advantage. The personal qualities of transformational leaders are consistency, integrity and openness to ideas. They are decisive and risk taking, charismatic, inspiring, analytical, creative and entrepreneurial. Transformational leaders pick up an organisation by the scruff of the neck and change it. They leave a fingerprint on the club.

Transactional leadership is different, more about management than leadership. Transactional leaders concentrate on the management of specifics – 'We need to work on those handling drills so the set plays work properly on Saturday.' These leaders will 'tell them, watch them, correct them'. They will concern themselves with issuing instructions and monitoring performance.

Steve Bull has watched Clive's work. 'It's classic transformational leadership stuff,' says Bull. 'He's got "turn-around leadership" down to a fine art – you go in and totally transform a set-up then move on to the next one. If you look back at his career, that's what he's done – gone in, made the big-hitting changes and moved on. I suspect he's the sort of person who gets bored easily and likes fresh challenges.'

The business of winning

Clive's aim when taking over the England rugby team was to use his business skills on the 'business of winning'. In fact, he brought unique, left-field business skills into sports management. It would be naïve to think that Clive was the first person in history to bring business skills into sport – others before him had worked in a business-like fashion. Rod Macqueen was bringing professional standards into the Australian team a long time before Clive brought them to England but, with all respect to Macqueen, never before had someone brought such a cutting-edge, vibrant, 'throw the rule book out of the window' mentality that Clive brought. His business methods would have been challenging enough in any small business, let alone in a newly professional sport. The important thing was the way in which Clive used those business skills in rugby. Organisations are now studying his management of the England rugby team to find clues about how to improve their businesses.

Another thing that Clive did when coaching England was to believe that victory was more important than his own personal standing. This was thrown into question by his planning for the Lions tour, when his selection of Alastair Campbell led many observers to conclude that he had made the appointment not for the good of the team, but for reasons of making himself look better and more important by association. Clive denies this absolutely. He says he appointed Campbell because he was the best media manager around.

If Clive did stoop to employing Campbell to bolster his own ego, it would be out of character. There's nothing in his background to suggest that he is a man with an eagerness to mix with the rich and famous in order to look good. Indeed, when it came to Henley, London Irish and England, Clive was willing to make himself look utterly ridiculous at times, just to ensure that the team had everything it needed to be a success. 'The man with the new idea is a crank until the idea succeeds.' That is what Clive was – the crank who was always out on a limb. Then England started winning, and suddenly he didn't seem so daft any more. The Lions lost and he was a crank again.

Sir John Harvey-Jones describes himself as a 'keen rugby fan' as well as being the former chairman of ICI who doubled the price of the company's shares within thirty months of his appointment and turned a loss into a £1 billion profit. He says, 'People want to work for an identifiable person and the values of that person are very important, but good leaders place overall success before personal glory always.' That's what Clive did. He never elevated himself beyond the team and his coaches. He sits like a spoke in a wheel, spindles extending beyond him and out into greatness.

Harvey-Jones presented *Troubleshooter*, the TV series in which he analysed ailing companies and offered advice. The series was shown in the late eighties and early nineties, when Clive was developing his business, and Harvey-Jones quotes crop up in some of the literature that he presented to his management team. Clive may be relieved to hear that the troubleshooter concludes that Clive did 'an excellent, consistent and patient managerial job. He showed good communication abilities as well as regard and affection for those being grown, coached and led.' Praise indeed.

'Clive's an exciting bloke to be with – an energiser,' says Fran Cotton. 'The RFU needed that – someone who wouldn't follow orders. I liked the things he said. They made sense. He was always bright and thinking of new ideas.'

Half madman, half genius

There have been a lot of intelligent, experienced businessmen consulted for this book, and all those who have worked closely with Clive have declared their enthusiasm for his abilities as a leader and skills as a businessman, but outside of the close-knit circle, people, by and large, think he's nuts. Where do the claims that Clive is half-madman, half-genius come from? People have called him a 'mad professor' and he has 'exploded' in press conferences before now. Clive is a journalist's dream because you never quite know what he will do from one minute to the next. Sometimes, after England had won convincingly, Clive would storm into the press conference without making eye contact. There would be no communication. He would take his place at the top table and grimace at the assembled gathering as if we were all personally responsible for the death of his first born. A simple statement such as, 'Clive, you must be delighted with the result today,' would provoke such an outburst that the questioner regretted getting up that morning, and those planning a more aggressive line of questioning would quickly reconsider in the interests of their personal safety.

On other days, Clive would wander in, smiling and laughing. He'd compliment journalists on their work and remark on the lovely weather. England had just lost. Madness – or it seems like madness until you understand how Clive works. Three aspects of Clive's character, in my opinion, have a bearing on his demeanour in these situations, and give rise to cries of 'he's mad'. The first is that Clive's definition of winning is bigger than just scoring more points than the opposition. Think back to London Irish when Conor O'Shea tried a move that he totally messed up. Clive responded to the error with delight because O'Shea had tried to play in the way Clive wanted him to. He'd raised his expectations of himself, done something different, tried to play a better class of rugby. Winning, Clive-style, means more than simply winning a one-off match. Clive wanted England to win always, but outside the big games, he yearned to see evidence that the team was moving towards his ideal style of play. Particularly against weaker opponents, just grinding out a narrow victory would never satisfy him.

The second point is that Clive does not respond well to people who are merely being nice to him. He demands honesty and integrity. So, in the press conference example, he would genuinely have preferred it if someone had said, 'Clive, you may have won today, but that was not a brilliant performance. There was no fluidity, no real style.' Remember, Clive is the man who told selectors they were 'insane' to select him for the Lions tour and leave Paul Dodge at home. He doesn't respond well to niceties. He's too detached from the minutiae of life around him. This has freed him to focus on what is important to him, but it can make him appear distant and ever so slightly mad.

The third thing to mention in relation to Clive's 'madness' is his way of doing things. If he wants to get from A to B, he just goes. If someone puts a series of obstacles in his way, he'll try to get them removed, but there will come a moment when he just decides he's fed up and needs to be at B. So he crashes through them, regardless of the consequences, causing havoc, but getting to B. To witness the charge without knowing how much was done to get the obstacles moved painlessly, and without understanding just how much getting to B means to him, is to witness the act of a madman.

'I can see where the image comes from,' says Jonny Wilkinson, 'but I don't think he's mad at all. I think he'll just do whatever it takes for England to be a better side. I remember he once told me to base my high game on how many dropped goals I could get in a game. That sounds like a daft thing to say – but what he wanted me to do was to see where the opportunities were for drop goals. When could you add another three points to the scoreboard? What ways were there in which I could put pressure on the other teams? It all made sense – everything he did made sense, but if you took things at surface level, from the outside without understanding what he was trying to achieve, then yes, I suppose he might have looked a bit mad.'

How does he compare?

As well as looking at the qualitative aspects of Clive's leadership, it's worth considering the quantitative. The most logical way of doing this is to compare him to the two head coaches who preceded him, Geoff Cooke and Jack Rowell. Cooke started with the England team soon after the first World Cup. He was in charge of England between January 1988 and March 1994. Under him, England played forty-nine games and won thirty-five of them, with one draw and thirteen defeats. Against the southern hemisphere, they won three out of twelve games. In World Cup matches they had four wins and two defeats.

Under Jack Rowell, England played twenty-nine games from June 1994 to July 1997. They won twenty-one and lost eight. They played six southern-hemisphere games and won two, and six World Cup games of which they won four.

Clive was in charge between September 1997 and 2004. England played eighty-three matches under him – an astonishing fact, indicative of how much more rugby is being played. He coached for only a year longer than Cooke, but England played thirty-four more games. They won fifty-nine games, drawing two and losing twenty-two. They won thirteen southern-hemisphere games out of twenty-nine played, and ten of 12 World Cup games.

What does all this mean? The easiest way to make comparisons is by the percentage of victories, because of the vastly differing numbers of games played. Assessed in this way, the total number of victories attained by each of the three coaches is quite similar. Cooke won 71.4 per cent of his games, Rowell won 72.4 per cent and Clive won 71 per cent. So, purely in percentage terms, Clive comes bottom of the pile.

Where things become interesting is in relation to the 'big wins' – victory over the Tri Nations and in the World Cup matches. Despite leading England to victory in back-to-back Grand Slams in the early nineties, Cooke won just 25 per cent of his games against southern-hemisphere sides. Rowell won 33 per cent against Clive's 45 per cent. In World Cup games, Cooke and Rowell won 67 per cent of their matches, and Clive won 83 per cent.

Cooke is sitting in the sun in Portugal, semi-retired and looking after the English first division from his home in Yorkshire and his holiday home in the sun. He says, with considerable honesty, 'Given these conditions [the conditions that Clive had], we'd all like to think we could have done the same as him, but we'll never know.

'Clive has done a tremendous job. He was always enthusiastic and really wanted the job. After a hairy first couple of seasons, he lost his idealism and settled down. When rugby changed, it changed completely. It was chalk and cheese compared to what the sport had been like before, so it's impossible to sit here and say, "I could have done that" because the truth is – we'll never know.'

Jack Rowell says, 'If you look at the World Cup, it all boils down to the fact that one of the big five are going to win it and so England would have a chance. But you have got to have good players and a phenomenon called Jonny Wilkinson, and I would say Martin Johnson for his leadership qualities, and stacks of world-class players with experience, such as Lawrence Dallaglio. If you add in Clive's ideas, then it became a particularly heady cocktail for England – not just in the World Cup but also in the time leading up to that.'

There are two other ways in which to examine the impact of Clive Woodward. First, in terms of the public's perception of him and second, in terms of his legacy – how did he change rugby union? What was the long-term impact on rugby of his period as England coach?

The people's view

For the purposes of this book, I conducted a survey of 5,000 people. Major national organisations gave me access to their databases to send a questionnaire by email to 3,500 people, and 1,500 people were handed leaflets in the street in Surrey, London and Birmingham. There were 2,740 email responses and 543 responses to the leaflet, giving a total of 3,283, which is a response rate of 66 per cent.

The aim of the survey was to canvass public opinion of Clive as a coach and to investigate the perceived importance of a coach. The questioning was done following victory in the World Cup but before the Lions tour, so does not include any views of Clive post-Lions. I tried hard, in the production of the questionnaire, to disguise the fact that I was doing the research for a book on Clive Woodward.

The questionnaire asked for basic details, such as ages, addresses, rugby knowledge and whether respondents had seen, or were at, the 2003 World Cup – 8 per cent of those who responded were actually at the Rugby World Cup, a high percentage presumably because those who received an unsolicited questionnaire in their email in-boxes one morning were more likely to reply if they had been to the tournament and knew something about rugby. This was reflected in another way – 20 per cent regarded themselves as knowing nothing about rugby, 60 per cent said they knew something about rugby and the remaining 20 per cent suggested they knew a lot about rugby.

The questionnaire asked respondents to name the one individual who contributed most to the World Cup victory – 15 per cent thought that Clive contributed most. By far and away the highest percentage went to Martin Johnson, who won 51 per cent of the votes. Jonny Wilkinson came second with 24 per cent. Clive's percentage put him in third place. Other players' contributions were well spread, with most getting just 1 per cent (for example, Richard Hill) or 2 per cent (Matt Dawson, presumably because he had a hand in the winning drop goal). As a comparison, I asked about other sports. In answer to the question who was the most important character in the England cricket team, not one respondent mentioned Duncan Fletcher, the coach. Asked about the England football team, no one mentioned Sven-Goran Eriksson. In short, it was quite unusual for so many people to single out a coach as the defining character in a winning sports team.

Another statistic worth noting here is that those respondents who declared they knew a lot about rugby voted for Martin Johnson and Clive Woodward exclusively with the vote split 70:30 in the captain's favour.

When presented with a list of names of famous sports coaches and asked to choose the top three – 39 per cent picked Clive on their list. The most highly regarded coach was Sir Alex Ferguson, whom 70 per cent of respondents regarded as one of the top three coaches. Of course, one would expect that higher-profile football coaches would attract more votes than those less well known. Arsene Wenger received 58 per cent of the vote, and Clive was joint third with Jurgen Grobler, the Great Britain rowing coach. Groebler is very successful but infinitely less well known than the others.

The survey also looked at how important respondents considered the role of the coach to be – 60 per cent thought it vital to the effective performance of a team, and 40 per cent said it was important but no more important than any other factors. Interestingly, when I asked the same question about business, 100 per cent thought it was vital, the most important factor in a team's success. It should also be noted here that 100 per cent of those respondents who claimed to have a 'very good knowledge' of rugby said that a good coach was vital.

The final question asked was about Clive's future. How did respondents think he would cope in football? Not one respondent thought that Clive 'wouldn't last a minute in football'. The vote was split – 39 per cent thought he would be able to 'coach a professional side' and 39 per cent said he would 'coach a decent club side'. Almost a quarter of respondents (22 per cent) thought he would end up as coach of the England team.

The legacy

Since the World Cup, has there been a real uplift in the sport? Certainly, I can sense a renewed interest in rugby – children play with rugby balls in parks where once they all carried footballs. Rugby seems a 'sexier' concept somehow. Friends who knew nothing about rugby before the World Cup and had little interest in my job seem suddenly overwhelmed with interest in the characters but, my casual observations aside, has the World Cup made a real difference?

Twelve months on, 33,098 new players had taken up the sport. Indeed, the RFU say there was a 16 per cent growth across all age groups, taking the total playing club rugby to more than 230,000 people. The really good news is that the biggest increase comes in the Under-7 to Under-11 age range, with an additional 15,293 children now playing the game – 32 per cent growth. Those already playing have had their numbers bolstered by the tournament. Five hundred clubs reported at least one extra team.

As well as players, an additional 3,135 coaches and 783 referees were recruited in the twelve months following the World Cup, bringing the totals to 22,469 and 6,060 active in the game respectively. The number of volunteers rose by 8.6 per cent, from 33,225 to 36,081. More than half of these were aged between twenty-five and fourty-four.

Those not actively involved in the sport have still shown an interest. Revenue in the RFU's 'Rugby Store' rose by over 90 per cent to £7.7 million in twelve months. This figure includes sales of over £1 million in one calendar month in December 2003 when goods worth £1.7 million were sold.

Martin Johnson sits back in his seat and puts his big hands behind his head. I have just asked him whether England would have won the World Cup without Clive Woodward.

'That's a horrible question,' he says. 'A horrible, horrible question.'

Yesterday, Johnson played his final game of rugby ever. Today, he is reminiscing about life with Clive. The good times: 'He was so passionate, so enthusiastic, and so keen to try everything and shake everything up. He created a great environment for the team. Some of the guys have said that now he's gone, they realise how much he did and just what England has lost.' And the bad times: 'We didn't always agree. He could be easily led. He's stormed out of arguments with me in the past, and there have been times when we just could not agree at all.'

But, back to this crucial question – could England have won without him? 'There's no question that England were vastly improving as a side when Clive took over. We'd played well in the 1997 Five Nations and there were signs of real improvement. Then Clive came in as the first full-time coach and was able to devote all his time to it. If you're going to ask whether England would have won the World Cup with any other coach in charge, you have to ask who could have done it? One name stands out – Ian McGeechan. Could England have won the World Cup with Geech in charge? I don't know. It's impossible to say whether Geech would have got all the politics right like Clive did. I guess when you think about it like that, you'd have to say that it's unlikely that England would have won the World Cup without Clive in charge.'

And the Lions? Could the Lions have won the Test matches against New Zealand with another coach in charge? 'New Zealand were more skilful and better prepared than the Lions. You can't wave a magic wand and make the Lions better. It takes years to develop a winning side, not a couple of weeks. Clive took most of the country's best coaches with him. If that group of coaches couldn't do it, it's hard to see how it could be done by anyone.'

Back in 1995, Clive Woodward was the coach of London Irish, trying to keep hold of his job in an increasingly hostile environment. Ten years later, he had been praised for being the greatest coach in the world and criticised for being the worst. It's very difficult to assess someone as complex and fast-moving as Clive Woodward, but there is no question that, given time and resources, he has the ability to turn teams around. Given talented players, he is able to create an environment in which they can flourish and become the best in the world. Few things about Clive are certain except that the story is far from finished. His immediate future is in football, but there is so much more out there that will doubtless capture his attention. It is impossible to predict where he will end up, but one thing is certain – whatever he does, whatever plans he makes or businesses he seeks to lead to success, the last words in his philosophy, as the last words in this book, will always be *Think Differently*.

Index